MOVING BEYOND ASSESSMENT

MOVING BEYOND ASSESSMENT

A PRACTICAL GUIDE FOR BEGINNING HELPING PROFESSIONALS

Melissa D. Grady

AND

Eileen A. Dombo

OXFORD
UNIVERSITY PRESS

OXFORD

UNIVERSITY PRESS

Oxford University Press is a department of the University of Oxford. It furthers the University's objective of excellence in research, scholarship, and education by publishing worldwide. Oxford is a registered trade mark of Oxford University Press in the UK and certain other countries.

Published in the United States of America by Oxford University Press
198 Madison Avenue, New York, NY 10016, United States of America.

Library of Congress Cataloging-in-Publication Data
Grady, Melissa D.
Moving beyond assessment : a practical guide for beginning helping professionals / Melissa D. Grady and Eileen A. Dombo.
    pages cm
Includes bibliographical references and index.
ISBN 978–0–19–936701–6 (alk. paper)
1. Social service—Practice. 2. Social service. 3. Counselor and client. I. Dombo, Eileen A. II. Title.
HV10.5.G695 2016
361—dc23
2015030193

9 8 7 6 5 4 3 2 1

Printed by Sheridan, USA

We dedicate this book to our students and our clients, past, present, and future. We have learned and continue to learn a great deal from them, and are honored to be part of their learning and growing experiences. Thank you to our families, without whose unwavering support over the years our work would not be possible. And finally, to our colleagues who continue to inspire us with their dedication to improving our world around us.

CONTENTS

MOVING BEYOND ASSESSMENT

CHAPTER 1

INTRODUCTION

A client walks into the room. He looks sad, disheveled, and hopeless. He has come to you for help—to "fix the problem." He states he wants you to help him "make his life better and to feel better." Your job, or so you feel, is to alleviate his struggles and instill in him hope and a sense of empowerment, right? Or so you ask yourself.

Most new practitioners feel an overwhelming sense of pressure to know what to do in every practice situation. Whether it is meeting with an individual client in an agency setting, engaging with a family for a home visit, or working in the community, new practitioners often feel that they ought to know exactly what to do, even at the beginning of their training. People choose to enter professions like social work, psychology, counseling, nursing, medicine, and other helping professions because they want to help people and, in turn, make the world better and more just. Yet, the feeling of being at a loss regarding how exactly to accomplish those goals comes quickly, often right at the beginning of graduate school. Good intentions only go so far. In addition to having good intentions and a passion for and commitment to the work, practitioners need to have skills and knowledge *and* be able to use them appropriately and discriminately depending on the situation at hand.

We want to emphasize from the start of this book that you will develop the capacities described through a lifelong learning process. We know you have heard that before, and that does not help you now as you are starting out and need some tools to succeed today. Yet, we feel compelled to mention it here because often beginning practitioners feel frustrated by the pace of this learning process and want to gain knowledge more quickly. Part of what makes working with people so engaging is their complexities. When these complexities are then paired with individual, family, group, or community circumstances, it can feel overwhelming to believe that you will ever have adequate skills and knowledge to help create a change in someone's life or community. However, with each iteration of your training, you will continue to gain more knowledge. By pairing your knowledge with an increased understanding of how to mobilize and utilize this ever-growing set of skills, you will feel more confident in your professional capacities.

This book was designed to be part of the beginning phase of this lifelong learning process. It is written to assist new helping practitioners feel less anxious and more prepared to approach and work with the clients and communities they desire to help. It is not designed to be a comprehensive guide to your training as a practitioner but rather to help you take the initial steps in your own journey.

As practitioners and professors, we have received numerous requests from students and novice practitioners to find a book that is clear and easy to understand and helps them feel more prepared for the initial stages of working with clients. As such, we have written each chapter to be a reference guide that is easily readable and accessible. Combined, we have over 30 years of practice experience plus over 15 years of teaching social work graduate students about practice, theory, and research. In writing this book, we used knowledge from our own practice experiences in conjunction with years of working with graduate students to address here what beginning practitioners need at the initial stages of working with clients. The book is meant to be user friendly and to address many of the issues of concern for beginning practitioners, as well as address other practice-related issues that they have yet to ponder. This book is primarily intended to help practitioners who will be working in direct practice settings rather than in communities or macro practice. While some of the concepts and principles may apply, this book is aimed at helping those beginning practitioners who will be working with individuals, families, or groups. In addition, although we include a chapter on the diagnosis of mental health disorders, this book is meant to extend beyond mental health or clinical practice. We hope that the book will be applicable to multiple practice settings.

We believe that before individuals can even start to think about working with clients in a direct practice way, the first step is to think about developing their professional style and way of working. Therefore, Chapter 2 addresses the working alliance as well as the professional self and issues related to taking care of the self in doing this work. Chapter 3 focuses on exploring and understanding the role of cultural and identity issues in practice. Chapter 4 addresses the context in which practice occurs and understanding how the setting guides your role. Following Chapter 4, the book is divided into three sections. The first section focuses on assessment and the beginning stages of working with clients. The chapters in this section address the first session, assessment, the importance of asking difficult questions, and safety assessment for both the client and others involved with the client, including the worker.

The second section focuses on issues related to preparing for and implementing interventions with clients. It is designed to help you prepare thoughtfully for your work with clients, including the use of the evidence-based practice process, the role of theory in treatment planning, preparation of a treatment plan, preparation for termination, and how to create an ongoing assessment process of your work with clients. In other words, how will you know whether what you are doing with your client is working? This section also includes chapters on how to work with clients in the "middle phase" of an intervention. It is not designed to be a toolkit on how to work with every client, and it will not provide examples of practice models. These issues are beyond the scope of this book. This section is meant to provide some guiding principles and to address some basic issues related to intervention.

Finally, in the third section we address the changing landscape of practice. The chapters in this section address finding a supervisor and getting the most out of your supervision; provide considerations related to the use of technology and social media; and provide a beginning understanding of some of the biological, medical, and neurobiological issues related to practice. These chapters provide some guidelines on these complex issues that will certainly evolve over time as the world changes—and you change as a professional.

We conclude the book with some parting advice and tools that will be useful as you begin your journey as a helping professional. We include well-established resources in these areas with the hope that they will remain helpful to you throughout your career. However, we encourage readers to remain aware of new and evolving resources in their particular areas of practice.

In the end, we hope that this book provides you with a bit more confidence and knowledge as you enter the first stages of your training and career. Working with clients provides an exciting journey but can be a bit daunting at the same time. Our intention is to help keep the excitement about the work alive, simultaneously helping to reduce the anxiety so that you can be present and available to your clients as you join them on their own journey, which has the potential to enhance your own as well. After all, this journey is what keeps us engaged in this work.

CHAPTER 2

WHAT TO KNOW BEFORE YOU START

It is the first day of your internship or the first day of your new job in social work or a related helping profession. You are getting ready to begin a new stage of your career. You may have a number of questions about what you should wear or how you should introduce yourself. You may also have a number of concerns about what others will think of you or how you will answer tough or personal questions from your clients. In addition, there may be other issues that you may not have even thought of that are important to consider, such as how this work will have an impact on you or change you in some way. This chapter is designed to help you think through some important preliminary issues so that you are as prepared as possible when you start this new phase of your career.

THE DEVELOPMENT AND CARE OF THE PROFESSIONAL SELF

For most of us, when we are with certain individuals or groups we act in a particular way; we share more or less compared to when we are with others, we let down our guard or put it up, and we even dress in a particular way based on who we are with at the time. In each situation, we have a way that we act or present a different "self," which is often dependent on a variety of factors.

A professional social work setting is no different, as there are different ways that we should and do act in such contexts. Social workers need to present a *professional self* in their work with clients and in their interactions with colleagues. While this statement may seem obvious, in our experience as professors and supervisors, the concept of a professional self is not always adequately explored by social work students. As such, we believe it is essential that future social workers think through what it means to have a professional self and what this self would "look like" for them. We believe there are several essential components to a professional self, namely: dress and physical appearance, how to work with interdisciplinary teams and other professionals, communication factors, and consideration of how the National Association of Social Workers' (NASW, 2008) Code of Ethics informs how social workers should behave as professionals.

DRESS AND PHYSICAL PRESENTATION

Whether someone has completed training or is still in the midst of it, social workers must present themselves professionally. We do not in any way mean to imply that social workers or trainees should run out and buy an extensive or expensive wardrobe. It also does not mean that your personal style needs to be altered significantly. We simply mean that the way you dress should reflect the respect you have for your role and for those with whom you work. Table 2.1 provides some general guidelines to consider as you are thinking through how to present yourself in a professional setting.

Remember that everything you have on your body is a form of self-disclosure and may be a topic of interest to your clients. Items such as jewelry (e.g., a cross or star-of-David necklace, a wedding/commitment ring), a tattoo, and piercings might all be topics that are of interest to your clients. We are in no way suggesting that you do not wear them or show them; we are simply encouraging you to be prepared to hear questions about such items. We suggest that you speak to your supervisor before you start about what is

TABLE 2.1: Dress Guidelines

Guideline	Explanation
Clean clothes—not clothes that are stained or have marked holes	May communicate to the client that you cannot take care of your own clothes, so how will you take care of them?
For women: skirts that are at least to the knees	This is especially if you will be sitting down on the floor, such as with young children.
For women: ensure that the tops you wear do not show inside your shirts when you bend over	Many social workers will be bending over paperwork or doing other related activities, and you should wear a camisole or closer-fitting clothing if this applies.
Be cognizant of the setting with regard to the expense of the clothing or other accessories	Professional does not have to mean fancy or expensive. Be conscious of what message it sends to clients in your setting to appear in expensive clothing or jewelry.
Wear clothes that consider safety	In some settings, safety may be a factor. Consider shoes that allow for easy running or clothes that are not too loose and could be grabbed.
Avoid clothing with messages on them	Clothes that communicate your affiliation with a particular group other than the agency should be avoided, as it is a form of self-disclosure and could send unintended messages to the client(s).
Avoid clothing inappropriately tight	Tight-fitting clothes can be distracting and too revealing.
Wear clothing that is consistent with those of the other workers	Use your colleagues as your guide in terms of appropriate clothing. Observe others and try to follow their lead as much as possible.

appropriate attire for your setting and to plan how to respond to clients when they do ask questions about your personal appearance. It is best to be clear about the expectations and norms before you start and to feel prepared for such questions or comments from clients ahead of time. When deciding what to wear, whether it is clothing, jewelry, or other items, reflect on the balance between the importance of the item to you and the potential of its distraction of others from the work at hand. This process can help you discern which items are essential to your authentic presentation of self and which you may want to choose to bring out in a different setting.

WORKING WITH INTERDISCIPLINARY TEAMS

The majority of practice settings will require social workers to work with professionals from other disciplines. These professionals could be individuals with similar training as you (i.e., a psychologist or other mental health worker) or completely different training from you (i.e., a vocational trainer or teacher). Regardless of the composition of the team, there are two key points we want to make about social workers' roles on these teams.

The first point is that social workers should be active members of the team. Our message here is that if you do not speak up, then neither the profession nor the needs of your clients are represented. It may seem intimidating to speak up in a group with others who appear to be or who actually are more experienced or educated than you. However, the fact that they have more experience does not mean that they should be the only members to have an opinion or a perspective. It is possible that the social worker knows something that the other team members do not. It may be that the client has shared something with the social worker that he or she has not shared with the rest of the team (i.e., the client does not like taking his medicine because it makes him feel nauseous). In addition, some teams may be focused on the struggles or deficits of the client and not as focused on the strengths or capacities of the client. Because social work training emphasizes the strengths perspective, social workers can bring this important perspective to the team. For these reasons, we encourage you to be a vocal presence on the teams in which they are involved.

The second point we want to make is that, as team members, social workers should present themselves as professional and competent. Again, just as with dress, this statement might appear obvious. However, we have some specific points we feel are important to consider. The first is that while we believe social workers should be a presence on the team, they should provide *relevant* feedback as opposed to speaking only to have something to say. Therefore, be thoughtful about what information you want to share before you share it. If possible, take some time to plan what you want to say so that your thoughts are organized and clear.

Next, with whatever ideas you have that you want to present, provide a rationale for those ideas. It is important that these opinions be based on research, theory, client feedback, or some other credible source. There have been studies that have reported that social workers are perceived by their colleagues as not having a strong basis for their opinions and have even been referred to as "airy-fairy" in their approach to working with clients (McCracken &

Marsh, 2008, p. 134). Therefore, it is important that social workers explain the rationale for their professional opinions and that these points are based on credible sources.

COMMUNICATION

One of the ways of expressing and presenting the professional self is through oral and written communication. With written communication, social workers may use multiple methods to communicate with colleagues, other professionals, clients, and family members, such as paper or electronic means. We spend more time in Chapter 17 discussing social media and other issues related to technology, but we want to discuss a few issues here concerning communication in general and to offer some general guidelines to follow with regard to how to communicate in a professional manner.

WRITTEN COMMUNICATION

What is essential to remember about written communication is that once you write it, it is available for everyone to see. Check with a supervisor about rules concerning communication. Otherwise, remember the following:

- Anything posted online can be sent to anyone or anywhere else.
- Write everything as if you know that the client will be reading it.
- If writing is not a strength of yours, make sure you have someone review/edit your work. You are representing the social work profession, and the work should be professional. Anything you write can be part of a permanent record that could be around for years.
- In any form of written communication, use a professional style of writing, such as opening with "Dear Ms. Jones" or "Dear Dr. Jones." Remember the tone of e-mails should be as if you were writing a formal letter and not just an e-mail to an acquaintance.
- Think about the clients and whether they are more likely to respond to one form of communication compared to another.

ORAL COMMUNICATION

- Be sure that with oral communication you ask others to repeat back to you what they have heard because often your meaning can be misunderstood.
- It is often prudent to follow up on oral communication with a written note in the file or email to document that the communication took place and the message that was conveyed.
- Speak clearly and avoid fillers such as "um" and "like" as they detract from the message and the professionalism of the communication.
- Use formal communication unless instructed to address the person informally.
- Be aware of your nonverbal communication, which may contradict your message.

Finally, social workers on teams and in professional settings need to be always cognizant that they are representing a profession that has a core mission and values. Therefore, the comments and opinions expressed by the workers on teams and in meetings should be consistent with the profession's values and ethics. In addition, the actions of the worker should be in keeping with the principles that guide the profession, such as maintaining boundaries and the roles to which they are assigned. We have unfortunately been on teams where some of our social work colleagues, in their desire to help their clients, have made suggestions that cross boundaries (e.g., by the workers offering to provide a service outside of his or her role). We have also witnessed our colleagues describe a conversation to other professionals in which they have disclosed confidential information from the client—indicating that they do not uphold confidentiality agreements. Therefore, we strongly recommend that the readers be familiar with the NASW (2008) Code of Ethics to better understand the behaviors associated with our professional standards. We encourage you to review them as soon as possible if you have not already done so. They can be easily accessed online (https://www.socialworkers.org/pubs/code/default.asp).

USE OF SELF

Throughout your professional career, you will most likely hear the term *use of self*. The definition is somewhat elusive, in that it is used differently to describe various aspects of how you use yourself in your work with clients. These aspects can refer to personality or behaviors, such as sense of humor, body language, and others (Dewane, 2006; Edwards & Bess, 1998). In these instances, the phrase is used to capture what many people think of the art of the work you do with clients (Cameron, 2014; Graybeal, 2014). Just like a cook, musician, or painter, for example, the personal style influences how you execute whatever task you are doing with your clients. In this way, you will be developing your own style or fine-tuning the "instrument" you will be using in the relationship with the client: yourself. (See Chapter 4 for more information on the relationship.) If you think about different medical care doctors you have had, there may be some who had a great "bedside manner" compared to others who did not. Those who you liked may have shared a bit about themselves, leaned in when they talked to you, asked you questions that appeared to go beyond your "presenting problem," or had other characteristics that you noticed. Two different providers can be providing the same "intervention," but their styles may be quite different; these examples represent one interpretation of the use of self.

Another way of defining use of self is derived from the theoretical orientation that is used by the social worker. Different models of intervention in micro, mezzo, and macro social work as well as different modalities of treatment (i.e., individual, group, or family interventions) describe the role or stance of a social worker in those contexts. We discuss more about how different theories inform our work with clients in Chapter 11. For now, it is important to know that, depending on which theory you are using to help inform your work with a client, theory may guide you to be slightly different with the client than if you were using a different theory. For example, let us compare two different individual models. One might have you focus more on your reactions to the client and what those reactions tell you about the client and then purposefully and with careful intent articulate to the client those reactions to help facilitate change. Another model might have you be more of a coach to the client, with your focus on teaching skills. Using this model, your reactions to the client are irrelevant to the skill-building focus and would not be shared at any time with the client. Each of those stances asks something different of the worker. These differences are driven primarily by the underlying assumptions of the model and what is assumed will facilitate change.

For us, the phrase *use of self* is a combination of both of these definitions. Social workers need to attend to, notice, and use their personalities to engage with clients. As social workers evolve professionally, their own styles and comfort levels with what they bring to the relationship with clients grow and change (Schneider & Grady, 2015). Good supervision can be a useful tool in helping newer social workers reflect on how their own styles have an impact on all clients as well as with certain subgroups. This topic is covered in more detail in Chapter 16. In addition, social workers need to be aware of the assumptions of the model they are using and how those assumptions lead to a particular stance or style of working with clients. Both of these definitions or descriptions of the use of self are essential for workers to attend to in their work.

SELF-AWARENESS

A key factor in the ability to purposefully use ourselves with clients is our own level of self-awareness. One of the most critical aspects needed for a competent social worker is being self-aware. If we are unaware of how we come across to others, such as how our sense of humor can be "off-putting," our discomfort with eye contact, or the tone of our voice, then we will not be cognizant of how those personality styles or traits are affecting our clients. We also need to know our own triggers for when we might be upset or offended or when we might be more likely to cross a boundary with a client. We need to be aware of which clients we are more likely to avoid versus those we eagerly seek out. We need to think about what we gain by doing this kind of work with clients and what toll it might be taking on us. Without self-awareness, we can make professional judgment errors that can have lasting consequences, both for ourselves and for our clients (Safran, 2011).

There are many ways to gain self-awareness. Some social workers have advocated for all students studying for the master's in social work to participate in therapy (Mackey & Mackey, 1993) as a way to have future workers gain some insight regarding who they are and what their vulnerabilities are as well as their strengths. However, requiring social work students to attend therapy has garnered criticisms, including the associated costs and that some students may identify a preference for a path to self-awareness (Mackey & Mackey, 1993). Other methods to increase self-awareness besides therapy include journaling, spiritual guidance or counseling, use of supervision, or personal relationships. We are not advocating for any one particular pathway. What we are advocating is for every reader to find an ongoing useful method that enhances their own self-awareness so that the clients are receiving care from social workers who use themselves in a professional, cognizant, and intentional way.

SELF-DISCLOSURE

Also tied to use of self is the use of self-disclosure with clients (Burkard, Knox, Groen, Perez, & Hess, 2006; Dewane, 2006; Edwards & Bess, 1998; Katz, 2003; Schneider & Grady, 2015). Self-disclosure can take many forms. The most commonly thought of form is the worker sharing some type of information about him- or herself with the client (Burkard et al., 2006; Dewane, 2006; Edwards & Bess, 1998; Katz, 2003; Schneider & Grady, 2015). However, as we discussed previously in this chapter, self-disclosure can also take the form of the jewelry or tattoos that a worker shows. In this section, we focus on the first type of self-disclosure. This focus is not to dismiss the importance of being thoughtful about what you wear on your body or other forms of self-disclosure, such as the car you drive or the bag you carry. We encourage all readers to be cognizant of what messages are being sent to clients and colleagues by how we present ourselves. In our work with students and recent graduates, we have found the most challenging aspects of self-disclosure tend to be centered on information that they are being asked to or choose to share about themselves. Therefore, we have chosen to focus on this aspect of self-disclosure.

What appears to be most challenging in our experience is that in most every other relationship (professional or personal) a way to connect with another person is to relate something about ourselves to the other. For example, when meeting someone who is from a different part of the country, it is common to reflect on your own experiences, or lack thereof, and enter into a dialogue about these experiences in relation to the others'. Or, if someone is frustrated with a colleague, it is socially acceptable to share a similar story to demonstrate to the other that you can relate because of a similar experience. While both of these scenarios may be focused on relatively mild topics, there are three important points we want to make regarding why these seemingly innocuous approaches may not be appropriate in a professional social work context.

First, by talking about yourself, you are taking the focus off the client. The social worker is not and should not be the focus of the work; the client is the focus of the work—always. We are there to connect, engage, and empathize. We are not there to be friends or to have a conversation that implies mutuality. While you want to do as much as you can to eliminate the power differential that will inevitably exist between you and your client, this relationship is not mutual as only one person's needs in the room should be addressed, and those are not the worker's.

The second point is that by disclosing some information about yourself, it can potentially set up an expectation by the client that you will share more. If you answer one question and then refuse to answer another, the client may wonder: What has changed? What is it about the current question that you are uncomfortable sharing? This line of thinking again shifts the focus away from the client and to you, shifting the direction of inquiry to the worker rather than to the client.

Finally, it is important to consider that once that information is shared, you cannot take it back. There is a confidentiality agreement often made between you and the client, but *this agreement is one directional.* You, as the worker, cannot disclose information about your client, but there is no rule that the client cannot share what you have said to others. We have had colleagues, for example, who discovered that information the worker had chosen to share with the client ended up on a blog that the client had written. Other colleagues and clients saw the blog and now that information about the worker was on the Internet, able to be found with a simple Google search.

We are not trying to state that social workers should *never* disclose any information. Social workers often do share information. In some settings, there is more of an expectation that information will be shared (such as your religious faith if you are part of a faith-based center). It is also more common in some cultures to share information about yourself, especially if two individuals are from the same culture. However, any information that is shared should be done purposefully, thoughtfully, and *always in the service of the client.* It is important to be thoughtful about what impact a piece of information has on the clients themselves, as well as the work itself. Without knowing why the client wants to know the information or how your sharing the information will further the work, disclosing information could be potentially damaging. A phrase that you will hear throughout this book to help you think through your choices is: Why are you doing this particular thing with this particular client at this particular time? If you cannot clearly identify the reason, then it is likely a good idea to pause and reflect some more in supervision. When it doubt, don't!

I (M.D.G.) was in a peer supervision group several years ago when a colleague was describing an encounter she recently had with a new client. (I have received permission to share this story in the book, but her name and the name of the client are withheld for confidentiality reasons.) The client came to see her about receiving therapy as she was struggling with issues concerning infertility and was looking for some help to manage her grief and other feelings. She was interviewing several different therapists in the area (which is common and we both encourage it), and the client was asking each therapist about whether they had children. My colleague was the only one who chose not to answer the question. She explored with the potential client what she hoped to gain from having that information, how it would affect her knowing that a therapist did or did not have children, how she felt it would enhance the work together, among other questions. The client was shocked that she did not respond, experienced it as odd and withholding, and left angry. Much to my colleague's surprise, this client returned to her and asked to start treatment with her. What the client realized was that, based on what she had learned about the other therapists' parental status, she was spending much of her energy and thoughts on what she imagined was going on in the lives of those other therapists. With my colleague, however, because she did not know the parental status, the work felt more about her and not about her fantasies about the therapist.

We think this example is a powerful one in helping to understand how a piece of information once shared can have a profound impact on the client. Therefore, self-disclosure should only be done after thoughtful consideration. Again, our rule is "when in doubt, don't."

There are ample ways to buy time so that you can think more about a question, possibly consult with a supervisor, and then return to the client with a thoughtful response. Some useful phrases are the following:

- Tell me what would be helpful to you if you knew this information?
- I hear that this piece of information is something that you want to know. Before answering your question, I would like to think more about it and get back to you the next time I see you.
- Can you tell me a bit more about how knowing this information would help you?

It can be common for clients to ask you about your own personal experiences related to something they have gone through themselves, such as substance abuse or sexual abuse. Often, in those situations they want to know if you will "get it." Will you understand their experience? However, what is always important to remember is that even if you have had "on paper" the same type of background or history, this apparent similarity in no way can be assumed to be the same experience. This statement can also be said for people who come from the same family who have lived through the same event. If you think about your own family and a critical event that occurred in your family, your *experience* of that event and your reactions to and memories of it will most likely be different from your other family members'. Therefore, we encourage you not to disclose whether you have or have not had a similar background because your story is in many ways irrelevant for understanding what that event or life story meant to your clients or what significance it plays in their current life. In some cases, when clients know that the practitioner had a similar experience, the clients may begin to have feelings of pressure or even a sense of failure as they compare their lives to yours. Of course, these comparisons are based on their own assumptions and perceptions, which may or may not be accurate. Regardless of their accuracy, the focus again shifts away from them to the social worker.

Your experience can inform your questions and possibly help you to be more empathic, but it is always important to keep in mind that your job is to understand *the clients'* experience so that you help them in the best way possible. How you use your own history to inform your work is a critical piece of the concept of use of self and one that will evolve over time as you develop as a social worker (Schneider & Grady, 2015).

ROLE OF THE WORKER

One final aspect of the use of self is the role you have with your client. Social workers have many different roles with clients, including advocates, brokers of services, clinicians, investigators, supervisors, hospice or medical discharge planners, intake/triage workers, community organizers, and many more. We expand on the role of the worker in Chapter 4. However, here we want to emphasize that with each of these roles comes a different set of expectations as well as ways that we use ourselves. For example, if you are only going to be working with a client one time as a triage/intake worker, your goal is to focus on getting the information that will most help you identify the needs of the client so you can determine the most appropriate type of service for that client. In contrast, if you are working in a clinical role with the client, you may be more focused on building a relationship rather than being as purposeful in fact gathering on the first service.

In both of these scenarios, it is essential that social workers conduct themselves in a professional manner and use their personality in ways that help make the clients feel at ease and comfortable. However, the pacing of the time with the client, the types of questions that are asked and even details like whether you are in front of a computer or holding a clipboard are all aspects of how the worker presents and uses him- or herself.

Given the variety of roles that social workers can play, it is essential that workers who are new to an agency or to a position within the agency ask supervisors and other colleagues about their styles in engaging with clients. How do they engage with clients given their roles? Can they give some examples of times an interaction with a client was tricky? What happened? How did they handle it? Depending on the role those individuals have with clients, they will respond differently. Therefore, it is important that workers new to that setting have a clear understanding of the expectations, scope, and limitations of their roles.

THE IMPACT OF THE WORK ON THE SOCIAL WORKER

> Milton Erickson used to say to his patients, "My voice will go with you." His voice did. What he did not say was that our clients' voices can also go with us. Their stories become part of us—part of our daily lives and our nightly dreams. Not all stories are negative—indeed, a good many are inspiring. The point is that they change us.
>
> Mahoney, 2003, p. 195

The work that you will do as a social worker will have an impact on you in profound ways. We hope and have every expectation that the work will have mainly positive impacts as you grow and develop as a professional. However, both of us have worked a significant amount in settings and with clients where trauma or other profoundly painful events have affected clients. We have experienced changes in our own lives as a result of this work and believe it is essential for social workers to use their self-awareness to notice such changes and address them should they begin to negatively impact their ability to stay resilient and engaged in the work. For example, I (M.D.G.) have worked with adolescents who have sexually abused other children. At one time, I was facilitating a treatment group for female adolescents who were adjudicated for molesting children. In this group, four of the five girls had been babysitting at the time of their offense. As a result of this experience (and my other work with this population), I have always been particularly wary of babysitters with my own children. For example, I have always felt more comfortable with them going to a group care setting where there are multiple eyes rather than having a babysitter, which for me feels too scary. However, many of my friends have always preferred the nanny option as they feel their children are cared for in their homes and obtain more one-on-one attention. Of course, rationally I know that the vast majority of caregivers are safe and will not molest children. I know this statistically and factually. However, my experiences in the field have changed my perspective, and I behave differently as a result.

COMPASSION FATIGUE

It is important for social workers and other professionals to pay attention to the different reactions that they might experience in the field. There is a large body of literature that describes the various ways that practitioners may react when working in challenging settings. We provide more information in the Resource Guide as we do not do justice here to the literature and resources on this topic. This chapter focuses on the concept of compassion fatigue (CF), which is a phrase used to capture the toll that the work can take on the worker (Figley, 1999). CF can be seen as the strain experienced by the therapist to remain empathic and connected to clients who are relating their traumatic stories.

There are many ways that a social worker can begin to experience CF. For some practitioners, hearing the stories of their clients can shift their perspective, as I (M.D.G.) described previously in this chapter regarding my own practice experiences. This shifting is referred to as *vicarious trauma* (VT) and refers to a shift that can occur when practitioners have repeated exposure to "clients' traumatic experiences [that can] cause a shift in the way that trauma counselors perceive themselves, others and the world" (Trippany, Kress, & Wilcoxon, 2004, p. 31). In other words, as you begin to hear the stories of your clients, your views of the world change (McCann & Perlmann, 1990). Maybe you feel less safe or maybe you feel guilty with your increased awareness of privilege or maybe you become more cynical about the level of humanity in the world.

Another path toward CF is when a practitioner has experienced secondary traumatic stress (STS). For those who experience STS, their symptoms or reactions closely resemble those who have experienced the trauma firsthand. These symptoms or reactions are similar to those who have shown signs of post-traumatic stress syndrome, which might include jumpiness, hyperawareness or hypervigilance of their surroundings, flashbacks, difficulties sleeping, or intrusive memories or dreams (Figley, 1999). The changes as a result of VT are primarily focused on the cognitions of the worker, whereas STS reactions mimic trauma reactions and the biological and psychological symptoms of having been exposed to trauma via their clients.

BURNOUT

Compassion fatigue can then be the result of the worker's experience with either VT or STS, leading to a high level of fatigue and struggles to remain present with clients. Many individuals are familiar with the term *burnout*. It is often used to describe someone who appears not to care anymore about their job, does not seem engaged, and is cynical or apathetic at best regarding what happens as a result of their work. This view of burnout is similar in those who are in helping professions and is seen to be "a result of the general psychological stress of working with difficult clients versus having a traumatic reaction to a specific client-presented information" (Trippany et al., 2004, pp. 31–32), such as can occur with VT and STS. Also, burnout generally happens gradually, whereas VT and STS can have a sudden and acute onset. Burnout also does not tend to have the changes associated with VT, such as changes in trust or intrusive memories, yet it is possible that burnout can result from VT and STS. Burnout can be the result of the ongoing stress involved in helping those in challenging situations, which is often paired with feeling hopeless or helpless to do more.

COMPASSION SATISFACTION

What is also important to remember is that there are also some positive outcomes that come from this work. Compassion satisfaction (CS) refers to the positive experiences of being in a helper role (Stamm, 2002). If working with people who have had traumatic experiences or major life difficulties was so hard *all* the time, no one would do it. There is a sense of reward or accomplishment that comes with serving those in need. What draws us to social work or other helping professions is a desire to see people overcome obstacles or transcend traumatic experiences, or to help communities reach their potential. Caring brings a level of satisfaction from these experiences, and helping others carries rewards that serve as protective factors against CF (Stamm, 2002). CS is the reason we keep doing our jobs, even when it is hard or overwhelming, because we see growth, healing, recovery, and success in our clients.

THE IMPORTANCE OF SELF-ASSESSMENT

By now, you are probably catching on that a critical theme throughout this chapter is the need for self-awareness, which includes an awareness of how we affect clients and how the work directly affects us. Just as with the other areas we have discussed previously, it is important for workers to have self-awareness regarding how the work may be having an impact on us in our professional lives as well as how those reactions spill into our personal lives. Conducting self-assessment concerning how your work is affecting your professional and personal lives should take place on an ongoing basis, even when you feel "fine." Using standardized tools or checking in with colleagues and supervisors about your work should be integrated regularly into your professional life. In settings where supervision is not the place to address the impact of the work, think about finding a "self-care buddy" with whom you can meet regularly and talk to about ways to take care of yourself in the work. To help you get started, the Resource Guide at the end of the chapter lists some useful resources for assessing yourself and where you can find more information on these topics.

WAYS TO SUPPORT SELF

Remaining resilient in this work requires daily attention to self-care. If you wait until your vacation or until you have enough money for a spa day, it will be too late. Daily attention

TABLE 2.2: General Guidelines for Protecting Self Against VT, STS, Burnout, and CF

- Remember that treating trauma patients is not for everyone.
- The issue is managing VT rather than totally avoiding it.
- Emphasis should be on early identification and treatment, reducing the long-term negative impact of VT.
- Interventions need to be multilevel and should not be left up to the individual.
- A psychotherapist or helper should not feel ashamed or guilty about experiencing VT.
- The attitude should be on validating and normalizing such reactions.
- Reframe VT as a sign of being a committed and a sensitive therapist.
- Nurture awareness, balance, and connections.

Source: Adapted from Meichenbaum (2006).

to what may seem obvious—eating regular meals, sleeping well each night, and leaving work on time—is important as a first step. Each person will need to find personal strategies to help prevent or minimize these potential negative reactions to the work with clients. There is no one way. However, Table 2.2 offers some guidelines from Meichenbaum (2008) that we have adapted regarding his discussion of VT.

Also, we encourage social workers to consider the importance of looking at multiple levels of their work. Implementing a multilevel self-care model is one way of accomplishing this goal (Dombo & Gray, 2013). This model requires looking at self-care on all levels: individual, departmental, and organizational. In this model, self-care is not only the worker's issue or responsibility but also the responsibility of every member of the organizational system. In this multilevel model, organizational leadership is responsible for exploring how the environmental factors play a role in worker health, program directors and supervisors explore ways team meetings and other group forums can be used to normalize the effects of the work and provide education and support, and finally the worker is provided with education and tools to address the individual experiences of CF or VT (Dombo & Gray, 2013).

ENDING ON AN UPLIFTING NOTE

While we have just described a number of potential challenges that can arise from your work as a helping professional, we want to end this chapter with some words of encouragement. As practitioners, we have found that we are inspired, awed, amazed, and profoundly moved by our work. We have found this work to be challenging emotionally and intellectually, and through these experiences, we have grown personally and professionally. Neither of us can imagine any other career where we would have the privilege of hearing someone's story, being part of their journey of reaching whatever goal that they may have, and seeing changes occur in all levels of society as a result of social work efforts.

We truly believe that social work's perspective of valuing the complexities of our clients' lives does have the risk of being overwhelming, as our profession considers poverty and issues of social justice that have an impact on our clients along with mental health and family dynamics. Yet, because social work attends to these multi-level issues, we are trained to and can intervene in multiple arenas in our society. We are not limited to any one level (micro, mezzo, or macro) of social work practice. This unique perspective of social work is a perfect way to remain balanced in our professional lives. We can work one-on-one with clients and then also think about systemic issues and work with teams to create those changes. As a result of this diversity of roles and ways to intervene, not only can social workers diversify their work to remain fresh and invigorated, but also this diversity provides opportunities for us to make changes in a multitude of ways.

We are excited that you have chosen social work as your profession. We hope that by thinking through some of these issues before you start your professional career or near its beginning, you will have the opportunity to be as prepared as possible so that you have a long and fulfilling career as a social worker. It is a rewarding profession, and we hope that you will gain as much from it as we have.

CHAPTER 2 RESOURCE GUIDE: ASSESSING YOUR SELF-CARE (RICHARDSON, 2001)

This self-care assessment is designed to measure how well you are balancing your own needs with the needs of those you serve. It is recommended you reassess yourself on a regular basis and use the results to adapt your self-care plan as needed. It is designed to be used as a tool to help you gain **AWARENESS** about your own needs and limitations, maintain **BALANCE** between your work self and personal self, and deepen your **CONNECTION** to this work.

Use the following scale to rate the frequency with which you engage in these self-care activities:

5 = Frequently
4 = Occasionally
3 = Rarely
2 = Never
1 = It never occurred to me to do this!!

A. PHYSICAL SELF-CARE

_____Eat regular meals
_____Eat healthy foods
_____Exercise
_____Get regular medical care
_____Take time off when sick
_____Get massages
_____Do fun physical activities
_____Take time to be sexual

_____Get enough sleep
_____Wear clothes you like
_____Take vacations or day trips
_____Get away from telephones
_____Other:_____

B. PSYCHOLOGICAL SELF-CARE

_____Make time for self-reflection
_____Engage in your own therapy
_____Journal
_____Read about topics unrelated to work
_____Try not to be in charge
_____Decrease stressful experiences
_____Listen to your inner experiences
_____Let others see different aspects of you
_____Practice receiving from others
_____Be curious
_____Say no to extra responsibilities
_____Other:_____

C. EMOTIONAL SELF-CARE

_____Spend time with those whose company you enjoy
_____Stay in touch with old friends
_____Give yourself affirmations and praise
_____Love yourself
_____Revisit favorite books and movies
_____Identify comforting things
_____Allow yourself to cry
_____Find things to make you laugh
_____Express your outrage via social action
_____Play with children
_____Other:_____

D. SPIRITUAL SELF-CARE

_____Spend time in nature
_____Connect with a spiritual community
_____Be open to inspiration and hope
_____Connect to the nonmaterial
_____Be present, not the presenter

_____Identify what has meaning for you
_____Meditate/pray/sing
_____Spend time with children or animals
_____Have experiences of awe
_____Contribute to causes you believe in
_____Read literature that inspires you
_____Other:_____

E. WORKPLACE AND PROFESSIONAL SELF-CARE

_____Schedule breaks in your workday
_____Take time to chat with colleagues
_____Make quiet time to complete work
_____Identify projects that are rewarding
_____Set limits with clients and colleagues
_____Balance work/caseload
_____Arrange a comforting workspace
_____Get regular supervision
_____Negotiate your needs
_____Have a peer support group
_____Develop nontrauma areas of professional interest
_____Other:_____

A SPIRITUAL PRACTICE OF MEDITATION FOR ADDRESSING VICARIOUS TRAUMA

By infusing spiritual practices into one's self-care, the social worker can address the reactions to the work in a simple, portable, and inexpensive way. This process focuses on taking off what has been taken in from your time with the client. It is a three-step process, using meditation, to let go of or not take on the reactions to the client's pain and suffering. It can be done briefly between appointments to be ready for your next client or in a longer meditation after the day is done. We have developed this specific meditation based on the loving kindness meditation practices used by many meditation teachers.

Practice 1 addresses compassion for self as "helper" in trauma work. As the clinician becomes the vehicle for client healing, he or she must use mindfulness as a relational concept, where the clinician models self-compassion through personal practice and behaviors. Practice 2 surfaces reactions to what the client brought up in session or the clinician's reactions to the client. It provides an opportunity to cleanse the mind and emotions from the interaction. Practice 3 addresses the clinician's own issues that surface through trauma work. Using this meditation, one can focus on letting go of ego attachments to the role of "helper" or status in the community. It helps one let go of resentments held from feeling "put upon" by others' pain and suffering. This enables clearer focus on what is gained from helping trauma survivors, how the work is purposefully and mindfully engaging. Created using breathing meditation (Salzberg, 2011b) and adapted from the Buddhist practice of loving kindness meditation (metta), the meditation we offer for addressing VT is as follows:

Find a calm place, without distractions. This can be a certain chair, or a corner of a room. Sit comfortably. At first, simply observe the breath. Notice it going up and down, in and out. Take a few cleansing breaths. Notice "I am breathing in"; "I am breathing out."

After a minute or two, slowly say the first phrase of the compassion meditation to yourself. Do this on an "in breath." Breathe in and out contemplating the phrase. You may want to repeat it.

After several breaths focused on the first phrase, continue on to the next phrase of the compassion meditation. In a similar manner, slowly say each phrase of each practice. As you end the practices, take a few cleansing breaths to end the meditation.

Practice 1: Compassion meditation.
"May I be gentle with myself in my work."
"May I be attuned to those I help."
"May I forgive the imperfect nature of my work."

Practice 2: Letting go meditation.
"May I let go of my client's pain."
"May my client know peace."
"May I let go of my reactions to my client's pain."

Practice 3: Reflection mediation.
"May I heal from my own pain and suffering."
"May I give thanks for being able to do this work."
"May I transcend my ego attachment to my role/my client's progress."

Excerpted from "Engaging Spirituality in Addressing Vicarious Trauma in Clinical Social Work: A Self-Care Model," by E. A. Dombo and C. Gray, 2013, *Social Work and Christianity*, 40(1), 89–104.

CHAPTER 3

CULTURAL AND IDENTITY ISSUES IN PRACTICE

In helping relationships, the differences between practitioners and clients are often the elephant in the room. This chapter addresses ways to bring these differences into the relationship in an effort to enhance the working alliance, build rapport, and deepen your understanding of your clients' lived experiences. We discuss how elements of difference and similarities can impede or enhance the work and offer some guidelines to help overcome these barriers. Practitioners are encouraged to honor difference, not make assumptions when either differences or similarities are noted, and learn about their clients through a stance of *not knowing*.

To operate from a stance of not knowing is to utilize the techniques and tools discussed in the assessment section related to ethnographic interviewing and to approach each client as a unique person with his or her own distinctive identity. This approach allows practitioners to engage in culturally competent work through curiosity about *clients'* unique lived experiences. The goal of the curiosity is to create the opportunity for clients to share the following with the practitioner: the clients' identity, experiences of oppression, and meaning made of these experiences.

INCREASING YOUR AWARENESS OF OPPRESSION AND POWER

To truly understand your clients' worlds, you need to gain a deeper understanding of their experiences of oppression and powerlessness and the potential impact of those experiences on all aspects of the bio-psycho-social-spiritual domains. Throughout the course of your professional education, you have probably heard the term *isms* (e.g., racism, sexism) used to describe the multiple dimensions of identity that form the basis of marginalization and discrimination (Corneau & Stergiopoulos, 2012). Virtually every dimension of a person's identity is subject to norm/other categorizations that leave some identities more privileged than others (Rosenblum & Travis, 2008). This idea sets forth the notion that there are identities that are considered the norm by mainstream culture; therefore, those are categorized as not the norm are considered different or other. If you reflect on the US culture, people in the norm categories are those who are Caucasian, male, Judeo-Christian, able bodied, mentally healthy, and so on. Therefore, those who fall in the other categories are people of color, women, people with physical disabilities, people with mental illnesses, and the like. Most of the individuals, families, and communities with whom you will work experience multiple forms of oppression and marginalization based on race, ethnicity, socioeconomic status, religion, gender expression, sexual orientation, age, disability, mental illness, and other dimensions of identity. A crucial aspect of how we work with our clients is our own self-awareness regarding power and how we view and value difference (Schmitz, Stakeman, & Sisneros, 2001; Spencer, 2008; E. Williams & Barber, 2004).

OPPRESSION

One way to think about the experience of oppression is to think about freedom. Is the client able to act out of free will, or are restrictions placed on the client due to some dimension of the client's identity? Is the client able to accomplish the personal goals he or she has set out, or are their seemingly insurmountable obstacles in the way? Oppression limits a person's ability to act freely by closing certain options to them (Dybicz, 2010).

For example, imagine you are working with a client named Joe who is a 34-year-old man from Nicaragua. He immigrated to this country when he was in his teens and was later diagnosed with schizophrenia. Joe has been living in a halfway house since being released from prison. His previous arrest was for assault with a deadly weapon while under the influence of drugs and alcohol. He is attending Narcotics Anonymous (NA) meetings to try to stay clean and is striving to adhere to his medication regimen to manage the symptoms of his mental illness. Your job is to help Joe find a job and housing. Joe has been on several interviews but has not been selected for a job. In the interviews, he has been asked if he has "papers" to prove he is in this country legally, has been told that his English is not good enough for the job, and has been asked questions about his criminal background and mental health status that revealed that the interviewer was not comfortable with Joe. On multiple occasions, you have found an apartment for him, but when he showed up to look at it, the landlord told him that the apartment was no longer available.

One way to look at Joe's inability to find a job and a place to live is to explore what he does in the interviews and give him skills to improve. Another way to look at it is through the lens of oppression. Is Joe being discriminated against because of some aspects of his background and identity? To help Joe, it will be important to explore how these experiences feel to him and the meaning that he is making of them. If we focus solely on enhancing his functioning and performance in job interviews, we miss the larger sociocultural experience of discrimination. When we are able to help Joe see that he is not "failing" in these tasks but rather the lack of success is due to discrimination, the formulation of the problem shifts.

Rather than viewing the lack of success as a personal failure, you see that discrimination is infused in the societal structures related to employment and housing. This shift in understanding creates a counterstory to explain what is happening (Dybicz, 2010). The narrative shifts from being a problem with Joe to a societal problem. While this understanding does not help Joe get the job or the apartment on a particular day, it does show Joe that you do not blame him for not reaching these goals. In addition, you can communicate that you and he will plan together to shift the focus of your work to overcome these obstacles. It puts you and Joe on the same team: squaring off against oppression and discrimination.

POWER

Power is another force in our society that, while often invisible, has a strong influence on our lives. Most students and novice practitioners do not feel as if they have much power in their work settings. More likely, in your setting, you feel more like the *least* powerful person there. However, to your client, you have a great deal of power. You have power by virtue of your role, knowledge, and access to resources. Although it may be hard for you to believe that you do in fact have this power, we encourage you to think about times when you have gone to a provider, anyone from a mechanic to a physician, for a service. In these cases, you are often dependent on the other for knowledge of the problem, the solutions and skills for resolving it, and information about how much the service will cost. The provider holds the power to help you or not, as well as to tell you how much such help will cost.

One of the reasons we love our profession is that we recognize the existence of power within the helping relationship. In addition, we work hard to simultaneously minimize the power imbalance while using our power (i.e., knowledge, skills, resources) to help clients achieve their goals. To assist in this process, we recommend that you have a direct discussion with your client about power and oppression in the life of the client, as well as in the working relationship, which will open honest discussion about ways to work together (E. Williams & Barber, 2004).

ADDRESSING ISSUES OF OPPRESSION AND POWER IN PRACTICE

When initiating a helping relationship, it is important to place the awareness of the experience of oppression and power front and center in your mind and include a desire to understand through the lens of the client. This awareness relates directly to our ability to work competently across cultures because "cultural interaction is a fluid process that is dynamic" (Lee, 2011, p. 190). When we use the term *culture*, we refer to a range of identities, recognizing that families, communities, individuals who share a particular identity, and other groups have their own sense of a culture. Simultaneously, we must always keep in mind that each individual within that group has an experience that is unique to him or her and may be outside any perceived norm for that group. Therefore, it is essential in our work that we consistently seek to understand the individual's experiences and perceptions rather than impose our own.

This understanding of the clients' experiences develops and evolves over time as we communicate our desire to understand them more fully. It also comes through a greater level of trust as clients opt to share more with us. We cannot emphasize enough that while you may have received information about the experiences of a certain population from journals, books, movies, or other sources, keep in mind that the client will have his or her own personal experience that is unique. If you attempt to show that you "understand" based on your academic learning or stereotypes you hold rather than communicate that you truly want to understand the *clients' lived experience*, you risk alienating them.

Often, what prevents us from truly understanding our clients is the reality of being in a subjective state in cross-cultural work. The client is an "ethnic stranger" to us, and this causes anxieties and discomforts that can lead to problems forming a strong working alliance to reach the client's goals. How we feel about clients is informed by our

- Culturally based life values (influenced by our culture)
- Theoretical beliefs and practices (shaped by academic training)
- Emotionally charged prejudices (rooted in personal experiences)
- Biases about own ethnic identity (shaped by family of origin and personal experiences) (Perez Foster, 1999)

Our self-awareness about these factors allows us to see when they are getting in the way of the work. When we can take the perspective of those we are working with, we are less likely to act out of our own biases (Yoon, Moulton, Jeremie-Brink, & Hansen, 2012).

You will frequently be working with clients from other cultures who do not understand how people with power in the dominant groups view their behaviors. By using the AWARE model, you can bridge cross-cultural work:

Accept the other person's behavior without judging it against your culture
Wonder what the behavior means in their culture
Ask what it means to the person, showing respectful interest
Research and read about the culture
Explain what the behavior means in your culture and give examples so the person can learn new behaviors that will help the person function in your culture

Returning to the discussion of Joe, perhaps you could use the AWARE model to explore how his behavior in the job interviews and visits to apartments to rent is interpreted in this culture. You can provide the opportunity for Joe to explore how his behavior has meaning in his culture that does not come across in that way in this culture. In working cross culturally with Joe, you have an opportunity to honor his culture and help him strategize for success.

HONORING DIFFERENT VALUE SYSTEMS

In our everyday life, we encounter people who have different beliefs and values from our own, so it makes sense that this is true in our role of helping others as well. Our reactions to these occurrences in our professional experiences must be guided by the social work principle of *starting where the client is*. We have to remember to place the client's world-view front and center, not our own (Blow, Davis, & Sprenkle, 2012). Our value systems come from our identity, which is influenced by culture, community, social group, religious teachings, family, and other sources. These values often guide our decisions and behaviors, and when we act in opposition to them, it often causes feelings of shame or guilt (Schmitz et al., 2001).

We all carry biases. Expecting that you will be bias free is unrealistic. What is expected is that you will value the belief system of your client and not impose your own beliefs on the client (Smith, Li, Dykema, Hamlet, & Shellman, 2013; Walker & Staton, 2000; D. Williams & Levitt, 2008). For example, imagine you are working with a single mother grappling with no financial resources. She tells you that, even though she lacks any form of financial support from the father of her children and is having trouble putting food on the table, she feels strongly that she should not work so she can be at home with her children. You may hold a bias that women should work to support their families and therefore judge the client for not putting forth the goal of finding a job as part of her work with you. What you come to find is that the client places great value on staying home to raise her children and being home for them when they need her. This value is rooted in her childhood experiences as a latchkey kid and feeling that her mother was never there when she needed her. If you attempt to impose your own belief regarding work onto her, your bias will most likely create a rupture in the working alliance (Safran, 2000), and you will be devaluing the (unpaid) work she is doing in raising her children. Instead, you could honor her value system by cocreating a goal with her to address family finances and means of financial support.

Clients will often make choices or set goals that go against your values and beliefs. We have had many conversations with supervisees and students about these practice situations. We have had these feelings myself as well. The task is to separate out what "I" would do from what "the client," using their values and self-determination, must do to be true to their value system. Should your client leave his or her marriage or stay for the children? Do your client's religious beliefs influence what the client is and is not willing to do to address family planning or fertility issues? Does your adult client continuing to live at home derive from "failure to launch" or a practice that is culturally normal or even economically prudent? When you work with the client's values and beliefs, you will have a clearer answer.

WORKING WITH SIMILARITIES

Sometimes, it is not the experience of working with those different from us that is most challenging; working with people who share similar experiences, identities, cultures, and values presents its own difficulties. Some research explored the effectiveness of matching clients and workers based on identity similarities. This research generally showed that outcomes tended to be no different, or just marginally better, when there were similarities than when differences existed (Bryan, Dersch, Sterling, & Aredondo, 2004; Coleman, 2006; Erdur, Rude, & Baron, 2003; Farsimadan & Draghi-Lorenz, 2007; Hall, Guterman, Lee, & Little, 2002; Murphy, Faulkner, & Behrens, 2004; Taber, Leibert, & Agaskar, 2010; Zane et al., 2005). Working across similarities can create its own risks or problems.

First, we run the risk of assuming we "get" the client's experiences when we really do not. As mentioned, the client may not see you as similar to them. If you want to reassure the client that you understand them and their situation without directly exploring it, you will most likely have to say why it is you think you do.

Many of you may know what it is like to struggle financially, be a person of color, be a descendent of slaves, come out as gay, hold religious beliefs that are not widely held, experience neglect as a child, have a mental health diagnosis, or have many other lived experiences. Yet, those experiences are personal to you. If you then perceive your personal knowledge to be universal by assuming that you "know" what any of those experiences feel like, you may choose not to explore what those experiences were like for the client. When you assume you know, you shut down dialogue. When you act from the stance of not knowing, you are fully aware that you do not know. Also, remember that even if you think you have experienced the same form of oppression as your client, this is not a short-cut to understanding how it felt for him or her.

TO SELF-DISCLOSE OR NOT SELF-DISCLOSE—THAT IS THE QUESTION

Our desire to connect our own experiences to our clients' is understandable. It is also understandable that clients would want to know about us as well. In many other situations when we engage with people who have similar experiences, it is common to connect in relation to those similarities. These experiences can involve something that is seemingly benign, such as having visited the same geographic area, or they can be more personal, such as sharing the same cultural heritage. However, as we discussed in Chapter 2 on boundaries and self-disclosure, the relationship that we form with our clients is not a typical relationship, and our efforts to connect to them by sharing our stories can often shift the focus away from the client and on to us. In addition, the client may see the experiences as different from his or her own, begin to compare you to him- or herself, or have a range of other reactions; in the meantime, you may end up disclosing more information about yourself than is appropriate.

For example, when I (E.D.) worked at a rape crisis center, clients frequently asked how I could help them if I did not know what it was like to experience sexual violence. They would often directly ask if I had similar experiences to theirs. When I was new to the work, I was anxious about the many differences that existed regarding race, ethnicity, socioeconomic status, gender, religion, sexual orientation, age, and others. But, here was an experience that crossed all groups. My clients wanted to know how I thought I could help them if I did not know what it was like to be them? I decided to never directly answer that question. If I answered no, then I ran the risk of losing credibility; if I answered yes, then I ran the risk of invalidating their experience by creating an assumption that I knew what their experience was like. In reality, that question was not about similarity or difference, but about whether I knew how to help them. When I would ask, "What is it you really need to know about me to work with me?" the answer was typically, "I need to know that you understand what I am going through and can help me." The answer to that question was always yes.

We do not mean to imply that you can *never* share a lived experience with a client. If a client is traveling to or from a particular area where we have been, we can share our experiences of that place. If a client mentions his or her love of a type of food, then we can also discuss our feelings about that food. While these may appear to be silly examples, they are meant to illustrate that even as we are careful and intentional in this relationship, it is still a relationship. Being a complete "blank screen" or neutral to the point of having a nonpersonality is not helpful.

For example, in my (M.D.G.) work, I often use metaphors to help illustrate a point I am trying to make. Sometimes, sharing a common interest can help you use metaphors more effectively as it is a common language that you both "get." At one point, I had a client who participated in a similar hobby as I do. I found that sharing that I also participated in this hobby was helpful as I was able to use the hobby as a metaphor for some of the points we were discussing. I believe that the metaphors and "lessons learned" were more meaningful and had more credibility because the client knew that I understood that world.

In thinking about what to share, we encourage you to be intentional, purposeful, and deliberate about what you disclose regarding any similarities *and* differences that you perceive between yourself and the client. Part of this reflective process is to consider *very* carefully why you feel it would be helpful *to the client*. Whose needs are you serving? Remember our motto of self-disclosure—when in doubt, don't!

FINAL THOUGHTS ON IDENTITY AND DIFFERENCE

As you contemplate how you want to convey to your clients a desire to understand their lived experiences, including how experiences of oppression, power, and marginalization have had an impact on their lived experiences, remember a few key points:

- Be alert to social identity and norm/other differences.
- Seek to learn more about that which you do not know.
- Always assume your world is different from your client's.
- Realize you are not bias free.
- Know your own cultural lens and what you are likely to project on others.
- Identify and focus on the most salient cultural aspects at the moment.

- Gain knowledge of the dynamics of oppression, power, racism, discrimination, and stereotyping.
- Be open to learning from your client.
- Become comfortable with discussing difference, oppression, and power openly and honestly.

Also, be aware that the client–practitioner relationship will be marked by a variety of combinations of differences and similarities. In some cases, as the worker you will feel that the client has had more privileges and power than you, and this can make it difficult to own your role. Much of the writing about working across differences with clients assumes that the worker comes from privilege and the client from an oppressed or marginalized population. This may not be the case, so keep in mind that the experience of difference will vary based on the identities of client and practitioner.

CHAPTER 3 RESOURCE GUIDE

LINKS TO SELF-ASSESSMENTS AND ONGOING LEARNING TOOLS IN RELATION TO DIFFERENCE

Association of American Medical Colleges. (1995–2014). *Tool for assessing cultural competence training*. Retrieved from https://www.aamc.org/initiatives/tacct/

Harvard University. (2011). *Project Implicit*. Retrieved from https://implicit.harvard.edu/implicit/

Management Sciences for Health Organization and US Agency for International Development. (n.d.). *Quality and culture quiz*. Retrieved from http://erc.msh.org/mainpage.cfm?file=3.0.htm&module=provider&language=English

National Center for Cultural Competence. (n.d.). *Self-assessments*. Retrieved from http://nccc.georgetown.edu/resources/assessments.html

YOUR ROLE AND RELATIONSHIP WITH YOUR CLIENTS

In our opinion, one of the best parts of our profession is the number of roles social workers can hold as professionals. Social workers can be found virtually everywhere people are in need of support. They are in hospitals; schools; community mental health clinics; psychotherapy practices; jails; local, state, and federal government departments; community organizing agencies; spiritual communities; homeless shelters; and other places too numerous to count. Within each of these settings, social workers hold a number of different roles that influence their responsibilities to the agency and the clients. To describe each and every possible role a social worker can take in a professional career would be impossible. Therefore, this chapter was designed to have you think through some questions to help you better understand your role in your setting so you can be as effective as possible.

In addition, the role you have with your clients will influence the type of helping relationship that you may form with them. The social worker–client relationship is an important aspect of the helping partnership that you will create with your clients. This chapter also explores some of the critical elements that encompass an effective relationship as we keep in mind the role you and your agency play in lives of your clients.

SOCIAL WORK ROLES

As just stated, it would be impossible to adequately describe every possible social work position and its corresponding role and responsibilities within an organization. Yet, there are some broad categories often used to describe social workers' roles within agency settings. Hepworth, Rooney, Dewberry-Rooney, and Strom-Gottfried (2013) described broad categories of direct practice roles and the specific functions of those individuals within them (see Table 4.1).

It is important to note that some of these roles are perceived as more in line with social workers who work to create social change on a macro level. However, many social

TABLE 4.1: Social Work Roles

Role	General Description	Possible Position
Direct provision of services	Meet face to face with clients to provide services	• Individual caseworker or counselor • Couples and family therapist • Group work services provider • Educator/disseminator of information
System linkage roles	Link clients to people and other resources	• Broker—an intermediary who assists in connecting people with resources • Case manager/coordinator—assesses the needs of a client and arranges and coordinates the delivery of essential goods and services by other resources • Mediator/arbitrator—works to eliminate obstacles to service delivery • Client advocate—works with or on behalf of clients to obtain services and resources that would not otherwise be provided
System maintenance and enhancement	Evaluate structures, policies, and functional relationships within agencies that impair effectiveness in service delivery	• Organizational analyst—identifies factors in agency structure, policy, and procedures that have a negative impact on service delivery. • Facilitator/expediter—plans and implements ways of enhancing service delivery • Team member—contributes knowledge to an interdisciplinary team • Consultant/consultee—provides expertise on a particular topic as a consultant; assumes a consultee role when expert knowledge from another is needed • Supervisor—assists staff in linking assessment with intervention plans and evaluation
Researcher/ research consumer	Select interventions that can be evaluated; evaluate the effectiveness of their interventions; and systematically monitor the progress of any intervention	• Researcher—evaluates effectiveness of an intervention • Research consumer—uses research to select appropriate interventions
System development	Improve or expand agency services based on assessments and research	• Program developer—develops services in response to emerging needs of clients • Planner—works formally and informally with influential people to plan programs that respond to unmet and emerging needs • Policy and procedure developer—formulates and modifies policies within agencies that primarily serve clients • Advocate—joins client groups, other social workers, and professionals in advocating for legislation and social policies aimed at providing needed resources and enhancing social justice

Note: Adapted from *Direct Social Work Practice: Theory and Skills* (9th ed.), D. H. Hepworth, R. H Rooney, G. Dewberry-Rooney, and K. Strom-Gottfried, 2013, Brooks-Cole, Belmont, CA, pp. 30–34.

workers, regardless of their identified role, may work in multiple systems and hold multiple roles. It is for this reason that some authors have referred to the functions of social workers rather than to a designated role, as many of these functions cut across different roles within any one agency (Gambrill, 2013). According to Gambrill, the major functions of social work include "1) relief from psychological distress and material need; 2) social control (e.g. maintaining social order and regulating the labor market); and 3) social reform (altering the conditions related to the psychological distress and material need)" (p. 8). What Gambrill meant by social control is "encouraging adherence to social norms and minimizing, eliminating, or normalizing deviant behavior" (p. 8). She provided many examples of formal functions of social controls, such as laws, public health regulations, and institutions that are concerned with social control, such as educational, criminal justice, and social welfare agencies. Each of these functions can be carried out within multiple roles that social workers hold within their own agencies or organizations and may at times appear to be in conflict with each other. Therefore, while we have presented different categories of roles here, it is important to remember that social workers may be responsible for many different functions even within one described role.

WHY IT MATTERS

Given this range of possibilities, you may be asking yourself why it matters so much to define your role when it may change moment to moment. There are actually multiple reasons why you need clarity regarding your role.

The first reason is that being clear about your role *protects you personally and professionally.* This clarity increases the likelihood that you will be successful in your position as you gain a solid set of skills and knowledge that are specific to your position. Being clear also increases the likelihood that you will not cross boundaries with clients by making promises you cannot keep or set up unrealistic expectations that you and your agency cannot meet. Many of these potential situations may seem obvious (e.g., providing individual therapy where you ask personal questions to a client versus when your role is limited to gathering demographic information for a form), yet many of them are less obvious. For example, less experienced social workers may feel that given their therapeutic role with a client, it makes sense to be the one to investigate an accusation of sexual abuse rather than referring the client to someone in a forensic role. However, an investigator has different responsibilities than a therapist. If you are seen as unable to stay within your role, you could set yourself up for ethical or legal violations that jeopardize your ability to continue to practice.

The second reason to be clear about your role is that it is protective to the clients. Many clients have lives that are chaotic and unclear. It is important to be clear and consistent with them regarding what you can and cannot do for them. This clarity provides a sense of predictability that is important for safety and security in a relationship. It is helpful to be clear up front so that the boundaries of your role are clear, ensuring that their expectations of you are in line with your role.

The final reason for you to be clear about your role is for the benefit of your colleagues and organization. If you think about any agency as a beehive, everyone has a job to do and if everyone does his or her job, the beehive works well. When different people begin to duplicate the work of others, not only is this style of working inefficient, but also it can create tension and frustration among those who work together. An attempt to be "helpful" by taking on the role of another colleague could be interpreted as a lack of trust in that person to do his or her job or that you believe you can do it better. These interpretations can lead to multiple conflicts and challenges within the workplace. As mentioned, when multiple individuals carry the same duties, there can be a great deal of inefficiency that occurs. Therefore, it is important for the agency and your collegial relationships to be clear about what your specific contributions are to the organization.

We would like to put forward a caveat before moving on to the next section. We have both worked in organizations where employees became the "jack of all trades" out of necessity. There are many agencies where employees do a little bit of everything in order to keep the agency afloat. We are not saying that social workers should be rigid about any one role that they assume. It may be that the expectation *is* that each employee will take on multiple roles within one context. This phenomenon is actually common. Therefore, it is important whether you wear one hat or multiple hats in one setting to gain as much clarity as possible in identifying what your specific roles are within that setting.

HOW TO DEFINE YOUR ROLE WITHIN THE AGENCY

One of the best sources to start understanding your role within the agency is your supervisor. We cannot emphasize enough the importance of having clear conversations with your supervisor to help you clarify your responsibilities. For example, if one of your major responsibilities is program development (i.e., developing a new aftercare program at a school), then little of your time may be spent working with the children in the school in a therapeutic manner. The majority of the time with the students and their families may be focused on understanding what the needs and wishes are for this group so that you can design an effective and responsive program. If in the same setting, however, your responsibilities are to counsel the children, then you might spend much of your day in sessions with them either individually or in a group. Both of these roles are well within the purview of social work but require different knowledge bases and skill sets. Therefore, it will be important for you to gain clarity regarding your role so that you can utilize or develop the appropriate skills and knowledge needed for that role. Another reason to focus on your own role is to ensure the work is completed. If you spend much of your time outside your role doing other tasks, then the work that is your responsibility is not being done.

To be most effective in your position, we encourage you to ask your supervisor questions that will help to clarify these aspects of your role. The list that follows provides guiding questions that might help you in this conversation. These questions are meant as options and may feel slightly redundant because they are all designed to ultimately gather the same information. We provide here a range of options so that you can identify which ones feel more appropriate or more "your style" than others.

- What would a typical day look like for me?
- How would you describe my primary responsibilities?
- On what criteria will I be evaluated on any performance reviews?
- What specifically are you hoping I will accomplish by "X date"?
- What are the limits of my role? Is there anything I should *not* focus on in my position?
- What skills do you anticipate I will need the most to be successful in my position?
- What knowledge do you anticipate I will need the most to be successful in my position?
- Are there particular individuals within the agency who it might be useful for me to shadow or observe to better understand my role and responsibilities?
- How will I know if I am carrying out my role well?
- Are there particular outcomes of my work that you would like to see?
- Who will be giving me feedback about my roles and responsibilities?

THE SOCIAL WORKER–CLIENT RELATIONSHIP

The relationship that social workers form with their clients is a critical component in the change process (Hubble, Duncan, Miller, & Wampold, 2010; Teyber & McClure, 2011; Walsh, 2013; Wampold, 2010). Numerous studies over the last two decades have evaluated the impact of the practitioner–client relationship on outcomes with clients (Lambert & Barley, 2002; Walsh, 2013; Wampold, 2010; Weinberger & Rasco, 2007). The majority of these studies have concluded that two primary elements account for positive outcomes in direct practice more than anything else: "(a) the therapeutic alliance and (b) the practitioner's ongoing attention to the client's perspective about the intervention" (Miller, Duncan, & Hubble, as cited by Walsh, 2013, p. 7). Given these findings, it is critical for social workers to learn to develop relationships that will be effective in contributing to the change process.

THE DODO VERDICT

The importance of the alliance in relation to skills, resources, or tools that practitioners provide to their clients using specific models of intervention has long been debated (Weinberger & Rasco, 2007). The debate about the importance of particular techniques or models and their role in outcomes is often referred to as the "dodo verdict" (Duncan, 2010; Weinberger & Rasco, 2007). This phrase owes its origins to the story of *Alice in Wonderland* by Lewis Carroll (1865/1962), which presents a famous race among different animals. The animals scatter around the field, and at the end of the race the dodo bird asks, "Who has won?" Dodo Bird quickly responds, "Everybody has won, and all must have prizes." This story has been used as a metaphor in outcome research of different intervention models to explain the controversy between those who believe that there are specific and discrete approaches or models of intervention to address certain issues, otherwise known as empirically supported interventions (see Chapter 10), versus those who believe in what is known as the common factors (CFs) (Duncan, 2010).

This debate among practitioners from multiple disciplines stems from the CF research that indicated that the outcomes for different models of intervention are similar; in other words, no one model of intervention is superior to others (Duncan, 2010). To help understand this finding, researchers began decades ago to look across all of the different models and concluded that there must be "pantheoretical factors in operation that overshadow any perceived or presumed differences among approaches" (Duncan, 2010, p. 9). The idea with these pantheoretical or CFs is that different interventions work because of what they have in common, rather than what makes them different from each other (Weinberger & Rasco, 2007). There is now a large body of research to support these CFs and their important role in influencing the outcomes in direct practice.

COMMON FACTORS

The research on the CFs in client outcomes boils down to four primary domains. Past research on the CFs has listed the four domains as client characteristics, therapist qualities, changes processes, and techniques (Bogo, 2006; Hubble et al., 2010). However, more current research has shifted these domains a bit, placing more emphasis on the alliance that is formed with between the practitioner and the client (Hubble et al., 2010). These domains, while independent of each other, are also interdependent, meaning that each influences the other to some degree (Hubble et al., 2010).

Extratherapeutic or client factors: These factors are the clients' internal and external resources. These factors include the "clients' readiness for change, strengths, resources, level of functioning before treatment, existing social support network, socioeconomic status, personal motivations, and life events" (Hubble et al., 2010, p. 35). Other characteristics within this factor are the clients' expectations, help-seeking activity, and distress level (Bogo, 2006).

Models and techniques: The use of models and techniques plays a critical role in improving outcomes, but not necessarily because one approach is better than another (Hubble et al., 2010; Wampold, 2010). They are important because they activate the feelings of hope and expectancy and increase the placebo effect (Hubble et al., 2010). The placebo effect is when clients demonstrate improvement simply because of their expectations that whatever they are doing will improve their condition or situation (Kirsch, 1985). In addition, models and techniques engage the client in "healthy and helpful actions," and they "offer the client an appropriate explanation for his or her difficulties and set forth strategies for problem resolution" (Hubble et al., 2010, p. 36). In a sense, models and techniques provide structure to the work. In fact, research shows that when there is a lack of road map or theory to explain and organize the course of the plan for change, the outcomes are worse (Hubble et al., 2010; Wampold, 2010). It is essential that the practitioner has a plan reflecting a rationale for what is being done, and that the plan makes sense and has meaning to the client (Wampold, 2010).

Therapist factors: "Available evidence documents that the [practitioner] is the most robust predictor of outcome of any factor ever studied" (Hubble et al., 2010, p. 38). Although the research strongly indicated that the practitioner heavily influences the outcome, what specifically the practitioner does is less clear. In other words, the specific actions taken or characteristics shown by the practitioner that influence and improve outcomes have not yet been identified. However, what appears to play a central role is their ability to form a strong alliance with their clients (Hubble et al., 2010; Wampold, 2010). What matters is the practitioners' ability to demonstrate "caring aspects of empathy, warmth, acceptance, and validation that create[s] safety" (Bogo, 2006, p. 96) and ultimately *how* they deliver a particular treatment rather than the specific treatment that they deliver (Wampold, 2010).

Therapeutic relationship/alliance: The relationship or alliance is "a partnership between the client and therapist to achieve the client's goals" and is "one of the best indicators of outcome" (Hubble et al., 2010, p. 37). Research continues to show that there is a causal relationship between the quality of the relationship and the outcome of the intervention with clients, meaning that strong alliances lead to better outcomes (Weinberger & Rasco, 2007). What is important to remember about the alliance is that it is the practitioner's ability to form a collaborative partnership with the client that influences the outcome (Hubble et al., 2010).

SO WHAT IS THIS THING CALLED
THE WORKING ALLIANCE?

As discussed, the alliance is the factor most written about in outcome research with regard to social work and other disciplines' interventions with clients (Weinberger & Rasco, 2007). Essentially, the alliance is the connection that you have built with the client. Although it may seem like it is a nebulous concept, there are valid instruments that can measure this construct and in turn the strength of this relationship (see resource guide for listing of sources). While there are many different variables that contribute to the alliance, there are three main characteristics that define this relationship (Lambert & Barley, 2002).

The first characteristic is *tasks*. These are the behaviors and processes within the intervention itself that make up the actual work that occurs between the worker and the client (Lambert & Barley, 2002). It is important that both the client and the worker see these tasks as important and relevant to the client's life. These tasks might include deciding how often the meetings between the social worker and the client might take place or they might involve what types of activities occur in addition to deciding each person's roles and responsibilities in the work together (Bogo, 2006). For example, if a client living in a homeless shelter comes to a social worker in the hopes of finding safe housing, it will be important for the worker and the client to agree on who will do which tasks to reach this goal. In addition, it is important for the social worker to clarify what he or she is able to do within his or her role, as well as what the social worker is unable to do within that role to ensure that the client is clear on the limits of the social worker's role in helping to secure safe housing.

The second characteristic relates to *goals*. Both the client and the practitioner must endorse and value the goals and purpose of the work they are doing together (Lambert & Barley, 2002). Here, it is important to remember the social work principle of "starting where the client is." This principle means that social workers give priority to the client's stated goals, their views of the issues with which they are struggling, and their capacities to manage those issues. (See Chapter 13 on creating goals and planning for treatment with clients.) While goals may be established at the beginning, it is important to remember that the goals may also change during the time social workers work with clients. Regardless of the content of the goals, it is essential for the alliance that the worker and the client agree on the direction of the work together. For example, using the case mentioned, if the worker believes that the client should not look for housing until he or she has learned anger management skills and begins to form a plan to address those skills rather than housing, the alliance will suffer. The process of cocreating the goals helps cement the bond of the working alliance.

Finally, the alliance also must include a *bond* between the practitioner and the client where there is "mutual trust, confidence, and acceptance" (Lambert & Barley, 2002, p. 25). This bond is formed when the worker is able to demonstrate attunement and understanding of a client's thoughts and feelings, as well as be able to hold a nonjudgmental stance (Bogo, 2006). In the example of the client who is seeking housing, it is possible that the client could become frustrated with the process and feel that the worker was not doing enough for him or her. If a bond existed between the worker and the client, then the client could feel comfortable expressing frustrations because the client knows that instead of rejection, the worker will listen to her concerns and feelings and work with the client to redefine their tasks together. Without such a bond, the client might become hopeless and give up on the process.

TAKE-HOME MESSAGE ON THE RELATIONSHIP

What we hope is abundantly clear from this discussion about the relationship is that your relationship or the working alliance that you form with the client matters greatly. Regardless of your setting and your role within the setting, your ability to form a strong working alliance with your clients is a significant factor in helping them to reach their goals. Therefore, we encourage all readers to focus on building relationship skills through coursework, supervision, modeling, role playing, and practicing with clients. To summarize some of the research we discussed, beginning practitioners should focus on learning to

- Demonstrate empathy, genuineness, authenticity, and a nonjudgmental stance
- Create mutually agreed-on goals that start where the client is
- Clearly articulate the intervention approach they will take with clients, including the tasks, roles, and responsibilities of each person involved in helping to achieve the clients' goals

- Provide a rationale for their approach that links the explanation to the suggested plan for intervention
- Provide a space for clients where they feel accepted and validated
- Use reflective listening skills effectively
- Attend to client factors, such as their motivation, and modify their approach accordingly

CONCLUSION

Due to the varying roles social workers can have within different organizations, it is critical for social workers to understand their specific roles and related responsibilities. The best method to define these roles and responsibilities is through conversations with the social worker's supervisor. Many issues can be avoided or minimized when social workers are clear regarding the specific expectations held for them within their agencies.

Regardless of the role that social workers hold with clients, the most critical factor in helping to improve outcomes for their clients is to learn how to form strong working alliances. To strengthen these alliances, social workers should pay attention to the internal and external resources of their clients, be able to provide the rationale for the intervention approaches they are suggesting might be helpful, use relationship skills to create a bond with their clients, create mutually agreed-on goals that start where their clients are, and clearly articulate the tasks, roles, and responsibilities that each individual will have in the work together. These relationships exist regardless of whether you will work with your clients for an hour in an emergency room or in a group home setting where there may be hours of interactions over several months. One of the aspects of our work with clients that makes this work so rewarding is the unique relationship that you have the privilege of forming with your clients.

CHAPTER 4 RESOURCE GUIDE

We have provided below a list of two of the most commonly used instruments designed to measure the relationship between the client and the social worker in social work practice. There are others beyond this list, but we have included the two that we feel are most well known and that are available for free.

1. The Working Alliance Inventory (WAI © A. O. Horvath 1981, 1984, 1992)
   a. Available for free from http://wai.profhorvath.com/
   b. Measures the quality of the relationship between the practitioner and the client.
   c. Both the client and the practitioner complete the forms.
   d. It has undergone numerous evaluations and is considered a useful instrument to measure this aspect of the work.

2. Session Rating Scale (SRS © 2002, Scott D. Miller, Barry L. Duncan, & Lynn Johnson)
   a. Available for free from https://heartandsoulofchange.com/
   b. This instrument is designed to evaluate the client's views of how well the practitioner is addressing his or her goals, as well as the fit of the practitioner's style to his or her needs.
   c. It is designed to be used at the end of the session and allows for "real-time" evaluation of the fit between the client and the practitioner.
   d. It is completed by the client.
   e. The SRS has been used internationally and when used has demonstrated that client's report significantly better outcomes.

PART I

BEGINNINGS

THE FIRST SESSION

Starting new relationships of any kind can be a little unnerving. This is certainly true of professional relationships that have a lot riding on our ability to connect with clients and engage them in the process of setting goals and achieving the change they desire. Both you and the client may find a first meeting a little awkward, as it is a different sort of first meeting than you might typically have in another social or professional setting. In addition, some people are more comfortable with initial interactions than others may be. However, we can assure you that you will get better at navigating first sessions over time. In this chapter, we offer a set of guidelines to help students and new practitioners address some of the common concerns that may arise in these initial meetings, but understand that there are agency and organizational guidelines and parameters that may influence different aspects of these encounters. We also provide some legal and practice guidelines regarding how to address these concerns.

PREPARING FOR THE INITIAL ENCOUNTER

Often before the first meeting, you or someone else from your agency may have interactions with the client, such as phone discussions or e-mail exchanges to discuss scheduling. Other clients may just walk in or have been placed at your agency, such as a hospital or school setting. It is important to remember that these first encounters with either you or your agency can set the tone for how the clients might perceive you and your ability to help them. We strongly recommend that you understand early on in your field placements or your jobs how clients come to the agency. What is the process for clients to gain access to your services? How welcoming is the process? How difficult is the process? It can be helpful for you to walk through the experience as if you were a client to see what it feels like to engage with the agency. Here is where you can put on your macro/organizational hat and view the process through a systems lens to see if there are ways to improve the process to ensure that clients feel welcomed and attended to, starting with their initial contact with the agency or the individual with whom they will work.

Once the first session is scheduled, you will also have to navigate the initial greeting before settling into the space you will be using for the meeting. These exchanges should be given a great deal of careful thought; they can set a tone for how the rest of the meeting will feel. For example, if you are greeting the client in a waiting room, do you call out his name? Do you refer to him as Mr. Smith or use his first name? If coming into a client's hospital room or home, do you walk right in or ask permission to enter and inquire about where you should sit? When greeting a client for the first time, do you initiate a handshake? These questions contribute to feelings of nervousness.

It is helpful to discuss these questions with your supervisor to help navigate these microinteractions. If you do not have this opportunity, it is best to abide by confidentiality and not call out a client's name in a waiting room. Instead, you could ask the group of clients waiting which person has an appointment with you. Also, it is a good operating principle not to initiate a handshake or other touch with a new client. There may be cultural norms that prohibit this kind of touch, or you may make the client feel pressure to shake hands when the client would not otherwise. Take the lead from the client and let the client set the pace.

You will also need to introduce yourself to the client. While this may seem like an obvious statement, it is actually a complicated interaction and one to explore with your supervisor. In some settings, such as in a school or some shelters, the expectation will be that you will use your last name and be called Ms. Smith or Mr. Jones, for example. In other settings, you and the other staff may be called by your first name only. Again, it is important that you talk with your supervisor regarding how other staff members are called. It is much more difficult to backtrack than to start off on the right foot.

Beyond your name and role at the organization, there will be questions the client may have about who you are and what qualifications you have; in other words, the client wants to know, How can *you* help *me*? Here is the first test of your honesty as well as your confidence. Be sure to directly address your role as a student intern or new professional. There is a fine line between being honest about your lack of experience and instilling confidence in your abilities. You may want to consider rehearsing a statement about yourself in supervision or with a peer. Spend time role-playing a first session to generate ideas of authentic statements. Perhaps you could say something like, "My name is Eileen, and I am a student intern here at XYZ Services. I will be meeting with you once a week to work on your goals, and I will be meeting weekly with my supervisor, who will help guide our work together. Do you have any questions for me about my role here or this process?" Handling these questions openly and honestly will help develop trust. If the client has any reservations about working with a student or new practitioner, be sure to let the client know that you understand their concerns and reassure them that you have the necessary education and skills to help them. When a practitioner has close supervision like you will, clients actually haves more agency resources focused on them and their goals, and this can be seen as a benefit rather than a deficit.

To calm your jitters and focus on the meeting with this new client, take a few moments to center yourself. Breathe, clear your head, and get ready to listen. You have learned about listening skills in your coursework, so have confidence in what you already know and the skills you are beginning to hone. Be curious and without judgment about *this particular client*. The client may be similar to people you know or have worked with in the past or even yourself, but there is much you do not know about *this client*. The client is the expert on his or her life and situation. You have a set of skills and techniques that you can use to help the client as you work together toward setting and achieving the client's goals. Know you are capable of "being with" clients and that you cannot solve a client's problems today. It is possible that much of what he or she is coming to the agency to address has been an issue for years and cannot be "fixed" or resolved in one or two meetings. Keep in mind that there are three main tasks for the first session:

1. Create a safe environment for you and the client.
2. Establish a trusting relationship.
3. Set the frame of the work and attend to intake forms, treatment plans, and other paperwork.

CREATING A SAFE ENVIRONMENT

Your ability to create a safe environment in which you and your client will meet is influenced by your role, the organizational setting, and many other variables. In some settings, you will be meeting with clients in the same space every time. In this case, ensure that you have soft lighting, tissues, visible clocks, and comfortable seating that is neither too close nor too far apart. In other practice arenas, you will be working in a host setting, where mental health services are not the main focus and are seen as adjunctive to the mission, such as in hospitals and schools. In these settings, meeting space may be hard to come by and less than ideal for your purposes, as it may be difficult to create quiet spaces where you will have privacy. In these situations, it can be helpful to let those around you know why your work requires privacy and request their help. You may want to consider keeping a "do not disturb" sign, tissues, a clock, and other items with you for use in any space.

Finally, when your work requires you to enter hospital rooms or go on home visits, you never know what the environment will be like. In these situations, talking with the client about why turning off the television or meeting in private will be helpful to the work you are doing together and can establish understanding that you are both responsible for this work. Regardless of your setting, it is important for you to keep in mind both your and your client's physical safety. We spend more time addressing this issue in Chapters 8 and 9. However, in the context of your first meeting, it is important for you to keep in mind a few issues:

-   Notice where you and your client are located in relation to exits.
-   If your client is known to have a history of violent behavior, make sure that another staff member is aware of when and where you are meeting.
-   If you are conducting home visits or working in the community, request specific safety training before you begin making visits.

ESTABLISHING A TRUSTING RELATIONSHIP

Trust is an essential component of helping relationships. To share details of their lives, clients will need to feel that they can trust you. You may be the first person with whom they have ever shared their story, and there may be parts of this story about which they feel some collection of difficult emotions, such as shame or guilt. We mentioned that it is important for you to learn to be curious, nonreactive, and nonjudgmental. As clients begin to share their stories in the initial meeting, it is essential that you practice these skills to establish trust from the beginning of the relationship.

Let us pause for a moment to address this concept of being nonjudgmental. It is not really possible to be without judgments. We are all human, and it is natural to have initial impressions or judgments (which can range from very positive to very negative) about your clients, just as they will have their initial reactions to you. For example, clients might remind you of someone in your past; you might have initial judgments based on perceived social identity differences or from reading about the clients in their case file. It is important to notice your reactions and discuss them with your supervisor to prevent them from being felt by your clients or interfering with the professional relationship you are building with them.

Confidentiality is another crucial component of the professional relationship. In your role as a professional social worker, you will not be sharing what clients tell you with friends and family members. While you have heard this many times before, it is important to clarify what confidentiality means in the context of this relationship with your clients as this knowledge can help them to feel more comfortable being open and honest with you. However, even with this knowledge, you cannot assume that a client will feel safe enough to trust you right away.

Trust is typically earned over time, and with some clients you will really have to earn it. Some clients may say or do things to test whether you are trustworthy. For many clients, given their own personal histories, their reluctance to trust you and to first determine if you are trustworthy are completely understandable. Take a moment and think back to a time when someone broke your trust. This type of experience can be painful and can make you wary of trusting others in the future. The more extreme trust violations are, the more self-protective and mistrustful we can become. It is important not to judge clients who do not trust you right away. Know that this can be a healthy process of evaluating another's trustworthiness; in other words, this is a strength that can be reflected back to the client. You can normalize the process of building trust in relationships and ask clients what they see as barriers to trust or indicators that they can safely open up.

As part of building a trusting relationship, it is important to be honest with clients about confidentiality and its limits. It is normal to want to reassure clients that "everything you say will be kept confidential." However, this is not the case in most practice settings. You share what clients say with supervisors, administrators often review case notes, and there are situations for which you are required by law to break confidentiality. Confidentiality often extends to others outside your practice setting, so let clients know that you receive supervision where you may discuss your work with them so you can obtain the best guidance to help them. Be clear about the situations for which you need to break confidentiality, such as when they are a danger to themselves or someone else. As a mental health professional, you are a *mandated reporter*, which means that there are laws that require you to report information about physical and sexual abuse of a minor or vulnerable adult. These laws vary by state, so familiarize yourself with the laws in the state(s) or jurisdictions where you are working. It is common for neighboring states to have different laws, and it is your professional responsibility to understand these differences. This topic is covered in more detail in Chapters 8 and 9.

SETTING THE FRAME AND ATTENDING TO PAPERWORK

In addition to introducing yourself to the client and working to establish a sense of safety and trustworthiness, you have some business to which you often must attend. In many settings, you will be required to complete an initial intake, fill out insurance forms, review informed consent documents, and attend to other paperwork. It can be challenging to balance the relational part of this meeting with the administrative requirements; let the client know at the beginning of the meeting what you have to accomplish. If you start with "tell me what brings you in today … " and spend 30 minutes listening to the client's life story, you may be rushed at the end of your time together to complete all the paperwork and not do a good enough job of validating and responding to what you just heard. Consider beginning this first session with, "We have a couple of things to do in our meeting today; I have some paperwork we need to fill out and forms for you to sign, but I also would like for us to spend a little time getting to know each other and for you to tell me what brings you in today. Where would you like to start?" This way you set a tone of honesty, openness, and partnership. By laying out all the tasks that you have to accomplish together, you are transparent, and by asking where the client wants to start, you are putting the client in the driver's seat. Most helping relationships feel unbalanced, with you in the powerful role of helper and the client in the help-seeking role. Efforts like this one can help create more balance in the relationship and set the frame to be one of collaboration.

One of the key pieces of paperwork is asking the client to give his or her *informed consent* to treatment. While this is often seen as a formality in some settings, it is a key part of establishing trust and setting the frame of the relationship. It is your opportunity to spell out the benefits, as well as any risks, associated with receiving services. Ideally, you will point out the informed consent document to clients and ask that they read it carefully and take time to answer any questions they may have about the services they will receive. This step is vital to ensure that your clients understand what they are agreeing to in this process.

Setting the frame for your work together also requires you and the client to review the ground rules for the meetings. How long will each meeting last? Will you meet once a week? Where will the meetings take place? Will the location be the same for each meeting, or will it vary? It is also important to address the boundaries of the relationship, like what limits there are on contact outside of meetings. These include how you will communicate with each other, such as the use of phone or e-mail. The use of technology in providing services is addressed in more detail in Chapter 17. We encourage you to be careful about establishing rules consistent with your setting; you do not want to set up an expectation with clients that you then have to change. In addition, if there is a possibility that you might see a client outside the agency, you will want to think about how will you handle such encounters.

For example, I (M.D.G.) worked with an adolescent client who lived near my home and my office and in fact did swim practice at my same gym. We discussed ahead of time what she would like to do if she saw me in the community. She decided that she would like to be the one to acknowledge me first as there may have been a time when she was with someone with whom she did not want to share who I was. It was good we discussed this plan ahead of time as we saw each other several times outside the office. It is important not to assume that the client will be familiar with the culture and norms of mental health services in general or your practice setting in particular and to socialize them to this unique relationship.

If the client has received services before, it is helpful to explore what this experience was like and how he or she felt about it. This discussion can be a good opportunity to process what the client needs from you and to address his or her expectations of your organization or program. It is also important during this discussion to be clear about and obtain a mutual agreement on the frame of the work and clarify the policies concerning missed appointments and any scheduling constraints. This initial meeting is also a good time to explore what the client considers a good outcome from your work together. How will the client know when personal goals have been achieved? What will ending the work together look like? It may feel too soon to discuss termination, but this is an integral part of setting the frame, as you and the client are embarking on a professional helping relationship that has a beginning, middle, and end. It is helpful to keep the end in mind as you proceed and plan for it to be a positive experience for you and the client. Further in this book, we discuss establishing clear goals and planning for endings, as well as how to evaluate whether the work you and your client have done has been effective in reaching the client's goals.

Finally, it is essential to leave enough time to explore any questions the client may have. If the client is particularly nervous, he or she may not have heard all the information you have shared. It is important to keep in mind any cultural norms that may influence the client's willingness to ask you questions. In some cultures, you may be seen as "the doctor" or someone with power who should not be questioned. In addition, the differences or similarities between you and your client in terms of gender or age may influence the client's comfort level in asking you questions. Other clients may look for physical signs on you or in your meeting place to see if you are a "safe" person so they can speak freely. For example, they may look for a religious symbol, such as a cross or star of David on a necklace, or look for a pink triangle or rainbow in your office before feeling safe to ask additional questions. For other clients, these same symbols may deter someone from asking questions. As discussed in Chapter 2, "What to Know Before You Start," there are no hard-and-fast rules for what to wear or what to have in your space. It is just important to be cognizant of the symbols with which we surround ourselves and the impact that these can have on our clients.

Finally, allow time to summarize what you have heard and discuss the plans moving forward. For some social workers, the initial meeting may be the only time that they will ever see a client. Regardless of how long you will be in the life of this client, it is helpful to summarize the initial session and review with them the time for their next meeting if one is to occur. Be sure to clearly state with whom the meeting will take place, where they should go for it, and who they should contact (it may be you but could be someone else) if the client has any questions about the appointment.

DIFFERENCES AMONG CLIENTS

It is important to make note of how different clients influence the initial encounters. For example, a client who is *voluntary*, or is seeking services of his or her own desire, will, and volition may engage with the practitioner differently from someone who is *mandated* to receive services. Mandated clients are typically those who would not otherwise seek services but are being told they *must* receive services. In some cases, clients are mandated by the courts or their employer or are receiving pressure from a friend, family member, or partner to obtain help (or else). Be sure to make note regarding whether the client has chosen to be there or not as you begin the work.

If someone is reluctant or resentful, they may not be so forthcoming with information and may be slow to engage with you and the work. It is also important not to make the assumption that a mandated client will be difficult to work with as some may actually embrace the experience. We encourage you to empathize with the situation they are facing and find a mutual goal or hope for the work. When you convey to the client that you understand why they resist change, you actually join together in the process instead of setting up a struggle for power. For example, you could acknowledge their frustration and make a statement such as, "Having to come in to XYZ Services each week for services you don't feel you need must be frustrating and feel like a waste of your time." After you have acknowledged their frustration, you can then follow up with a question such as, "Since we need to meet each week for 6 weeks, is there some way to make this time feel valuable to you and not just check off a box for the court system?" This type of exchange may help the client feel more engaged.

In the same vein, it is also important not to always assume that voluntary clients will be easy to work with. For example, although your client "Jane" knows she needs to make changes or engage services to help her establish and maintain sobriety, this knowledge does not mean she will be without ambivalence or resistance to the process or outcome. Often, there are secondary gains to the status quo of people's lives. When Jane makes changes in herself, it will have ripple effects to the rest of her life. So, while Jane may have voluntarily committed to sobriety and wants to stop drinking alcohol, this decision will mean changing where she hangs out (bars) and the people she hangs out with (drinking buddies). While she knows that drinking has been unhealthy and has caused other problems, she also knows on some level that it allowed her to avoid facing difficult emotions that stem from an abusive childhood. The secondary gain to drinking for Jane is the avoidance of deeper emotional work. By giving up her drinking, she is also giving up her safe and established, albeit unhealthy, coping strategy. It can be helpful to acknowledge to clients that ambivalence is normal and empathize as much as possible what it must feel like to make changes in their lives.

FINAL THOUGHTS ON THE FIRST SESSION

The first meeting marks the beginning of a big step for clients. Whether the client is mandated to receive services or comes voluntarily, starting a change process requires courage. It is hoped that the first meeting will help the client feel more at ease with this process and help to engage them in the working relationship when you reflect this sentiment of courage back to them in a genuine and authentic manner. When you show interest in the client and the client's particular circumstances and goals, you demonstrate that you value them. Remember that this work can be challenging and difficult at times, but it is a privilege to be able to help clients on their path to growth and change.

Ten Tips on Preparing for the First Session

1. Review client information for correct spelling and pronunciation of name.
2. Take a few deep breaths and clear your mind so you can be calm and focused.
3. Have all necessary paperwork with you—do not forget a pen.
4. Prepare the physical space as best you can for safety and confidentiality. A white noise machine can be particularly helpful in high-traffic areas.
5. Have a clock where both you and the client can see it.
6. Smile and keep nonverbal communication neutral.
7. Be aware of body language—yours and the client's.
8. Normalize nervousness and difficulty with trust.
9. Leave plenty of time for the client to ask questions.
10. Confirm the next appointment and give the client your contact information.

CHAPTER 5 RESOURCE GUIDE

REFERENCE GUIDE TO CONFIDENTIALITY LAWS

Child Welfare Information Gateway. (2013). *Disclosure of confidential child abuse and neglect records.* Retrieved from https://www.childwelfare.gov/systemwide/laws_policies/statutes/confide.cfm

Rape, Abuse, and Incest National Network (RAINN). (2012). *Confidentiality laws.* Retrieved from http://rainn.org/pdf-files-and-other-documents/Public-Policy/Legal-resources/2012/Privilege%20Database%20Summary.pdf

Robert Wood Johnson Foundation. (2012). *Health information and the law.* Retrieved from http://www.healthinfolaw.org/state

US Department of Health and Human Services. (n.d.). *Health information privacy*. Retrieved from http://www.hhs.gov/ocr/privacy/

US Department of Health and Human Services. (nd). *Summary of HIPAA Privacy Rule*. Retrieved from http://www.hhs.gov/ocr/privacy/hipaa/understanding/summary/index.html

US Department of Health and Human Services. (nd). *Summary of HIPAA Security Rule*. Retrieved from http://www.hhs.gov/ocr/privacy/hipaa/understanding/srsummary.html

ASSESSMENT

As mentioned in Chapter 5, in addition to creating a safe working relationship for the client, you must attend to the task of assessment in your first session. Assessment is a process that occurs over time with the client, and you are never truly "done" with it because new information about the client continuously emerges throughout the work together. Do not be surprised by new information, even in your last session. It is beyond the scope of this book to explore how assessment differs with families, children, couples, or other client systems, as this is not a book devoted entirely to assessment, and therefore it cannot address every issue in a comprehensive manner. This chapter focuses on assessment of individuals as we introduce you to the language and terms used in a social work assessment *in general*, knowing that your role within the agency, the theory you use, the mission of your agency, and the purpose of the assessment, as well as many other factors, will all ultimately influence what form your assessment with a client takes. Our goal here is to help you become familiar with what you may use at some point with clients and to understand what you may see in reports and treatment summaries when the assessment was conducted by another professional. This chapter addresses the different frameworks for assessment, as well as discusses some of their strengths and limitations. In addition, we aim to help you balance between assessing struggles and challenges and identifying strengths and resilience.

THE BIO-PSYCHO-SOCIAL-SPIRITUAL FRAMEWORK

You have heard that social work practitioners use a *person-in-environment* (PIE) perspective to assess clients using what is referred to as the *bio-psycho-social-spiritual* framework. This framework embodies what sets social workers apart from individuals in other disciplines. As social workers, we assess all clients holistically. A holistic approach means that a social work assessment considers how the biological, psychological, social, and the spiritual domains all intersect and influence one another. "In this approach, human behavior is considered to be the result of interactions of integrated biological, psychological, and social systems" (Hutchinson, 2013, p. 12). In addition, "developments in n͏ have generated new explorations of the unity of the biological, psychologica tual dimensions of the person" (Hutchinson, 2013, p. 13). Elements for cons a bio-psycho-social-spiritual assessment are listed in Table 6.1. Social work's of the interrelatedness of these domains and the importance of each of these elements sets our profession apart from others. Through this bio-psycho-social-spiritual framework, social workers look at the whole person within the context of their social environment, hence the term *person-in-environment* or *PIE perspective*.

As part of the holistic perspective, it is essential that social workers assess for *both* the struggles and risk factors that the individual(s) is experiencing *and* the individual's strengths and resilience. Within this PIE framework, the total picture of the client's life is assessed as social workers aim to understand clients and their needs on multiple levels. It is through this framework that social workers can assess the challenges clients are facing, as well as their capacities to manage current and past stressors holistically and therefore more effectively.

As social work practitioners, we assess for areas of health as well as problems in social functioning on the assumption that difficulties emanate from the challenge of effectively managing the internal and external stressors in life. The World Health Organization (WHO, 2014) stated that

> Mental health is a state of well-being in which an individual realizes his or her own abilities, can cope with the normal stresses of life, can work productively and is able to make a contribution to his or her community. (para. 2)

TABLE 6.1: Elements of the Bio-Psycho-Social-Spiritual Assessment

Physical	Psychological	Social	Spiritual
Bodily elements	Gender	Roles	Spiritual beliefs
Diagnoses	Sexuality	Culture	Organized religion
Health concerns	Personal experiences	Values	Values
Genetic predispositions	Significant others	Economic elements	Meaning making
Prescribed physical characteristics, including sex, race	Habits/behaviors	Race and ethnicity	
Abilities and disabilities	Relational patterns	Community connections	
Timing, such as aging process	Language	Stereotypes	
	Personal history	Physical spaces	
		Access to services	
		Historical events	
		Agency setting	
		Political situation	
		Institutions	
		Legal status	
		National origin	

ᴛhe severity of the client's distress is often a result of the discrepancy between both the number and the intensity of stressors and the client's ability to cope effectively. A professional social work assessment is the process of understanding the client's situation through the bio-psycho-social-spiritual framework. These areas of assessment are consistent with WHO's (2014) understanding of the determinants of mental health that there are "multiple social, psychological, and biological factors [that] determine the level of mental health of a person at any point of time" (para. 4).

In addition, another critical task during the assessment phase is to be able to answer the question, "What is going on?" The answer to this question will determine your product, which could be how you will frame the planned change process that you and the client will begin together, or it could be that the result is a referral to another agency or practitioner. As stated previously, the purpose and outcome of the assessment are determined by multiple factors.

Each practice setting has its own set of forms and information to gather, but most follow a general framework of gathering and organizing data on the client's life history to formulate a case theory within the context of the current circumstances. In other words, it is the linking of the client's past with the present and future that creates a map that organizes the social work practice by shaping the relationship and communication and determining the intervention (Bisman, 1994). Therefore, in most settings assessment includes

- Collecting facts about the client's past
- Making observations of the client in the present
- Considering the impact of differences and similarities on the client's life
- Forming hypotheses about the client's presenting problems
- Formulating questions to test these hypotheses
- Applying theories and models of practice to make inferences about the presenting problems
- Being aware of your own feelings and reactions in working with this client
- Formulating diagnoses based on the assessment

It is crucial to distinguish between "facts" and judgment. A *fact* is an observation stripped of assumptions of meaning or attributions of cause. A fact, for example, is that a child came to your office for a session with messy hair and dirty clothing with stains. A judgment, or assumption, is that the child is being neglected. There could be many alternative explanations regarding the child's appearance. A thorough assessment process helps you answer the question regarding what is going on with the child. If you jump to a conclusion to answer the question without all of the facts, then you have short-circuited the process and run the risk of reaching an inaccurate conclusion. In your assessment, you may find that the child is going through a developmentally normal stage of gaining more independence and wants to groom and dress by herself. In doing so, she did not do a great job of brushing her hair and took her favorite top and bottoms out of the dirty laundry basket. The parents, in an effort to encourage this independence, chose not to fight this battle.

A GENERAL FRAMEWORK FOR
FACT GATHERING

The assessment process requires you to organize all data regarding human growth and development. You must ask questions, listen to the answers, explore complex issues, and observe the clients. We encourage you to always be curious. The facts that are included in the assessment will be determined in large part by your setting. What is most salient for your purposes? Working with young children will require you to obtain a lot of information about their early development and family situation. In school settings, you will be paying particular attention to the factors that relate to educational success. In hospitals and healthcare settings, there will be much more emphasis on physical health factors. Working with frail older adults will require you to gain more information about cognitive functioning, activities of daily living, and the level of care needed. Facts are gathered through client meetings, observation, collateral materials (meaning documents from or conversations with other agencies or professionals), and objective measures, all while keeping in mind social work values and ethics, strengths, and cultural norms and factors. In general, you will need to gather information related to these domains:

- Biological/physical
- Cognitive
- Emotional
- Affective
- Behavioral
- Social
- Familial
- Cultural
- Environmental
- Spiritual/religious
- Socioeconomic
- Food/clothing/shelter
- Medical/dental
- Vocational/educational
- Transportation
- Communication
- Child care/eldercare
- Leisure/recreational
- Life transitions/adjustments
- Traumatic experiences
- Interpersonal processes
- Communication issues

It is important that you discuss with your supervisor what specifically he or she would like you to focus on or emphasize in the assessment process. This will vary by setting and program focus.

In addition to gathering this information, you should be asking yourself, and the client, some form of a *Why now?* question. Why is this person coming in for help at this particular point in time? In other words, what prompted the person to seek help now versus any other previous time? How does the client describe the onset, frequency, intensity, and duration of symptoms? Finally, explore any previous successful or unsuccessful attempts to resolve the problem and any other providers and systems involved in helping the client resolve the problem.

BALANCING STRENGTHS AND PATHOLOGY

Part of the fact-gathering process is to attend not only to the problems in functioning but also to the strengths and evidence of resilience. In many cases, what is seen as problematic behavior now was once adaptive behavior to stressful or traumatic experiences. While focusing on strengths and resilience, ask yourself the following:

- Where do I see competence, capacity, and courage in this person?
- In what ways does the client focus on the potential possibilities and positive outcomes?
- What are some creative ways the client is using resources?
- Where do I see a sense of agency and the desire to influence the course of his or her life?
- Have I seen ways in which the client shows he or she values him- or herself and has taken steps toward self-care?

A thorough assessment focuses on *both* strengths *and* challenges, *both* risk *and* resilience. Two major perspectives used in social work are risk and resilience (Fraser, Richman, & Galinsky, 1999) and strengths (Saleeby, 2012). These perspectives ensure that assessment does not dwell solely on the pathology but strives to understand the environmental contexts that put the individual at risk for these problems in social functioning (risk factors) and explores the client's innate capacities (strengths) and ability to bounce back from adversity (resilience). As practitioners, you need to examine stratification issues of opportunity, power, privilege, age, gender expression, race, ethnicity, social class, sexual orientation, occupation, as well as physical and mental challenges. These factors are important in assessment, but if you lose sight of strengths and resilience factors, you are not seeing a full picture.

ETHNOGRAPHIC INTERVIEWING

A useful tool to ensure that you are not making assumptions during an assessment, and even beyond this phase, is ethnographic interviewing. As described previously, in a typical mental health assessment process the practitioner approaches the interaction knowing that he or she needs to gather facts and data using a set of questions to formulate the treatment plan or any other plan or action. In other words, the practitioner may think, "I know what I need to know." In an ethnographic interview, the practitioner follows the client's lead as he or she determines what information is necessary to help build an understanding of the client's situation—"The client will tell me what I need to know." Ethnographic interviewing techniques allow the practitioner to immerse himself or herself into the unique world of the client to allow for deeper understanding and a more authentic interaction (Berry, 2011). This technique allows you and the client to create a space and a language with which to speak freely and be understood (Riemann, 2005). In this way, you are not solely hearing what the client is saying; you are engaging in *participant listening*, which allows you take in the values, beliefs, meaning, and context of the client's world and, most important, not to make assumptions about the client's meaning (Forsey, 2010; Haight, Kayama, & Korang-Okrah, 2014). When asking questions during an assessment, the following are some ethnographic techniques:

- Use open-ended questions rather than yes/no questions.
- Show interest in the client's point of view.
- Express your not-knowing position and desire to understand the client.
- Restate what the client says by repeating the client's exact words.
- Summarize the client's statements and give the client the opportunity to correct you if you have misinterpreted something that was said.
- Avoid asking multiple questions back to back or multipart questions.
- Avoid leading questions that tend to orient the person to a particular response.
- Avoid using "why" questions because such questions tend to sound judgmental and may increase the client's defensiveness.

We hope that you are thinking that these are good interviewing techniques in general. Yes—they are. What is different about ethnographic interviewing is the focus on using *global* questions and listening for *cover terms* (Leigh, 1998). Global questions are open-ended questions that invite the client to share what the client believes is important for you to know. An example might be that you have met someone who comes from a different part of the country or world than you and you would like to know how a particular social issue, like gay marriage or the disciplining of children, is perceived within his culture. A global question might be, "I have never met anyone from or been to X Place. Can you tell me how children are disciplined there?" The client will then tell you from *his perspective* about his world.

Cover terms are terms that capture the meaning of the other through language (Leigh, 1998). There are many phrases in American English that would be considered cover terms, such as "down in the dumps," "I am beat!" "His hair is sick." Many of these phrases are time bound; in other words, they were used at certain periods of time, such as the term *sick*. Someone coming from another culture would not know what that means and could make an assumption that you literally mean that the guy's hair is not feeling well, which would not make any sense. When using ethnographic interviewing, rather than letting such a phrase go by, even if you think you might know what it means, you would come back to that question and ask the individual what *he* or *she* means by that phrase.

The client's meaning is what is important, and by listening for cover terms, you can be more attentive to those phrases without making an assumption about what the client is trying to communicate. The client's description of the cover term is referred to as the *descriptors* (Leigh, 1998). These descriptors help to express the meaning that the client is hoping to communicate.

Using ethnographic interviewing, the interviewer provides a summary of what he or she has heard from the client and, most important, what he or she has learned at the end of the interview. This part of the process helps communicate the message to the interviewee that the interviewer has been a beneficiary of the process. The closer statement also reinforces that the interviewer is a learner in this process rather than the expert.

It is worth mentioning two important final statements about ethnographic interviewing. The first is that this technique is meant to demonstrate that the interviewer is a student of the interviewee's experience *only*. We would never want the interviewee to feel that he or she was representing an entire group, as some individuals historically have felt they were being asked to do. In ethnographic interviewing, the interview is designed to explore one person's experience and how that person may make meaning of that experience.

The other important message we want to give about this technique is that it is a tool that can be used with every client and in every stage of your work with clients. It should not been seen as a technique that is used only when we perceive that someone is different from us. We have personally experienced this and have heard from other social work colleagues that they have also made false assumptions about clients who they perceived to be similar to themselves due to demographic or geographic similarities. *Every* client has a unique story, and it benefits us all when we do not make assumptions that we know the client's story without fully exploring it and consistently taking the stance of not knowing. By adopting ethnographic interviewing as the foundation for your interviewing style, you will be more likely to avoid assumptions and listen with a more open ear to those unique stories offered by your clients.

ASSESSMENT AND SCREENING TOOLS

In general, there are many tools that can be used by social workers in the assessment process. As with everything in our field, there are pros and cons to each of them. At the risk of being too repetitive, check in with your supervisor to be sure you understand the needs of your agency. This will help you identify and then utilize the most appropriate tools in your setting while avoiding asking clients questions they have already answered for your agency. When engaging mental health services, clients can often feel overwhelmed and exhausted by repeating information and answering the same questions over and over again. By asking, what information you really need now and what you can gather over time, you can avoid bombarding the client with questions.

Assessment and screening tools are designed to help practitioners gather information efficiently, but as a result, much information can be lost when they become the primary tools or focus of the interview. In addition, it is important to assess the appropriateness of each tool given the client's unique presentation and identities, as some tools may not be appropriate given someone's cultural, educational, or diagnostic background. As we cannot discuss each of these in depth, our goal here is to introduce you to some general tools that are commonly used in our field so that you are familiar with them and could practice using them if appropriate for your setting.

SOCIAL FUNCTIONING PICTOGRAMS

Social workers often use *social functioning pictograms*, the most common being the genogram and the ecomap (Sheafor & Horejsi, 2011). A *genogram* is a pictorial representation of ideally three or more generations of a family system. It is a visual representation of the biological, legal, and family structure or system. It is helpful for recording pertinent family information, such as demographic data, as well as functional information such as medical (i.e., health issues like diabetes), emotional (i.e., histories of depression), and behavioral functioning (i.e., use of substances or history of incarceration). Finally, it is useful for delineating family relationships, such as particularly close bonds between members, and relationships that are estranged or full of conflict. When working with families in which there are patterns of intergenerational trauma or histories of mental illness, a genogram can help you and the client track the history and patterns throughout a family's history to understand where it began and how to intervene in these cycles. Every genogram should include a key to help anyone looking at it understand the meaning of each symbol used to express a pattern.

An *ecomap* is a pictorial representation of the client within the client's social context. Often, the genogram is placed in the center of the ecomap when working with children and families. The ecomap provides a blueprint for understanding the PIE perspective (Sheafor & Horejsi, 2011). What is the lived experience? In other words, what are the communities to which the client is connected? Are there other personal, social, psychological, and spiritual influences in the client's life? Where are the resources and natural helping networks with which the client already interacts? The ultimate purpose of an ecomap is to give a visual image of the social supports available to the clients. Similar to a genogram, the ecomap should have a key to help decipher the meaning of each of the symbols.

You can see examples of genograms and ecomaps in most social work practice textbooks if you are not familiar with them already. Depending on your setting and your time, you may choose one over the other in an effort to gather particular information in the assessment. It is hoped that comparing both of these tools demonstrates how each provides useful information about the clients and yet, with each of them, other information captured by the other is lost. You must decide which instrument is appropriate given your goals in the assessment.

MENTAL STATUS EXAM

An assessment tool commonly used by medical and mental health practitioners in a wide range of settings is the *mental status exam* (MSE). This quick assessment tool allows you to note observations about the client in the following areas:

1. *Appearance*—general observations about age, gender, ethnicity, and physical appearance, as well as hygiene, mannerisms, and so on.
2. *Mannerisms and approach*—practitioner's experience of the client as they engage in the process of the assessment; the client's manner of interaction, eye contact, expressions, as well as rate and volume of speaking.
3. *Emotions*—observations of mood and affect with regard to range and appropriateness. This is also where you would explore suicidal and homicidal ideation, risk of violence, impulsivity, and other potentially dangerous emotions and behaviors.
4. *Thought processes, content, and orientation*—This part of the exam is where you explore cognitive functioning (orientation to person, place, and time); coherence of speech; ability to attend to and follow the thread of the discussion; the presence of any hallucinations or delusions; and intellectual ability.
5. *Insight and judgment*—evidence of the client's awareness of their situation and the ability to predict consequences of behaviors to make safe and healthy choices (Corcoran & Walsh, 2014).

The main goal of an MSE is to provide a quick snapshot of the person in the present moment. It is meant to be mainly descriptive, as if looking at a picture, not about inferences or judgments. This picture can then be compared to other points in time, which can be useful when trying to identify whether someone's functioning has changed. For example, an MSE is often conducted at the time of admission to a hospital or other setting. One would hope that through the services provided at the agency, the client would improve. By comparing the MSE at intake to the MSE after a certain time frame, the practitioners can assess whether there has been improvement in certain domains. Similarly, if a client is at risk of a rapid decline, such as someone with a form of dementia, the MSE conducted on a certain day can be compared to the last month's and the one that was conducted 6 months previously. Such information can be vital in understanding the stability or instability of someone's mental state or functioning.

Of course, the MSE is flawed like all other tools. It only includes a limited amount of information, and there is a risk of different practitioners judging certain areas differently, in spite of every effort to make this process as judgment free as possible. Therefore, as with everything in our field, it is always worth obtaining a consultation or a second opinion and to gather additional information so you do not make a judgment about someone based on one specific source of information.

STANDARDIZED INSTRUMENTS

In addition to the general assessment tools, there are many screening tools that are used for specific issues, such as depression, anxiety, and trauma. (See Chapter 15 on evaluation for some additional discussion on the use of standardized instruments as tools for evaluating intervention outcomes.) They are referred to as standardized instruments, which "have uniform procedures for administration and scoring and are accompanied by certain kinds of information, including data concerning reliability, validity, and norms (average scores of certain groups)" (Gambrill, 2013, p. 395). They are used to:

> (1) Describe populations or clients; (2) screen clients (e.g. make a decision about the need for further assessment or find out if a client is eligible for or likely to require a service); (3) assess clients (a more detailed review); (4) evaluate progress; and (5) make predictions about the likely futures of clients. (Gambrill, 2013, p. 395)

In general, these instruments have been evaluated to measure a particular construct, such as those listed, and to give a score that indicates an affirmation of the presence of a disorder and often its severity. They are, in theory, designed to take the bias out of both a client's self-assessment and the practitioner's evaluation. A client's score on such an instrument can then be compared to "the standard" so that the practitioner and client can see how the client's score compares to either the general population or others who are similar, based on a demographic characteristic, such as age, gender, or ethnicity.

While they can be useful to clients and practitioners because they provide a benchmark for the presenting problem and can also ensure that the practitioner has asked questions that will capture the essence of the issue, they also have drawbacks. One in particular is that these instruments are often normed using populations that are convenient to the developer of the instrument (Drisko & Grady, 2012). For example, the developer is often an academic who uses college students as the normative population. Depending on where the person is located, this group of college students may or may not accurately represent the general population in terms of diversity, levels of functioning, and many other differences. Therefore, it is important to learn about the instrument with regard to the populations with which it was tested and how closely the populations resemble your client. Remember, different cultures express different struggles very differently (Lambert et al., 2005; Lambert, Markle, & Bellas, 2001).

Another important consideration is the impact the assessment might have on the person's self-perception. For some clients, knowing that they are "clinically depressed" gives a label that is helpful in that it captures their experience, and they can now search for resources and answers. For others, such a label can be damaging as they may see themselves as damaged and flawed, which increases their depression. Therefore, it is important to consider why you might use an instrument and the impact such information might have on your client.

Finally, these instruments are designed to measure *one* construct, such as depression, trauma symptoms, or developmental achievements. It is worth noting that, as a result, they are limited—they assess *only* one aspect of the person.

Many standardized instruments are protected by copyright, but others are open access and can be found in books or on websites (see the Summary Guide for more information). Some specific tools require training to learn how to administer and score, while others are self-administered by the client and relatively easy to score. Your supervisor can help you determine which ones are appropriate for your setting and your client population.

PSYCHOLOGICAL TESTING

There will be times when you will need to refer clients for psychological testing or assessment to determine if a specific diagnosis or problem in social functioning is present. Although social workers regularly conduct diagnostic assessments in their work with clients, some cases are more complex due to neurological issues or medical concerns that might make the diagnostic picture a bit murky and unclear. Also, there are times when clients are seeking specific information that is outside our expertise. In such cases, it can be helpful to have another professional who is trained in administering specific diagnostic and assessment instruments to parse out the complex issues or provide you and your clients the information that they need to plan for an intervention.

Most often, for nonmedical assessments, social workers use the expertise of licensed psychologists who are trained to conduct the type of assessments described. We recommend that you ask within your agency or identify on your own competent psychologists in your community who can offer such services when needed. For example, you may be working with a child who wants to attend a private school that requires an IQ test. This test will most likely be part of a battery of tests that are administered by a psychologist. There are also personality tests (e.g., the Minnesota Multiphasic Personality Inventory), behavioral assessments, achievement tests for work, career-planning assessments, and many others that are used for a variety of purposes. There are tests to measure depression, anxiety, posttraumatic stress disorder, and a host of other problems in social functioning (Kline, 2013).

Finally, one specific reason to refer clients to a psychologist for testing is to conduct a neuropsychological test. This would be necessary if you need to obtain a measure of cognitive functioning in situations where you are working with someone who has had damage to the brain due to an accident, abuse, athletic injuries, or military service. These tests are often a crucial part of formulating a comprehensive assessment of your client, and you will need to work with the psychologist administering the test to be sure you receive an interpretation of the results for use in creating an appropriate course of treatment. Psychologists who conduct neuropsychological testing have specialized training to look at brain functioning; therefore, it is important to refer to the appropriate person depending on the information that you are seeking.

CLASSIFICATION SYSTEMS

Depending on your setting, a main component of an assessment might be to develop a mental health diagnosis. As you gain more experience in this work, this part of the assessment process will become easier. However, it is always important to consult a reputable classification system of mental health disorders, such as the *Diagnostic and Statistical Manual of Mental Disorders, Fifth Edition* (DSM-5), published by the American Psychiatric Association (2013); the *International Classification of Diseases, Tenth Revision* (ICD-10), which was put out by WHO (1992); or the theory-driven *Psychodynamic Diagnostic Manual* (PDM), created by a number of psychoanalytic groups (PDM Task Force, 2006).

Whichever classification system you use, it is important to be aware of the cultural influences of these manuals and the way in which your client's culture will play a role in discerning what is "normal" and "abnormal" behavior (Lee & Kleinman, 2007). All labels or diagnostic conditions are social constructions derived by the culture from which they originate. Conrad asserted, "Illness and diseases are human judgments on conditions that exist in the natural world" (as cited by Heller & Gitterman, 2011, p. 6). Some individuals who study the cultural influences on diagnoses believe that "culture shapes the way general psychopathology is going to be translated partially or completely into specific psychopathology" (Lee & Kleinman, p. 29). The importance of evaluating the impact of cultural influences in our work with clients is discussed further in Chapter 3. In spite of the potential cultural limitations, these manuals attempt to organize research and practice information about clinically significant behavioral or psychological patterns that occur in individuals in a way that causes problems in social functioning or psychological distress and is not culturally expected or anticipated. These categories of disorders are offered to create consistency across practitioners in the identification, diagnosis, and treatment of mental health disorders.

Despite these strengths, it is also important to consider the impact of such labels on the individuals with whom we work. For example, it is essential that we always use a "person-first" approach when discussing clients who have been diagnosed or labeled in some way (Heller & Gitterman, 2011, p. 6). A person-first approach means that we say "the person with schizophrenia" versus "a schizophrenic," which leaves out the fact that there is even a person in the discussion. Therefore, it is important to remember that "all people maintain multiple identities and describing an individual by the name of their 'disorder' or 'condition' elevates that condition to a primary descriptor, potentially obscuring both the complexity and essence of a human being" (Heller & Gitterman, p. 6).

Depending on your professional training and experience, you will become aware of these debates and others that exist in particular professions regarding the use of classification systems. For example, many social workers have criticized the *DSM* for being too focused on pathology and not strengths based (Probst, 2013; Wakefield, 2013). This creates a conflict for these professionals, as they must come up with a *DSM* diagnosis for use in assessments as well as for insurance reimbursement of services. One alternative that has been created to the medical model classifications systems like the *DSM* and *ICD* is the *Person-in-Environment System Manual* (Karls & O'Keefe, 2008). This manual is seen as more in line with social work values and places the client in the context of his or her environment. It also offers open-source assessment forms. Unfortunately, the PIE has not been well developed in the literature or adopted widely by mental health professionals in the field (Kondrat, 2008).

FINAL THOUGHTS ON ASSESSMENT

Remember that assessment skills take time to develop. As new practitioners, you are just starting to develop this knowledge, skill, and confidence. You are never actually finished with the assessment process, even though you may have completed an assessment product. The client situation is constantly changing. Learn to be comfortable with an ever-changing landscape and be open to new information that will change the course of the work.

CHAPTER 6 RESOURCE GUIDE

SCREENING TOOL REFERENCES AND WEBLINKS TO HELPFUL ASSESSMENT RESOURCES

American Psychiatric Association (APA). (2014). *Online assessment measures*. Retrieved from http://www.psychiatry.org/practice/dsm/dsm5/online-assessment-measures#Disorder

CSWE Gero-Ed Center. (2014). *Differential mental health assessment course materials*. Retrieved from http://www.cswe.org/CentersInitiatives/CurriculumResources/MAC/GIG/SLU/36890.aspx

International Society for Traumatic Stress Studies (ISTSS). (2014). *Assessing trauma: Assessment resources*. Retrieved from https://www.istss.org/assessing-trauma.aspx

Michigan State University: School of Social Work: Koehler for Mental Health Professionals. (2003–2012). *Assessment tools*. Retrieved from http://socialwork.msu.edu/koehler/for_mh_professionals/forms.php

Military Pathways. (2014). *Military mental health screening program*. Retrieved from https://mentalhealthscreening.org/programs/military/resources/a-different-kind-of-courage.aspx

PAR, Inc. (2012). *Mini-Mental State Examination (MMSE®)*. Retrieved from http://www4.parinc.com/Products/Product.aspx?ProductID=MMSE

SAMSHA-HRSA: Center for Integrated Health Solutions. (n.d.) *SBIRT: Screening, brief intervention, and referral to treatment*. Retrieved from http://www.integration.samhsa.gov/clinical-practice/sbirt

SAMHSA-HRSA: Center for Integrated Health Solutions. (n.d.). *Screening tools*. Retrieved from http://www.integration.samhsa.gov/clinical-practice/screening-tools

SMH: Screening for Mental Health. (2010). *Our programs*. Retrieved from http://www.mentalhealth-screening.org/programs/

Teen Mental Health. (2014). *Clinical tools*. Retrieved from http://teenmentalhealth.org/for-health-professionals/clinical-tools/

ASKING THE DIFFICULT QUESTIONS

What to Ask and How to Respond

New practitioners struggle with asking questions that can feel intrusive and personal. In addition, sometimes new practitioners may be afraid of what the answers to the questions might be and doubt their ability to respond effectively to the answers given by their clients. For example, many new clinicians are afraid to ask clients about their thoughts of suicide, believing that by asking the questions they will increase the likelihood of that person thinking more about it. In reality, there are real negative consequences of *not* asking such questions. To assuage such concerns, this chapter explores why these questions must be asked and debunks some of the myths of the risks associated with asking them. Examples of how to phrase such questions are offered in an effort to reduce the feelings of intrusiveness.

WHY MUST I ASK THESE QUESTIONS?

There is a scene in the movie *Kissing Jessica Stein* in which Jessica is talking with Helen about questioning her sexual identity:

> **Helen:** "What does your therapist say about all of this?"
> **Jessica:** "Oh I could never tell my therapist."
> **Helen:** "Why not?"
> **Jessica:** "Because it's private!"

This scene epitomizes the difficulty clients can have in feeling comfortable enough with us to discuss sensitive issues, even when they know that the information that is shared will be kept confidential. We also can feel uncomfortable asking a client personal questions or exploring difficult issues unless the client brings them up. These feelings of discomfort could easily lead to an impasse, with both client and practitioner waiting for the other to open the dialogue. Therefore, it is incumbent on us to ask the difficult questions to demonstrate to the client that we feel comfortable discussing these topics. The client can always decide that he or she is not ready to explore these issues or that there just might be nothing of significance to discuss. Yet, it is important to communicate that if there is a topic area that might be of significance to the client, you are comfortable exploring it.

When the practitioner asks the questions, it does three things. First, you are normalizing the concern. This normalization lets the client know that other people have concerns about these issues and that your work together is an acceptable forum in which to discuss them. Second, you are breaking the silence and any taboos about these topic areas. Many of us received messages from our families and our social settings that we *do not* "air our dirty laundry" or discuss difficult or personal matters in "polite company." The helping relationship is different, as this relationship may be the one where you *do* discuss these matters. We need to communicate that, within this relationship, these conversations are acceptable, and that providing a forum for these discussions is exactly what the relationship is for. We need to give the client permission to use the relationship if the client needs this kind of "space." Third, by asking these questions, we are directly confronting any shame the client may be carrying from not being able to talk about a subject. Shame is often the most significant barrier to discussing difficult issues. By giving clients an opportunity to talk about the topics about which they have feelings of shame, we hope to break down barriers built by their feelings of shame.

Not asking these questions can have some unintended consequences. Silence can send a message that you do not want to talk about sensitive matters. By avoiding questions that relate an experience (e.g., sexual abuse), it is possible that the client may interpret your silence as your way of letting him or her know that you would be too upset by a disclosure and cannot handle discussions related to these experiences. Another potential unintended consequence is that by remaining silent you may remind the client of others in his or her life who minimized or dismissed these issues, which can have an impact on feelings of trust and safety in the relationship. Finally, you may inadvertently convey to the client that he or she must continue being silent on these matters, leading the client to the conclusion that there is no safe place to discuss them.

MYTHS AND FACTS ABOUT ASKING DIFFICULT QUESTIONS

One of the reasons new practitioners do not ask questions about suicide, self-injury, abuse, and other sensitive topics is that they often hold misconceptions about what these behaviors mean or what the discussion will stir up in the client. Some common myths, and the more accurate understandings of these dynamics, are presented next to help you feel more comfortable asking these types of questions:

Myth: If I ask clients if they have thoughts about killing themselves, it will give them the idea that suicide is a way out of their pain.

Fact: When someone is not suicidal, you cannot "suggest" suicide as an idea by asking if they have thoughts about it. It is important to remember that when someone is having thoughts about ending their life, it can be helpful to discuss them and to explore other resolutions to the pain they are currently experiencing. It is also important to obtain information about previous suicidal periods and about any past attempts (Jamison, 1999). Such information will tell you about how lethal their attempts were and how they coped with such feelings in the past.

Myth: Asking a client if they have a history of sexual or physical abuse can cause a post-traumatic reaction in clients.

Fact: You can ask about whether a person has ever experienced abuse in the past without going into the details. If the client does have an abuse history or is currently experiencing abuse, you should proceed with great care in asking them to relate details or share memories. Practitioners who work with trauma survivors advocate for trauma-informed treatment approaches that lay the groundwork for coping skills to help the client manage the traumatic memories before sharing the narrative of the experiences (Courtois & Ford, 2012).

Myth: A client who self-injures is suicidal, so if I ask about their self-inflicted injuries, then I may be required to have them hospitalized.

Fact: There is a difference between self-injurious behavior and suicidal intent. Most people who inflict injury on themselves do not intend to end their life. Behaviors such as skin picking, hair pulling, and cutting or burning skin are often done in an attempt to relieve intense feelings. Such behaviors can be best understood as a coping mechanism to distract from or avoid feelings associated with distress or traumatic experiences (Walsh, 2006).

Myth: If I ask a client who is in recovery from substance abuse to discuss their history of use or desire to use again, it will cause a relapse.

Fact: Much like questions about suicidal feelings, discussing past problematic substance use or desire to use again does not cause clients to relapse. In fact, by helping clients discuss what causes them to feel like using (triggers), they can explore alternatives to that behavior. These discussions can help the client avoid relapse. Most clients who have already been through substance abuse treatment are open and honest about past behaviors and are invested in maintaining their sobriety (Witkiewitz & Marlatt, 2004).

Myth: If a client does not report problematic substance use, then you do not need ask any further questions about this.

Fact: If a client is using drugs or alcohol to cope with their distress, or if their use if feeling out of control, they may not be honest with themselves or with you about their current use. It is always important to explore if and how a client uses alcohol, illegal drugs, or prescription drugs and assess whether this use rises to the level of a substance use disorder (Tanner, Wilhelm, Rossie, & Metcalf, 2012).

ASKING THE QUESTIONS

As you begin to develop your own style of how to ask these questions, we offer you a few suggestions about how to approach these discussions and ways to handle disclosures.

TRAUMA HISTORY

Approaching the issue of trauma from a broad lens can be helpful in determining if the client has experienced significant life events that have overwhelmed his or her normal capacity to cope. Trauma is a subjective experience—what feels traumatic to you might not to someone else. One approach is to ask: "Have you had any experiences, recently or in the past, where you feared for your safety?" Or, you can ask: "Can you think about a time in your life when you felt overwhelmed by what was happening and unable to cope?"

If a client reports having experienced a traumatic event, you can let the client know that you are glad they felt comfortable telling you and that together you can work on exploring this experience when they feel ready. To ask specifically about sexual abuse trauma, you can ask, "Has anyone ever touched you in a way that made you feel uncomfortable?" or "Have you ever felt forced to do something sexual that you did not want to do?" You may be the first person who has ever asked these questions or the first person with whom the client has chosen to share this information, so be sure to respond to the disclosure with care and concern, using statements such as the following:

- "I'm very glad you told me about this."
- "I appreciate your willingness to share this difficult experience with me."
- "This never should have happened to you; I'm very sorry it did."
- "If you want to explore this in our work together, we can do that when you are ready."

If you do not feel able to help the client process these experience or if it is beyond the scope of the services in your practice setting, be sure to have referrals on hand to direct the client to someone who can help them. National and international resources can be found in the chapter summary guide.

SUBSTANCE ABUSE

There are various cultural norms concerning drug and alcohol use, and our own experiences may inform how and if we ask questions about substance use. However, asking clients about their use of alcohol as well as prescription and nonprescription drugs is crucial, as use of substances may be a sign of other struggles and can lead to a number of concerns related to physical and mental health, as well as social well-being and functioning. It can be difficult to "unravel" the threads of the mental illness and the effects of the substances, and trying to do so can feel like trying to answer that age-old question: Which came first, the chicken or the egg? Substance use can sometimes mask or alter the information related to other issues with which the person is struggling. For example, interactions with prescription medications can often complicate treatment and make it difficult to obtain a baseline of the client's functioning. Trying to treat an issue without understanding the full picture can make any intervention less effective.

When working with clients who are using alcohol and prescription or nonprescription drugs, it is essential to consider in your assessment process the potential impact these substances are having on brain functioning, emotional well-being, and their ability to be attuned with others in their lives, including you. Alcohol and other substances have an impact on the functioning of the brain's limbic system, cerebral cortex, and prefrontal cortex (Farmer, 2014). For more on the brain and neurobiological processes, see Chapter 18.

Clients who have both a substance use disorder and a mental health disorder are referred to as having a "dual diagnosis"; unfortunately, this combination is common in many of the populations social workers encounter (Drake & Mueser, 2000). Dual diagnosis treatments focus on addressing both substance use and mental health issues and combine or integrate mental health and substance abuse interventions. Integration involves not only combining appropriate treatments for both disorders but also often modifying traditional interventions. For example, social skills training interventions emphasize not only the importance of developing relationships but also the need to avoid social situations that could lead to substance use. Substance abuse counseling goes slowly, as there are multiple layers of challenges the client is facing related to both the mental illness and the impact of the substance use disorder. The goal of dual diagnosis interventions is recovery from two serious illnesses. In this context, *recovery* means that the individual with a dual diagnosis learns to manage both illnesses so that he or she can pursue meaningful life goals (Drake & Mueser, 2000).

To determine whether your client has a substance use issue, you must ask difficult questions that require the client to honestly evaluate whether his or her use has risen to problematic levels. Some questions to consider are the following:

- "Can you tell me about your use of alcohol, drugs, prescription medication, or other substances?"
- "Have there been any negative consequences from your use?"
- "Has anyone expressed concern regarding your use?"
- "Are you concerned about any behaviors that feel out of control?"

If these questions yield a disclosure about problematic use, respond with concern for the client's well-being and safety without shaming or chastising the client. There are many cultural stigmas concerning those who abuse substances, and you may hear others, including your colleagues, use derogatory terms to refer to clients such as "drug addicts" and "alcoholics." Not only are such phrases derogatory, but also they do not demonstrate respectful, person-first language (Heller & Gitterman, 2011). Such language often perpetuates society's negative views of individuals who struggle with substances, creating more barriers for clients who struggle with being honest and open about these issues. To convey your empathy, consider a response like the following:

> "Many people turn to drugs or alcohol to cope with stress. It seems like it worked for you for a while, but now it's not. Would you be open to talking more about how to find other ways to handle life's stress?"

Once you receive agreement from the client, you can then link them to some resources. The ones in the chapter's summary guide are a good place to start.

RELIGION AND SPIRITUALITY

A person's religious or spiritual practices are personal. We often do not discuss religion or politics in social settings because they can raise areas of conflict and differences of opinion between people. Practitioners who do not ask about a client's spiritual practices are often missing a big dimension of the person's life experience (Cunningham, 2012). If they are not religious or spiritual, that is also okay. But if you do not ask, you might never know. When you ask a client if they have a faith tradition or spiritual practices, it can open up a wealth of information about family history or how he or she makes meaning out of events, as well as provide a potential source of support or strength. Also, be aware that while for many clients their faith traditions are sources of comfort and pride, for others this topic may be an area of internal conflict. For some, faith traditions can be experienced as contributing toward feelings of shame or isolation due to a variety of factors. Therefore, it is important not to get into a discussion about your own personal beliefs or practices but to focus on your client. Should the client ask you about your own spiritual beliefs, it is important to explore why he or she is seeking to know this information so that you can best understand how to respond. It is a good idea to talk about these potential responses with your supervisor. For those social workers working at a faith-based organization, these issues may arise more often. As such, it is even more important to discuss with your supervisor how such conversations are handled at the agency.

When exploring spiritual practices or religious traditions, remember that these personal dynamics can change over time as the client grows and develops. Consider asking: "Does your family practice a particular religion?" You also want to follow this up with questions about changes in these practices over time. You can ask: "Have your beliefs or practices changed over time?" and "How does your spirituality influence your daily life?" If the client wants to tell you about his or her practices and beliefs, it is essential that your responses are nonjudgmental and affirming.

SEXUALITY

As noted with the scenario in the beginning of this chapter, it is normal for people to feel reluctant to engage in conversations about sex and sexuality. Your comfort level with asking questions about this dimension of human experience will depend on your own feelings about your sexuality and about having these discussions with others. You may want to spend time role-playing or practicing asking these questions with others with whom you feel comfortable to increase your skills. You can open up a dialogue by asking a general question: "Are you currently sexually active?" or "What sexual problems or concerns have you experienced?" This can begin a discussion about the client's sexual self. By asking a question such as "Overall, how would you describe your sex life?" you can also explore the level of satisfaction or dissatisfaction with this, along with any concerns about sexual health and well-being. It is possible that during this discussion, clients may chose to disclose any history of sexual trauma, so it is best to be prepared for such disclosures as well.

When exploring a client's sexuality and sexual health, you will often arrive at discussions regarding sexual orientation. If this does not arise naturally, you may need to ask a specific question, such as "How do you identify your sexual orientation?" Sexual orientation is on a continuum and can be fluid over the course of the person's lifetime, so you can also ask about any changes in sexual orientation over the life course. Be prepared for disclosures from a client who is grappling with sexual orientation. A client may tell you that they are unsure about their identity or that they are in the process of coming out and you are the first person they are talking with about it. Respond to any disclosures in affirming and normalizing ways. Statements such as "I am glad you felt safe telling me this" and "Many people find themselves questioning their sexual orientation over time" can reassure them that you are someone they can talk to. See the chapter's summary guide for resources for yourself, the client, and the client's family members.

SELF-HARMING BEHAVIOR AND SUICIDAL FEELINGS AND ACTIONS

Asking clients about self-harming behaviors can feel complicated for many reasons. Primarily, we can feel unsure about the severity of the behavior, as it can be difficult to differentiate between self-harm and suicidal intention. As noted in the myths and facts presented previously, distinguishing between a self-harming behavior and a suicide attempt helps practitioners obtain a sense of what the client needs. Identifying the differences between these two behaviors requires us to ask difficult questions about distress, self-injury, and any suicidal feelings and intentions.

You can begin to differentiate between these two by focusing on what is causing the behavior and what the client is intending in the outcome. People engage in self-injurious behaviors because of overwhelming intrusive thoughts or feelings; here, the desired outcome is relief from psychological distress or distraction from the unbearable affect (Walsh, 2006). Suicidal thoughts or feelings, on the other hand, typically stem from a sense of despair and hopelessness; the person is unable to see any resolution to the psychological and emotional pain he or she is experiencing. In these situations, the desired outcome is to end one's life to make the pain stop.

Questions about self-injury and suicidality should be both direct and empathic. Consider asking the following:

- "What do you do when your thoughts and emotions feel unbearable?"
- "Have you ever inflicted an injury on yourself?"
- "Do you ever cause yourself physical pain to alleviate emotional pain?"
- "Have you ever had thoughts about ending your life?"
  - If yes—"Have you ever acted on those thoughts?"
  - If no—"What keeps you from acting on those thoughts?"
- "How many times in the past have you tried to end your life?"
  - Ask follow-up questions here to gain information about the lethality of the methods used, for example, "What was the method by which you tried to end your life?"
- "Can you tell me about a time in your life where living felt unbearable?"

These questions are asked in an effort to understand the client's unique experiences of self-harm or suicidal feelings. Respond to disclosures calmly, demonstrating your concerns about your client's safety. If you convey a sense of fear or alarm, you will inadvertently send the client the message that you cannot handle these discussions. It is important explore multiple options regarding their next steps. Many clients may fear that you will insist that they be hospitalized, yet in most cases, self-injury does not require hospitalization. For clients who are suicidal, there is a difference between discussing feelings on which they do not intend to act and having a specific plan with lethal means on which they intend to act. These issues regarding client safety are explored in depth in the next chapter.

FINAL THOUGHTS ON ASKING DIFFICULT QUESTIONS

Asking these difficult questions may feel awkward at first, but as you have more practice, you will develop your own style that will feel natural and authentic to you and fit with your personality. Not asking these questions leaves crucial gaps in your assessment and therefore your treatment plan. It is often the practitioner's own concerns about his or her ability to effectively handle the answers to these questions that create a barrier as well as concerns about the questions feeling intrusive to the clients. The summary guide at the end of this chapter provides you with resources to help with these concerns. Remember, if you do not ask, not only will you not have the full picture of your client's situation, but also you may inadvertently communicate that such topics are uncomfortable or unacceptable in the relationship you have formed with your client. Therefore, it is critical that you explore, in supervision or in other forums, your own challenges with asking questions about difficult topics and find ways to communicate your openness and willingness to explore topics further. Your comfort with such topics will set the stage for a much more productive and it is hoped more effective relationship with your client.

CHAPTER 7 RESOURCE GUIDE: LIST OF RESOURCES

CHILD ABUSE

http://www.nationalchildrensalliance.org
   National Children's Alliance*: National resources
1-800-4-A-CHILD or http://www.childhelp.org
   National Child Abuse Hotline: National hotline for reporting, resources, and
   services

DOMESTIC VIOLENCE

http://www.thehotline.org
   National Domestic Violence Hotline: Online chat forums with domestic violence
   experts and counselors
1-800-799-SAFE
   National Domestic Violence Hotline

RAPE AND SEXUAL ASSAULT

https://www.rainn.org
   Rape, Abuse, and Incest National Network: Online hotline and national
   resources
1-800-656-HOPE
   National Sexual Assault Hotline

SELF-INJURY

http://self-injury.net
   National and international support communities
1-800-DONT CUT
   Information line for national resources

SEXUAL ORIENTATION AND GENDER IDENTITY

http://www.matthewsplace.com/hotline/glbt-national-youth-talkline
   Matthew's Place: National resources for gay, lesbian, bisexual, transgendered, and
   questioning youth
1-800-850-8078
   National Youth Support Line
http://www.glnh.org
   GLBT National Help Center: Free peer support and national resources for adults
   and youth

http://www.befrienders.org
   Befrienders Worldwide: International resources regarding sexual orientation and
      gender identity
1-888-843-4564
   GLBT National Hotline

SPIRITUAL ASSESSMENT

Canda, E. R., & Furman, L. D. (2010). *Spiritual diversity in social work practice: The heart of helping* (2nd ed.). New York, NY: Oxford University Press.

SUBSTANCE ABUSE

http://findtreatment.samhsa.gov
   Behavioral health treatment services locator: National resource for treatment
      programs and listing of self-help resources such as AA (Alcoholics
      Anonymous) and NA (Narcotics Anonymous)
1-800-662-HELP
   National Helpline for Substance Abuse

SUICIDE

http://www.suicidepreventionlifeline.org
   National Suicide Prevention Lifeline: Support in the United States
1-800-273-TALK
   National Suicide Prevention Lifeline toll-free number

CHAPTER 8

ASSESSING THE SAFETY OF THE CLIENT

In the previous chapters, we discussed different ways to gather information from clients. In this chapter and the one that follows, we offer guidelines about what social workers need to do with information that indicates that a client is experiencing abuse, neglect, suicidal feelings, or other potentially dangerous situations. While there are differences among the various states and jurisdictions regarding the legal mandates, we explain some universal principles that all practitioners must follow when learning about these situations, whether during an assessment or during the course of working with a client. We cannot emphasize enough the importance of consultation and supervision when there are concerns about a client. Supervision and consultation are important not only at the beginning stages of a career but also throughout its entirety.

MANDATED REPORTING

Social workers, like teachers, nurses, doctors, and other professionals, are mandated to report abuse or neglect of a child or of an adult who is over 18 years of age but considered vulnerable due to a cognitive impairment or mental illness. The specific issues of homicidal clients and social worker safety are explored in the next chapter. In this chapter, we address the issues of protecting our clients from harm by others or self-harm.

WHAT DOES IT MEAN TO BE A MANDATED REPORTER?

Being a *mandated reported* means that you are required **by law** to break confidentiality in specific cases involving abuse or neglect of vulnerable people (Ainsworth, 2002). The general language, with slight variations among each state or US territory, asserts practitioners who have a reasonable cause to *suspect* that a child or vulnerable adult known to him or her in his or her professional capacity has been or is in immediate danger of being mentally or physically abused or neglected are required to **immediately** report to either the police or the appropriate protective services agency (e.g., child protective services, adult protective services). While there exists a variety of state statutes on child abuse and neglect, harm of vulnerable adults, intimate partner violence (IPV), stalking, and protecting clients from self-harm and suicide (see summary guide for more information), there is no question that *all* mental health practitioners, whether they are counselors, social workers, psychologists, psychiatrists, hotline volunteers, substance abuse counselors, and others have a legal obligation to intervene (Reamer, 2006).

WHY ARE THERE DISCREPANCIES IN REPORTING?

In spite of this legal and professional clarity, there remains great ambivalence about mandatory reporting and a lack of adherence to the law among practitioners. Research showed that approximately 60% of professionals do not report under mandatory reporting situations because the practitioner

- Fears disruption of the therapeutic alliance
- Does not want to be involved in legal proceedings
- Fears liability if a report is unsubstantiated
- Sees no benefit to a client
- Fears intervention may be harmful for the client
- Believes that investigation does not always strengthen families
- Feels a lack of confidence in the social and legal systems to address the issue
- Thinks they do not have enough evidence to report
- Feels they can help the client better than the "system" (Zellman & Fair, 2002)

Another reason for the discrepancies is that there is little training and education for professionals beyond being told they are mandated reporters (Tufford, Mishna, & Black, 2010). While extreme or obvious cases, such as serious abuse or neglect of younger children, tend to be reported, many more cases do not. In addition, professional experience plays a role. Those with less training and those who have never reported tend not to report. Judgments about recognition and reporting are not made with consistency and typically result in underreporting (Webster, O'Toole, O'Toole, & Lucal, 2005). This underreporting becomes not only a professional training and education issue but also a supervision issue. Unlike many other parts of our role, these situations in our professional roles are not places for critical thinking; the law is clear about what is to be reported. It is also not the place for criticisms of agencies responsible for handling the reports to prevent the practitioner from executing this task. Protective services agencies are seen as screening out less severe cases of abuse and often face high levels of dissatisfaction with their performance by both professionals the community at large (Zellman & Fair, 2002). While these criticisms may be fair, they do not relieve the practitioner of reporting responsibilities.

The social work code of ethics (COE; National Association of Social Workers [NASW], 2008) has a number of ethical standards that address the role of *mandated reporter*. However, as with many ethical issues, the role of mandated reporter may make some social workers feel that carrying out this role puts them in conflict with other aspects of the COE. The core professional values of social justice, belief in the dignity and worth of the person, and the importance of human relationships are particularly relevant. The practitioner's responsibility to clients' self-determination ends at the point of risk, and the protections of confidentiality do not apply when it is necessary to prevent harm. Therefore, we must break confidentiality when we learn that a vulnerable person is being abused or neglected. The need to protect them outweighs the right to confidentiality. All people deserve to be safe from harm and neglect; this protection is a social justice issue and one that all professionals must uphold for the integrity of the profession.

A mandatory reporting situation is one in which you must have *reasonable cause to suspect* that there exists an abusive or neglectful situation (Reamer, 2006). In such cases, your role is not to be a detective and determine whether your suspicion is supported by evidence. It is the role of an investigator to determine whether there is sufficient evidence to support these suspicions. Your role is to report your suspicions, with support and guidance from your supervisor. With the mandatory reporting responsibility comes a protection for acting in good faith under reasonable suspicion. Professionals have immunity from civil or criminal charges that result from reporting in good faith (Reamer, 2006).

Finally, if the legal mandate to report, the ethical imperative to report, and the desire to protect your client are not enough, know that there are clear consequences for failure to report. These vary by state, but all include a fine, jail time, and loss of license to practice. Someone who is a mandated reporter obviously has important responsibilities and obligations. Clients should be made aware of this role at the beginning of your work together, especially the limits of confidentiality, the intervention options, and the policies of the agency. This process of reviewing this information with clients is referred to as obtaining their *informed consent*. This term is used as you want them to have all of the information about what they can expect so that they can be aware of their options, as well as any risks and benefits to them, and therefore make an informed decision when they give their permission to work with you and your agency. It is critical to clearly state under what circumstances you must report.

HOW DO I KNOW IF A CLIENT IS BEING ABUSED OR NEGLECTED?

Many practitioners find it difficult to navigate the gray areas of what constitutes abuse or neglect and whether what they are seeing or hearing meets that definition. Many social workers are told that they will "know it when they see it" without being given more training and information. Extreme cases are often obvious, but not all cases are extreme. In these circumstances, new practitioners benefit from supervision to help think through the details of each specific case and whether the situation rises to the level of needing a mandatory report. In fact, we strongly recommend that all social workers, especially those early in their careers, obtain supervision/consultation with a supervisor or colleague every time they suspect a client is experiencing abuse or neglect.

While not every case presents in the same way, definitions found in the broad categories of neglect and abuse are presented next (Briere & Elliott, 2003).
Neglect entails

- Educational neglect (failing to bring children to school)
- Failure to be protected from abuse
- Lack of proper care or control by parent or caregiver
- Danger of abuse from another person in the household
- Exposure to illegal drugs

Abuse entails

- Physical harm not caused by accidental means
- Sexual abuse or attempted sexual abuse
- Mental (emotional) harm
- Sex trafficking

Given that abuse and neglect are difficult to detect in vulnerable populations, screening for it in general populations is helpful. Research showed that children and vulnerable adults who experience maltreatment of some form tend to have marked shifts in behavior (a typically outgoing child is suddenly removed and shy), signs of distress and agitation with previously neutral situations (an older adult in a nursing home begins to become upset when the volunteer comes to take him to the park), and mental health issues such as depression, anxiety, suicidal ideation, dissociation, and hyperarousal (Donovan & Regehr, 2010; Lawson, 2009; Spinazzola et al., 2005). In any of these kinds of situations, screening for maltreatment should be part of an assessment.

INTIMATE PARTNER VIOLENCE AND STALKING

There will also be information you receive in an assessment or even in ongoing work with clients where you find that a client is being, or is in danger of being, harmed by someone else, but the client does not meet the criteria applied to individuals for whom mandatory reporting applies, as they are not considered vulnerable. These situations most commonly occur in relationships in which there is physical, emotional, or sexual abuse or situations of stalking.

ABUSE IN RELATIONSHIPS

Intimate partner violence (IPV), often called "domestic violence," is defined as

> a pattern of assaultive and coercive behaviors, including physical, sexual, and psychological attacks, as well as economic coercion, that adults or adolescents use against their intimate partners [current or former dating, married or cohabitating relationships of heterosexuals, gay men, or lesbians]. (Tower, 2003, p. 484)

Research on IPV revealed that approximately one in four women is physically abused by her intimate partner (Dass-Brailsford, 2007). Prevalence rates for men are mostly unknown, as most research is focused on women. This form of abuse can lead to death, physical injury, and mental health issues such as depression, anxiety, post-traumatic stress disorder (PTSD), guilt, shame, and the risk of revictimization in other relationships (Bennice, Resick, Mechanic, & Astin, 2003).

In addition to the direct mental health impact on the person experiencing IPV, if there are children who witness this abuse, this experience can have negative effects on their well-being. Children who witness IPV may develop PTSD, dissociative symptoms, distress, and increased aggression with peers. Witnessing IPV was found to be more harmful to the child than being the direct victim, as their helplessness in these situations caused great distress (Antle, Barbee, Yankeelov, & Bledsoe, 2010). This finding is even more remarkable given that approximately 70% of children who witness IPV are also victims of physical abuse, and yet in a study the IPV was more distressing to them (Dass-Brailsford, 2007).

It is common for people experiencing abuse in relationships not to disclose that the abuse is happening. For this reason and others, IPV is underdetected and undertreated by professionals (Tower, 2003). There are several barriers to professionals properly screening and then being able to subsequently effectively intervene with clients who present with experiences of IPV. Some of these barriers include

- Lack of education/training on abusive relationships
- Personal discomfort or experience with the issue
- Prejudicial attitudes toward victims "deserving it" or "provoking" their partners
- Lack of time to deal with disclosures
- Lack of institutional support to intervene (Tower, 2003)

Therefore, it is crucial that practitioners in all practice settings screen for clients who are currently experiencing IPV, or are survivors of violence in relationships, so the clients can be referred to the appropriate resources for support. In general, research showed that women who should be screened are those who present with severe PTSD, have children with PTSD, and are often isolated and lack social supports (Bennice et al., 2003). In general, asking all clients, male and female, if they have had physical, emotional, or sexual experiences in relationships that have felt abusive is a good place to start.

Another common challenge for practitioners is to understand the barriers that exist for victims when they contemplate leaving an abusive relationship. It is beyond the scope of this book to identify and explore these potential barriers, and we encourage readers to discuss these issues with their supervisors or participate in community trainings specific to IPV. As social workers, it is not our role to "convince" a client to leave an abusive relationship—we must value a client's self-determination. We must also become educated regarding the dynamics of power and control in abusive relationships and become familiar with those that are found in the "Power and Control Wheel" (see the summary guide). In addition, it is important not to communicate any judgments you might have about their choices but rather to strive to understand the complexities involved in an abusive relationship and help the clients to develop plans for them to remain as safe as possible given their situation.

In working with such individuals, one tool that social workers can use with clients is a safety plan. This tool can be used to help those in abusive relationships (and any children involved) think through and plan for a variety of scenarios with the ultimate goal of keeping all of the individuals in the home as safe as possible. The following are some of the topic areas (Dass-Brailsford, 2007) that might be discussed or addressed in a safety plan with a client:

- How to stay safe while living with abuser
- Identifying and reviewing guidelines for leaving
- Strategies for staying safe after leaving, as this a particularly high-risk time

See the summary guide for links to resources for creating safety plans with clients. It is important to check with the laws in the jurisdiction where you are practicing; in some areas, when children are exposed to IPV, social workers are mandated to report that IPV is occurring in the home.

STALKING

The behavior of stalking is typically understood to be a form of "obsessional following," as obsession is the basic element of stalking (Meloy, Davis, & Lovette, 2001). It is an abnormal or long-term pattern of behavior and interaction directed toward a specific individual constituting nonconsensual communication with or harassment of another person (Spitz, 2003). The type of relationship between stalker and victim varies from strangers to colleagues, acquaintances, or prior romantic relationship partners, to name a few. Research showed that 40–60% of stalking victims are prior sexual intimates of the stalker, and 90% of women murdered by intimate partners were stalked prior to their death (Cox & Speziale, 2009). If you are not sure if what a client is sharing with you meets the definition of stalking, the most common behaviors include, but are not limited to

- Repeated following
- Repeated phone calls/hang-ups
- Text messages
- Unwanted gifts/packages
- Acts of stealing/going through mail or garbage

- Commission of breaking and entering, vandalism, theft, arson
- Incidents of stealing underwear
- Harassment of and harm to others related to victim (including pets)
- Threatening items (e.g., dead flowers, cut up photos) sent to the victim
- "Coincidental" run-ins
- False rumors spread about the victim
- Stalking by proxy
- E-mails/spamming/instant messaging
- Connections in chatrooms
- Website "tributes" or blogs
- Personal data manipulation
- Tracking computer activity
- Blackmail (Sinwelski & Vinton, 2001)

One of important roles that social workers play when working with individuals who experience any of these scenarios is to help to identify that these are potential stalking behaviors. It is common for victims of stalking to downplay or minimize such behaviors and not take them as seriously as they should be. Many people minimize early signs of stalking as signs of a "jilted lover" or those stemming from a "harmless crush" at first. It is important to gather as much information as possible from the client and then discuss your concerns with your supervisor. It is critical that you and your supervisor identify what message to communicate to your client about your concerns for his or her safety.

If it does appear that the behaviors are not harmless but rather are consistent with stalking behaviors, then we recommend that the social worker discuss the identified experiences of stalking as serious and treat them as threats to the client's safety. During this discussion with the client, it is also important to strongly encourage and recommend to the client that he or she cease contact with the stalker after the client has clearly stated to the other individual to stop all communication and stalking behavior. In addition, many practitioners who have worked in these situations state that the client should never be alone with the stalker and to begin to build their own legal case by documenting in detail a record of stalking episodes. It is important to

- Catalog and document all items received from the stalker
- Report all incidents to police, even if the police do not take them seriously
- Secure a new phone number and use the old one only for the stalker (keep as evidence)
- Improve security at home, workplace, school, and all other environments
- Tell others they are being stalked and enlist their help in alerting the client to the stalker's attempts at contact or presence
- Develop an escape plan if you come face-to-face with the stalker
- Secure a restraining order when possible and safe to do so. (Spitz, 2003)

For more information about helping clients create safety plans and a stalking incident log, see the resources in the summary guide.

SUICIDE AND SELF-HARMING BEHAVIORS

The thought of working with someone who is actively suicidal has the potential to strike terror in the hearts of many practitioners, particularly new ones. Part of what leads to such a fear reaction is that these situations can be literally life or death, and we can feel powerless to prevent the worst case scenario from occurring. Yet, to help clients who struggle with such issues, it is important for social workers to respond proactively and learn as much as possible about these situations, rather than to retreat in fear. In her book *Night Falls Fast: Understanding Suicide*, Dr. Kay Redfield Jamison (1999) explored the history of practitioners' attempts to understand what causes people to want to end their lives and how to stop them. She stated:

> We have built hospitals to provide a sanctuary against madness and self-inflicted death, and developed psychotherapies to ameliorate pain and to help the suicidal navigate through the darkest times of their lives. We know a great deal about how to prevent suicide, but not enough. And what we know, we do not use as well or widely as we could. (p. 236)

The message to practitioners from Jamison and others who study and write about suicide and its prevention is not to be afraid. It is important that we do not avoid directly discussing suicidal thoughts, feelings, and intentions with clients due to our own fears, discomfort, or misunderstanding about the topic. Often, we avoid discussing suicide due to our fears that by asking about the topic, we will somehow plant this idea in a client's head and as a result avoid asking them if they have had thoughts of ending their life or have had previous suicide attempts. If someone has serious and consistent thoughts about ending his or her life, he or she will most often be honest about their history and be willing to discuss these situations with you. As we have discussed previously, by not discussing suicide with clients you may be inadvertently sending a message that you cannot handle the topic or do not take their concerns seriously. There will be some people who never discuss their intentions to end their life and do so quietly and without reaching out for help. For each of these people, there are many others who will try to get others to listen to their desire to end the emotional pain that haunts them.

Identifying risk factors for suicide in an assessment is crucial to client care as well as to reducing practitioner liability (Jobes, Rudd, Overholser, & Joiner, 2008). While mental health disorders such as major depression, bipolar disorder, PTSD, borderline personality disorder, and anxiety are commonly associated with suicide, so are a family history of suicide, major life stressors, and a prevailing sense of hopelessness about the future (Jobes et al., 2008). Practitioners should take all expressions of a desire to end one's life or simply "disappear" or "not be here anymore" seriously and document all discussions and resulting interventions (Reamer, 2005). Resources for conducting suicide assessments and ways to intervene are listed in the summary guide.

Distinguishing suicide attempts from self-injury is also an important part of a risk assessment. While self-inflicted injury is a real safety risk, it is not necessarily related to attempts to end one's life (Walsh, 2006). This topic was discussed in Chapter 7 on asking difficult questions, but bears repeating here. When a client has specific thoughts about ending his or her life, has a lethal method, and has a clear plan, these indicators raise a potential mandatory reporting situation and can frequently result in a period of hospitalization for the client's own protection. Someone who uses self-injurious behaviors, on the other hand, to discharge emotional pain or cope with distress does not necessarily require hospitalization but would benefit from risk-reduction strategies and learning alternative coping mechanisms. However, it is essential that before making such a determination of the risk levels, social workers seek supervision or consultation with other colleagues and document every piece of information that was used in making a decision. We provide more information in the summary guide at the end of Chapter 7 to help navigate these challenging situations, along with links in the summary guide in this chapter to the SAD PERSONS scale for assessment.

IF AND WHEN YOU DO HAVE TO REPORT

If you decide after gathering information from your client and consulting with your supervisor that you need to report that the client is in danger of harming him- or herself or that others are harming the client, we recommend having all of the information in front of you before you contact the appropriate authorities. When reporting, consider asking to speak with a supervisor because you will often get a more seasoned worker who can speak with you as a fellow professional. You will be asked to provide your name and professional identity and role and to provide all of the known information to establish the cause of the suspicion of abuse or neglect, including the identity of the person(s) responsible. You will need to provide the names, addresses, phone numbers, physical descriptions, and any other relevant information about the individual(s) who is at harm, as well as the individual(s) that you suspect is causing such harm. It is important at this time *not* to give your opinion or speculation. As stated previously, your job is simply to report the information that led to the suspicion; do not to pass judgment, editorialize, or draw conclusions.

While it may seem that social workers make reports of abuse separate from their clients, we encourage when possible to recommend to clients that they make a report themselves or with you. While it may seem counterintuitive, making a report together can be an empowering process, and in our own personal experiences, we have found that it can strengthen the working alliance. When you invite and encourage your client to be part of the process, you are reinforcing how you value the collaborative process and the partnership you want to maintain with the client. At a minimum, discuss with your supervisor how to tell the clients that you will be making a report. There may be some circumstances for which you do not want to inform the client ahead of time, but we believe that these situations are not the norm. Regardless of whether you and your client make the report together or how much you share with the client ahead of time, the ultimate responsibility for making the report still falls on the social worker and *not* the client.

FINAL THOUGHTS ON CLIENT SAFETY

Social workers can and should feel a great deal of responsibility for the well-being of their clients, rightfully so. While addressing safety from self-harm and harm by others is an important part of our job, we must remember that we cannot "save" our clients. Clients have the right to self-determination and can and will make decisions that create unsafe situations for themselves, such as remaining connected to people who we might determine are unsafe. It is extremely important that social workers do not blame the clients for their choices but seek to understand their choices so that we can better empathize with the complex nature of their realities. There are some behaviors and decisions that require us to report to the authorities to protect them or their children or vulnerable adults in their care. Other life situations will require us to help them navigate unsafe situations as best they can. Still other situations will call on us to highlight the situations in which they may not be safe. Balancing respect for client self-determination while seeking to protect them is a delicate balance to reach. As we have said throughout this chapter, we cannot emphasize enough the importance of using supervision to help navigate these challenging moments. It is important to consult, document, and know the laws governing your professional responsibilities where you practice. You must safeguard your professional integrity in addition to protecting your clients.

CHAPTER 8 RESOURCE GUIDE

The following are links to reporting laws, guides, procedures, safety planning resources, and links to assessment tools for suicide:

https://www.childwelfare.gov/topics/systemwide/laws-policies/statutes/manda/
  Child Welfare Information Gateway: Mandatory reporting laws by state for child abuse and neglect

https://www.rainn.org/public-policy/laws-in-your-state
  RAINN—Rape, Abuse, and Incest National Network: Mandatory reporting laws by state for sexual violence against children and vulnerable adults

http://www.acf.hhs.gov/sites/default/files/fysb/state_compendium.pdf
  Family Violence Prevention Fund: Compendium of state statutes and policies on domestic violence and healthcare

http://www.ncadv.org
  National Coalition Against Domestic Violence: Information on abusive relationships, the power and control wheel, and guidelines for creating a safety plan for clients in abusive intimate relationships

http://www.victimsofcrime.org/our-programs/stalking-resource-center/help-for-victims/stalking-safety-planning
  National Center for Victims of Crime Stalking Resource Center: Guidelines for creating a safety plan for clients being stalked

http://www.suicidepreventionlifeline.org/learn/safety.aspx
National Suicide Prevention Lifeline: Guidelines for creating a safety plan for clients who are suicidal

RESOURCES FOR ASSESSING SUICIDAL INTENT IN CLIENTS

Beck Scale for Suicide Ideation: http://www.beckinstitute.org/beck-inventory-and-scales/

Behavioral Research and Therapy Clinics: Reasons for Living Inventory and Suicide Attempts and Non-Suicidal Self-Injury Scales: http://blogs.uw.edu/brtc/publications-assessment-instruments/

Suicide Assessment SAD PERSONS assessment scale: http://www.capefearpsych.org/documents/SADPERSONS-suiciderisk.pdf

Suicide Status Form and CAMS Approach: Jobes, D. A. (2012). The Collaborative Assessment and Management of Suicidality (CAMS): An evolving evidence-based clinical approach to suicidal risk. *Suicide and Life-Threatening Behavior, 42*(6), 640–653.

CHAPTER 9

ASSESSING SAFETY OF OTHERS IN RELATION TO THE CLIENT

In Chapter 8, we addressed the importance of evaluating the client's risk of harm to him- or herself. In this chapter, we emphasize the importance of being aware of a client's potential to harm others, including the practitioner. While the risk of being injured on the job varies by the setting, we believe that, regardless of the environment, all practitioners should learn to do a safety assessment of their surroundings, their own personal safety, as well as the safety of others with whom the client may have contact. This chapter provides general guidelines on how to conduct an environmental safety assessment, with the caveat that each workplace setting will have unique conditions that must be considered.

WORKER'S PERSONAL SAFETY

From a broad lens, violence in the workplace is defined as any action, or threat of action, against a person in the course of carrying out their work, that creates a hostile or unsafe work environment and negatively affects the worker, either physically or psychologically. This includes all types of physical, sexual, and verbal assaults, threats, intimidation, bullying, and harassment. It also includes damage to property, stalking, and threats to harm loved ones, including pets (Occupational Safety and Health Administration [OSHA], 2004).

In a national study on safety in social service delivery, approximately half of those surveyed stated that their work presented safety concerns (National Association of Social Workers [NASW], 2006). In response to one of the questions on the survey, "Are you faced with personal safety issues in your primary employment practice," 44% of the respondents said yes. In addition, 30% of those who responded to the survey did not think that their employers adequately addressed their safety concerns. Although this study was focused on one type of practice setting, it is important to remember that personal safety issues are a concern in many different types of settings and should be taken seriously.

It is likely that many social workers and other professionals do not enter situations with clients focused on their own personal safety. Although there are individual factors that might influence a specific person to become unsafe or violent, there are community and systemic variables that have increased violence in places where social workers may work. These include

- Community-based psychiatric care for those who would have been in hospital settings prior to the deinstitutionalization movement;
- Involvement in family disputes, including child protection and domestic violence;
- Increased financial distress and cutbacks in services and public benefits;
- Growing substance abuse issues across populations;
- Growing cultural acceptance of violence and access to guns and other weapons; and
- Resistant or mandated clients who do not want intervention (Spencer & Munch, 2003).

Our intention with providing this information is not to scare new practitioners, but rather to encourage you to be a part of creating a culture of worker safety and work environments where workers are encouraged by supervisors and agency leadership to protect their safety while helping others. NASW (2006) reported that practitioners who encounter unsafe work situations are

- Novice workers (within the first 5 years of graduation)
- Workers in both public and private agencies serving the community
- Workers in primarily mental health and child welfare settings

In our opinion, these trends cover the gamut. Given that these trends could involve virtually any relatively new social worker, we believe strongly in discussing how you can be proactive in changing the culture of the workplace to attend to the safety needs of workers. To best serve the client, practitioners need to feel safe in their work.

Most troubling for those new to the field is the research finding of an inverse relationship between worker safety and years of experience (Spencer & Munch, 2003). In other words, the newer the worker, the higher the level of risk of being harmed by a client. This is because most new workers do not receive safety training and do not have the practice wisdom to know when situations are unsafe. They are more likely to worry than a more seasoned worker about getting in trouble for not completing a meeting with a client. While organizational leaders must attend to the task of addressing safety in the delivery of services, there are some concrete things each practitioner can do to reduce his or her risk of being harmed in their workplace. Social workers can deter some situations by being attuned to signs of danger and aware that the desire to help others does not protect you from being harmed by those you desire to help.

An important place to start for most social workers is to first acknowledge that violence can happen across all genders, classes, races, ethnicities, ages, religions, and contexts. We must never assume that a certain group or context is completely safe because of our assumptions or biases. With this acknowledgment comes attending to our own self-awareness and need for vigilance. We each have our own internal "alarm system" or gut feelings that a situation or person is not safe. Yet, we are often socialized to ignore these signals in an effort not to rush to judgment about people and work to talk ourselves out of our own instincts (de Becker, 1999). However, these signals are nature's way of letting us know when we are in danger. Therefore, it is important to pay attention to somatic signals of danger, such as a funny feeling in your stomach or the hair on your arms and neck standing up. Fear is sometimes viewed as a weakness, but it can be a gift that can save you from harm (de Becker, 1999).

To pay attention to your own danger cues and attend to your own safety while in the course of your work, we suggest you think about

- Being alert to risk without being hypervigilant.
- Preparing for potentially dangerous situations with tools and knowledge of agency policies and procedures.
- Learning to distinguish anger from rage—When is a client just expressing anger and does not have the potential to act it out?
- Identifying your subtle body cues that danger is imminent ("trip your alarm").
- Understanding some of the reasons why people may resort to aggression.
- Examining your own personal relationship to and feelings about anger—How do you react when people express anger or show nonverbal signs of anger (Smith, 2006)?

DE-ESCALATION TECHNIQUES

Some of the bullet points address being aware of your client's emotional state. With this awareness, it is possible that practitioners in some situations may be able to prevent a client from escalating from anger to violence. Weinger (2001) asserted that workers can increase their safety and reduce their risk of experiencing violence at the hands of clients by employing techniques to de-escalate violent behavior before it begins. She suggested that workers should

- Appear calm, centered, and self-assured
- Maintain a calm tone of voice as the client escalates
- Not argue with the client or become defensive
- Act respectfully at all times
- Validate client concerns while letting them know that their behavior is not acceptable
- Not engage in an analysis of the cause of the client's anger at this time
- Never turn their backs on an angry client or remain sitting if the client is standing
- Keep their hands where they can be seen and empty of objects
- Allow adequate physical space between them and the client
- Keep an eye on the client without appearing threatening to the client

As stated, be sure to trust your instincts. If you feel that the situation is unsafe, then there is a strong likelihood that it is. In these situations, you can let a client know that their behavior is creating an environment in which you are both unsafe. Let the client know that they will be choosing to end the meeting if their behavior continues. If the situation continues to escalate, be sure to keep that boundary. If the client will not leave, you should leave the immediate area and obtain help.

ASSESSING WORKPLACE ENVIRONMENT SAFETY

Addressing the worker's actions for safety is only one half of the equation. Whether practicing in a small agency, large organization or residential setting or conducting home visits, practitioners must attend to elements in the environment that relate to safety. While some research showed that residential settings are more risky than others (Winstanley & Hales, 2008), workers in all settings need to be mindful of safety issues. NASW (2013) stated that practitioners should be in work environments that are safe places for both workers and clients. To address these safety concerns, NASW recommended that

- Workspaces should have visible and easily accessible exits.
- There should be alarm systems to communicate to others and obtain assistance when the worker feels unsafe.
- Workers should be able to have another worker present when meeting with a client who may be dangerous.
- Workspaces should be free from objects that can be used to harm others, such as scissors, staplers, and the like.
- Buildings should have secure entry points and exits.
- Hallways, stairwells, and outdoor spaces should be well lit.
- Security cameras should be installed where appropriate.
- Mobile phones should be provided for those who work in the field.
- For workers doing field visits, risk assessments should be done prior to each visit.
- For those transporting clients in a vehicle, workers should receive specific safety training for risk reduction, and the vehicle should be in safe working order.

In essence, the environment in which the practitioner engages clients should be thoroughly reviewed through a safety and risk assessment lens. Whether the setting is an office, client residence, hospital, or residential treatment facility, the environment should be safe to enter and stay to conduct the work of the client meeting.

RISKS RELATED TO WORK TASKS

Many practitioners face other risks related to the type of work they are doing. Working in a domestic violence safe house, an inpatient psychiatric hospital, or a residential treatment facility for violent offenders and removing a child from the home are just some examples of high-risk activities for workers (Shields & Kiser, 2003). Working out in the community or in clients' homes is another area for consideration. Some safety tips in these situations include the following:

- Learn all you can about the family and community before going.
- Find out about the activities and whereabouts of gangs and other groups.
- Let supervisors or colleagues know your whereabouts and times of visits.
- Touch base with them at the end of each visit.
- Dress to allow for ease of movement and ambulation.
- Avoid wearing neckties, scarves, hanging jewelry, or anything that could be used to harm you.
- Avoid wearing religious or political symbols, sports team insignias, or anything that could incite conflict.
- Be aware of what is posted about you on social networks.
- Drive by meeting locations to see if there are any safety concerns before getting out of your car.
- Park in a well-lit area, close to the entrance, and back your car into the parking space.
- Do not leave valuables in the vehicle.
- Schedule visits during the daytime.
- Go on home visits in teams whenever possible.
- Do not enter homes where there is yelling or fighting.
- Scan the environment for weapons or dangerous pets before entering.
- Bring limited personal items with you (keys, phone, folder). Lock other items in the trunk of your car before arriving at your parking space (Harkey, n.d.).

The importance of trusting your gut feeling and danger instincts cannot be emphasized enough. If something does not feel right, respect that feeling and your internal alarm system. If you become uneasy about the situation in which you find yourself, leave and call your supervisor or the police. It is important to remember that when practitioners fear for their own safety in the work, they are unable to be effective in the task of helping clients. Worker safety is essential for quality and ethical client services and therefore should be a priority for every practitioner.

ASSESSING FOR POTENTIAL HARM TO OTHERS

Just like when a client is suicidal, when a client intends to harm someone else, there is a legal and ethical "duty to warn" the target of the violence or contact the police (Tapp & Payne, 2011). These situations can be challenging for all of the parties involved as the practitioner must break confidentiality and reach out to someone in the client's life and warn them. Therefore, the task at hand is to weigh the level of risk and threat against confidentiality and self-determination. This task means that even the most casual statements about a desire to harm another should be thoroughly explored. It is the practitioner's responsibility to determine the risk level for the present situation. This determination requires a comprehensive review of the desire, thoughts, fantasies, and wishes, as well as any clear plans and means to carry out any plans. The more specific the plan, the more readily available the means are available to the client, and the clearer the intent, the higher the risk of the client carrying out his or her plan.

The first step in ascertaining if the client is thinking about harming someone else is simply to ask. To gather this information, the practitioner should consider asking a question that is framed in a reflection on how upset and angry the client is, linking feeling to action, such as, "You sound very upset at Chris for how he treated you. It makes sense to me that you are angry and hurt. Sometimes when we feel that hurt we want the other person to feel hurt as well. Have you had thoughts of hurting Chris?" If there is a positive response to this statement, the next step is to explore with the client further to see if there is a plan, such as by asking direct questions like "How would you hurt Chris?" or "How would you see this happening?"

If there appears to be a plan, the next step is to determine whether the client has access to the means to carry out this plan and how likely the client would be to carry out the plan. To gather this information, practitioners can ask a question such as "You stated that you would like to see Chris feel your pain so much so that you'd hit him with a baseball bat. How likely are you to carry this out?" Practitioners can explore this subject further by asking the client if there are any reasons why he or she would not do this. What would prevent or hold him or her back from carrying out this plan? We also believe it is useful to explore what might happen if he or she went through with this action and if he or she can identify any negative consequences to him- or herself. If the client cannot identify any risk, practitioners can explore with the client if he or she could anticipate any legal or social ramifications or how hurting the other person would help your client alleviate his or her own emotional pain.

If the risk of your client harming someone else is low, you can validate the feelings while helping the client find alternative coping mechanisms to harming others. If the risk is midrange (the client cannot say for sure that he or she would not do it), then it is crucial to consult with a supervisor or colleague to review the level of risk and your decision-making process. Finally, if the risk is determined to be high, you should intervene immediately, as this is where your duty to warn comes in. For new practitioners, this intervention should be done under the guidance and direction of your supervisor or their designee. Attempts should be made to reach the intended victim by phone, e-mail, and any other means. When speaking with the intended victim, only information related to the threat may be shared. No other confidential client information should be given to the intended victim. If the person cannot be reached, then employ the assistance of the police. A police report should also be made at this time (Jongsma, 2004).

As a guiding principle, every interaction with a client and your actions pertaining to a client should be documented in the client's chart. It is even more important to document every conversation and attempt to explore a client's homicidal ideation or intent. In the records, we recommend that practitioners provide any client quotes and any client statements that pertain to the reasons for not carrying out the actions. In addition, it is important to provide detailed descriptions of any consultation sought in the case and follow-up conducted. Finally, be sure to document the interventions taken or when and if the homicidal ideation or intent ceases.

FINAL THOUGHTS ON SAFETY

Thinking about clients harming us or someone else is not comfortable, but it is essential to ethical practice. As with many uncomfortable tasks, it can be easy to be in a place of denial or avoidance of these tasks. As more workers require their practice settings to address the health and safety of the staff, it will not be incumbent on the practitioners to raise these issues themselves. However, in all work situations, to fully assess the health and well-being of our clients, we must explore our own safety and the safety of others in relation to the client. If we choose to neglect this task, we not only are being unethical, but also are putting ourselves and others into dangerous situations that could be avoided if we take a proactive stance.

CHAPTER 9 RESOURCE GUIDE: WORKER SAFETY PLAN AND CHECKLIST

WORKER SAFETY PLAN

According to OSHA (2004), there are five core elements to a safety plan for mental health practitioners. This should form the basic framework of any safety plan developed at your place of practice. They are as follows:

1. *Management-/leadership-driven efforts with employee involvement*—This should include a zero-tolerance policy for verbal or physical abuse, threats of violence, and bullying behavior. This should be communicated to all staff and clients.
2. *Worksite analysis*—A thorough inspection and analysis of physical workspaces should be undertaken to assess for potential threats to safety. This analysis should include a thorough review of previous incidents of violence, as well as identification of high-risk settings and clients. Workers who conduct home visits or work in residential settings should be given specific safety training for these settings.
3. *Prevention*—Actions should be taken to remediate any of the threats to safety identified in Step 2 and any course of action necessary to reduce risk of harm to workers. Common steps include installing alarm systems, "panic" buttons in consulting rooms, and adequate lighting outside the building for workers who leave at night.
4. *Safety training*—Safety training and risk reduction skills seminars should be provided for all staff, student interns, and volunteers, regardless of their service

provision role. This training is crucial for setting the issue as a priority for the agency. Supervisor training is also essential, as their response to a worker who feels unsafe or experiences violence can make a significant difference.

5. *Record-keeping and evaluation of the efforts*—Tracking incidents of violence or threats against workers is an essential part of worker safety. Each practitioner should know how to report these incidents and be aware of what happens to these reports. Debriefing of incidents with all staff is an important part of this process as well. In addition, ongoing evaluation of the effectiveness of worker safety programs will be helpful to make future improvements.

For more information about developing a safety plan at your program, visit https://www.osha.gov/SLTC/healthcarefacilities/violence.html.

CHECKLIST

For each individual practitioner, it can be difficult to determine when they are not safe with a client or are just feeling anxious or absorbing some projections or transference from the client. This checklist can be helpful to determine when you may not be safe. Remember that you should screen for safety risks with all clients, but pay specific attention to your safety with the client who

- ➤ Has a history of violence
- ➤ Has perpetrated violence against an intimate partner or child
- ➤ Has an active substance abuse problem
- ➤ Has a recent history of explosive anger
- ➤ Has a history of conduct disorder or antisocial personality disorder
- ➤ Appears agitated and difficult to calm
- ➤ Appears disoriented and dissociative
- ➤ Has made threats against you or workers in your organization
- ➤ Has access to weapons
- ➤ Has a history of psychosis and noncompliance with medications

PART II

PLANNING AND IMPLEMENTING INTERVENTIONS

CHAPTER 10

EVIDENCE-BASED PRACTICE AND HOW TO USE RESEARCH IN TREATMENT PLANNING

There are many aspiring social workers who enter their graduate programs paralyzed by fear at the thought of research. Words such as *statistics, probability,* and *significance levels* make their heads spin as they drudgingly head into their required research courses. As a result of this attitude, on completion of these courses, many master's of social work (MSW) students as well as those from other disciplines breathe a sigh of relief as they tell themselves they will never again have to think about research. However, the reality is that in today's world of practice, no clinician should or can practice without considering research in the clinical decision-making process.

In actuality, many social workers really do care about research; they just do not know it. They care about research because they care about finding out which is the best intervention for their clients' unique needs and circumstances. They care about making sure that what they are doing with their clients is working effectively toward achieving the goals of the intervention. For example, if you find yourself asking any of the following questions, you care about research:

- What is the best way to help my client?
- How will I know if what I am doing is working?
- What is the latest information on a particular disorder, mental illness, or health issue?
- What have other agencies or communities done to effectively address a particular issue on a macro level?
- What have other clinicians done previously to address a problem? Did it work? How so? If not, why not?

Our guess is that most of you ask yourselves at least one of these questions. More important, our profession believes that such questions are important. The National Association of Social Workers (NASW) Code of Ethics states that "social workers should base practice on recognized knowledge, including empirically based knowledge, relevant to social work and social work ethics" (NASW, 2008, 4.01.c).

This chapter's aim is to help new professional social workers see that research is not only critical to good practice but also does not have to be confusing and scary and therefore avoided. When we avoid understanding and utilizing research, we risk not offering the best available treatments for their clients. Finally, according to our own professional code of ethics, by not including research findings in our intervention decision-making process, we are not following the values of the profession or being ethically responsible as professionals (NASW, 2008).

RESEARCH AND SOCIAL WORK: WHAT DO YOU NEED TO KNOW?

While there are many different ways that clinicians can use research in social work, here we introduce one main approach, evidence-based practice or EBP. EBP is a *process* of using information that includes the clinician's expertise, the client's wishes and circumstances, and the best available empirical research, while considering the contextual factors, in the clinical decision-making process (Drisko & Grady, 2012). Each of these factors is important to consider when attempting to develop a potential intervention that you will cocreate with a client. EBP in social work is derived from and is related to evidence-based medicine (EBM) in the medical field. A widely cited definition of EBM in clinical practice was offered by Sackett, Rosenberg, Muir Gray, Haynes, and Richardson (1996):

> Evidence based medicine is the conscientious, explicit, and judicious use of current best evidence in making decisions about the care of individual patients. The practice of evidence based medicine means integrating individual clinical expertise with the best available external clinical evidence from systematic research. (pp. 71–72)

This definition has been expanded to include the clinical circumstances relevant to the client, which is more consistent with social work. Such circumstances might include the financial status, the work schedule, child-care requirements, or transportation barriers for the individual. As such, the model that we use in this book has four parts: (a) the current clinical circumstances of the client, (b) the best relevant research evidence, (c) the client's values and preferences, and (d) the clinical expertise of the professional clinician (Haynes, Devereaux, & Guyatt, 2002).

EVIDENCE-BASED PRACTICE

You might be asking, "So, what does EBP mean exactly?" or "What does this look like in practice?" What EBP emphasizes is that social workers need to follow a process of decision-making that ensures that all four of the areas mentioned are included. The idea is that if all four areas are considered, the worker and the client will be using a plan that is based on a holistic view of the client *and* one that is based on empirical support for its effectiveness.

As stated previously, EBP is a *process*. While the steps may vary slightly, the overall format is generally the same. The steps of the EBP decision-making process are as follows:

1. Draw on client needs and circumstances learned in a thorough assessment, identify answerable practice questions and related research information needs;
2. Efficiently locate relevant research knowledge;
3. Critically appraise the quality and applicability of this knowledge to the client's needs and situation;
4. Discuss the research results with the client to determine how likely effective options fit with the client's values and goals;
5. Synthesize the client's clinical needs and circumstances with the relevant research, develop a shared plan of intervention collaboratively with the client;
6. Implement the intervention (Drisko & Grady, 2012, p. 32).

A brief vignette follows to further illustrate this process. Please note that these are selected excerpts of a case, and that only segments particularly relevant to the process are shared here. Other areas of concern to social workers have not been shared, such as information about housing and socioeconomic issues, and the client's numerous strengths are not discussed at length. All of this client's identifying information has been changed.

Alice is 24-year-old who identified as a biracial, heterosexual, and agnostic woman. She came to a community mental health center at the recommendation of her primary care physician, who had performed a complete physical and could not find any medical explanation for her symptoms. She reported a number of gastrointestinal symptoms that included cramping, frequent bowel movements, and stomachaches. She had lost weight over the last 3 months. The social worker completed a thorough bio-psycho-social-spiritual history and asked questions about her strengths and the start of the symptoms, their severity, and their duration. An important part of her history that emerged in the assessment was that her parents separated when she was only 2 years old. Her mother was Caucasian, and her father, with whom she did not have a close relationship, was from Ethiopia. Her father had intermittent contact with her over the years, but she remained with her mother and felt that her stepfather was much "more of a real father" than her biological father ever was. Her father's family was a very close-knit family that remained insulated and close to other Ethiopian families in the area. She did not feel connected to them and felt anxious when she needed to spend time with them because she did not understand most of what they said and did not understand or participate in many of the cultural activities. She stated that she "always feels on the outside."

Step 1—Assessment: You need to learn strong clinical skills so that you are able to conduct a thorough assessment and identify clearly what it is your client is seeking in treatment (Grady & Drisko, 2014). It is important not only to identify what *you* think would be most helpful but also to remember to learn from the client what he or she believes would be helpful to address in your work together. Based on the assessment, you need to develop a good question from which to launch your decision-making process that is specific to the needs of the client. Examples of potential questions that social workers might ask in their work with clients (not necessarily the case of Alice) could include the following:

- How can attachment be improved in a recently adopted child?
- What are effective interventions for older women who are depressed?
- Is family therapy or individual therapy more effective in helping adolescents with substance abuse issues?
- Are some interventions focused on addressing anxiety more effective than others depending on the racial or ethnic identity of the client?
- What does a typical grieving process look like for children?

In Alice's case, the symptoms began after her biological father announced that he was going to be married in the summer and expected her to be in the wedding. He was marrying another Ethiopian woman from their community, and Alice was overwhelmed at the thought of being there and having to participate with "a bunch of people I do not know doing things I do not understand." In addition, she was picturing her father "acting like we are all one big happy family, which is FAR from the truth, and I am going to have to pretend like we are!" Her stress over this event appeared to have brought on the symptoms, and she was physically uncomfortable and had also missed work due to the physical symptoms. She stated that at the moment her boss was tolerant of her missed days to a point, but she really could not take more sick days. In the conversations with Alice, the social worker and Alice determined that a searchable question in this case would be "What are effective treatments for managing anxiety that manifest as physical symptoms?"

Step 2—Search: In Step 2, you need to be able to locate relevant research that will help you to answer the question you developed in Step 1. This is when you need to use the web-searching skills you learned through graduate school and in your library orientations. If you are not familiar with how to search databases to find information, this would be a good time to meet with your local librarian, either in your community or at your university. If you do not have access to academic search engines that are available through most universities, a suggested list of publicly available resources that you can use to search for potentially relevant information is in the Resources section of this chapter.

A quick search on the Cochrane Library (http://www.cochrane.org) for anxiety treatments with physical symptoms resulted in several hits. The top one was for a review called "Improving Return to Work in Adults Suffering From Symptoms of Distress." This systematic review addressed 10 studies focused on this issue. In this case, five of the studies used cognitive behavioral therapy and five used problem-solving therapy. Based on their review,

> *Our results showed that workers on sick leave because of an adjustment disorder can be helped with making their first step back to work (i.e. partial return to work) by treating them with problem solving therapy. On average, workers who are offered problem solving therapy start 17 days earlier with partial return to work compared to workers who receive no treatment or the usual treatment from their occupational physician or general practitioner. However, we also found that cognitive behavioural therapy or problem solving therapy does not help the worker return to work with full-time hours any quicker than workers who receive no treatment or the usual treatment from their occupational physicians or general practitioners. (Arends et al., 2012, para. 1)*
>
> *The authors noted that more research is needed on this topic to better understand what is helpful to this population.*

Step 3—Evaluate: Now that you have gathered some information, this step involves using the knowledge that you gained in your research courses to critically evaluate and appraise what you have found. Some of the questions you might be considering include whether a finding is statistically significant or if the sample that the researchers included in their study was similar to the client(s) with whom you are working. There will be many studies that are complicated and present information on statistics that you may not understand. While you will certainly not catch everything in the article, be a critical thinker while reading. For example, were the instruments used valid and reliable? Did the authors provide you enough information on the research process in general? Does the project even make sense to you? Is it clear from the article how to replicate the study or the intervention? In Appendix B is a guide developed by Bruce Thyer (1991) to help individuals use critical thinking skills while evaluating a research article.

> *The Cochrane Library is known for strong systematic reviews. The benefit of a systematic review is that the researchers have searched and evaluated the information for the reader. In addition, given that this review was done fairly recently (within the last year), the social worker felt confidence in these conclusions.*

Step 4—Collaborate: The important piece to remember in this step is the need to have a conversation *with* your client about what you have learned, rather than simply reporting what you found *to* your client. This conversation should be a dialogue that involves discussing the information *with* your client. It is important to clearly state what you found, as well as what your thoughts are about what you found. Also important is to keep in mind that you will need to tailor the information based on language, cognitive capacity, and other relevant considerations particular to the specific needs and characteristics of your client. This step occurs when you and your client come to some mutual understanding about what makes the most sense in terms of an approach to address the need identified in Step 1.

> *After finding this information, the social worker discussed these results with Alice. Together, they explored what problem-solving therapy was, whether this form of intervention made sense to the client in terms of her understanding of both the origins and potential resolution of the issue, and whether this form of intervention felt realistic to her. They also discussed the findings concerning cognitive behavioral therapy and reviewed similar information together. Alice believed that the problem-solving approach fit well because, although she had had anxiety-related symptoms in relation to her father in the past, she felt like this event was the main issue and felt like the approach would target that. This approach felt like a better fit for her.*

Step 5—Plan: Building on the conversation in Step 4, your job in Step 5 is to synthesize all of the information into a coherent plan considering all of the components included in EBP: client factors (i.e., wishes, interests, capacities); clinician factors (i.e., expertise, skills); research factors (i.e., what the literature reports might be effective); and contextual factors (i.e., culture, family context). Your expertise is involved in every prior step, from clinical skills in the assessment and in discussing information with the client to technical skills of being able to effectively search databases. In Step 5, though, your job is to bring all of this information together and to develop an appropriate plan that takes into account the conversation you had in Step 4.

> *The social worker now used the previous discussion with Alice in which Alice expressed her wishes and thoughts, in combination with the social worker's knowledge of both problem-solving therapy and cognitive behavioral therapy paired with the research, to create an intervention plan to move forward with problem-solving therapy. Here, the social worker needed to consider what Alice's wishes and preferences were, what the research said might be useful, and her own expertise, including her expertise that was outside what the research identified. In this case, the worker was in fact trained in the models that were identified by the research, and the client felt that such an approach, specifically the problem-solving approach, was a good fit for her, so no outside referral was needed. If, however, the social worker did not have that expertise or the client expressed a different wish, the outcome could have been different. For example, if the social worker in this case did not have any expertise in this model, it would have been appropriate for the social worker to have shared that information with the client and offered either to provide her with possible referral options or to state what she could offer and what empirical support, if any, she knew of regarding such an approach.*
>
> *In this case, they created a contract for 3 months with the overarching goal to increase Alice's coping capacities to effectively manage the stress and anxiety surrounding her father's wedding. These capacities would include a range of interventions in keeping with the approach, including defining the problem and generating alterative solutions and skills, such as relaxation techniques and visualization and self-monitoring.*

Step 6—Implement: After the process has been completed, it is now time to launch the plan. Depending on the client population or the agency where you work, the plans for each client may be very similar or very different.

> *Alice began to work immediately with the social worker using problem-solving therapy and began to address the concerns she had on entering the clinic.*

Although not included here, one additional step that is often included in the EBP process is the evaluation of the intervention. Social workers need to develop ways to assess whether what they are doing is working and be responsive when it is not. Because evaluating one's own practice is so important, we have dedicated a chapter to this process, Chapter 15.

LIMITATIONS OF EBP

EBP is meant to be a critical thinking process that encourages social workers to think broadly about how to approach different issues in social work. However, there are a number of limitations that should also be considered. Drisko and Grady (2012) provided a thorough summary of these limitations, and those interested in reading more on this topic are encouraged to refer to this source. However, the main limitations that they identified are summarized next.

SOCIAL JUSTICE CONCERNS

Much of the research conducted on social problems is focused on resolving individual functioning rather than structural issues. Many feel that this focus is

> at odds with some of the core values of social work. These include inadequately addressing structural issues that may contribute to social justice concerns and further pushing social work toward a limited medical model orientation rather than promoting biopsychosocial and interdisciplinary models. (Drisko & Grady, 2012, p. 242)

In other words, by studying interventions focused on individual functioning, the implication is that the cause of the problems originates from the individual, rather than contextual factors, such as poverty, crime, violence, and racism, to name a few.

LIMITATIONS OF THE RESEARCH

One of the limitations most often cited regarding EBP is the lack of research regarding a host of issues (Drisko & Grady, 2012). These include demographic characteristics, diagnostic profiles, as well as contextual issues such as research on alleviating poverty or reducing rates of community violence. For example, if you had a female client who recently immigrated from Ghana, experienced high rates of community violence, was a sexual abuse survivor, and was now pregnant and suffering from pregnancy-related depression, it would be difficult to find a study that included research subjects who fit her exact description. Therefore, practitioners must think about the most relevant question related to her specific needs at that time, as well as which demographic characteristics are most salient regarding her treatment. EBP argues for the use of the best available research. Therefore, social workers must use what they can find and then incorporate that information in to the other three factors considered in EBP. The field, however, is limited by what is available.

REALITIES OF REAL-WORLD PRACTICE

Another critique of EBP that clinicians have noted is that often the empirically supported interventions that are identified in the EBP process do not "take into account the 'messiness' of real life practice" (Drisko & Grady, 2012, p. 243). Clients and their lives are complicated, and like the client example presented in the preceding section, they face multiple issues. It is unrealistic that there will be a perfect fit between an intervention approach and the clients' needs. As stated previously, it is in these complex cases that practitioners must use their expertise to prioritize the needs of their clients and work with them to identify the intervention that is the best fit when possible.

OVEREMPHASIS ON THE RESEARCH

There have been some in the field who believe that EBP ignores the expertise of the practitioner, relying too heavily on the research, and ignores the art of social work practice (Drisko & Grady, 2012). We hope that it has been clear throughout this chapter that the social worker's expertise is critical through the entire EBP process. The critique mainly is concerning the fear that practitioners will simply search for an intervention and then implement it without really considering the client wishes, the importance of the relationship with the client, or the art of doing social work (Graybeal, 2014). We believe strongly that even models with the strongest level of empirical support must be provided in the context of a strong working alliance, as we discuss in Chapter 2.

LOGISTICS OF EBP

Another critique surrounds the logistics of completing the EBP process. It requires practitioners to have access to some research databases (although there are many publicly available) and relies on practitioners having some ability and confidence to interpret research findings. In addition, agency budget limitations exist that may prohibit a worker from receiving training in and supervision for implementing a new intervention. Finally, there may be a lack of community resources for any identified interventions.

CONCLUSION

In spite of the limitations of EBP, it provides a critical thinking process that infuses research into a client-centered approach to practice. We emphasized in this chapter the essential role research plays in our profession and in our work with clients. It is vital that social workers be able to articulate why they are doing what they are doing. The EBP process provides social workers with a concise method for answering such a question by allowing them to articulate their practice decisions in a manner that is consistent with both the person-in-environment approach used by social workers and with the code of ethics that addresses professional ethical behavior.

APPENDIX A: RESOURCES

This appendix is a list of resources available that are free to the public. For a more comprehensive discussion of the different available resources, refer to Chapter 5 in Drisko and Grady (2012), from which this list has been derived and modified.

- *The Cochrane Library*. This is a database of very high-quality systematic reviews (syntheses of available research) on single topics. The Cochrane Library is organized by disorder and medical model in orientation: http://www.cochrane.org
- *The National Guideline Clearinghouse*. This is a compilation of treatment guidelines derived by expert panels but based on research results. It is organized by disorder and medical model in orientation: http://www.guideline.gov
- *The Centre for Reviews and Dissemination databases* at the University of York includes the *Database of Abstracts of Reviews of Effects (DARE)*. DARE compiles over 15,000 systematic reviews, including those of the Cochrane Collaboration discussed previously: http://www.crd.york.ac.uk/crdweb/
- *The Centre for Evidence-Based Medicine* provides summaries from the Cochrane Database and weekly updates of new additions and changes to the Cochrane Database (which include many new titles at the beginning stages of research as well as newly completed systematic reviews): http://www.cebm.net/
- The UK National Health Service's *Clinical Knowledge Summaries* provide a source of evidence-based information about common conditions for the primary care practitioner. They include both medical and mental health disorders: https://www.nice.org.uk/about/what-we-do/evidence-services/clinical-knowledge-summaries
- The *National Mental Health Information Center* of the US Substance Abuse and Mental Health Services Administration (SAMHSA) offers "kits" to translate evidence-based programs into practice: http://store.samhsa.gov/list/series?name=Evidence-Based-Practices-KITs
- The *National Registry of Evidence-Based Programs and Practices*, which is part of SAMHSA. It is an online searchable database of over 250 programs: http://www.nrepp.samhsa.gov/
- The *National Implementation Research Network*. This website contains a series of briefs focused on children and on implementation lessons learned from an initiative in North Carolina to study whether postcare supportive services improved the long-term well-being of children exiting foster care: http://nirn.fpg.unc.edu/
- The *Center for Evidence-Based Practice* (CEBP) at Case Western Reserve University. The CEBP provides technical assistance—consulting, training, and evaluation—for service innovations that improve quality of life and other outcomes for people with

mental illness or co-occurring mental illness and substance use disorders: http://www.centerforebp.case.edu/

APPENDIX B: GUIDELINES FOR CRITICAL ANALYSIS OF RESEARCH ARTICLES

TITLE

1. Does the title include accurate identification of problem area, variables specified, and identification of target population?

INTRODUCTION

1. Did the report appropriately cite earlier, relevant studies drawn from the social work and other disciplinary literatures?
2. Was the research problem or question clearly stated?
3. Did the introduction conclude with one or more explicitly stated testable hypotheses?

LITERATURE REVIEW

1. Was adequate and relevant literature cited to acquaint the reader with the existing studies that had been found?
2. Was adequate and relevant literature cited to establish the need for the study and the likelihood of obtaining meaningful, relevant, and significant results?
3. Were the variables included in the study adequately supported for use with relevant literature?
4. Did the author(s) offer clear definitions of key terms and variables?
5. Were operational definitions used whenever possible?

METHODS

SAMPLING

1. Was a clear, potentially replicable description provided of the sampling procedure used to recruit clients for the study?

2. Were the criteria for inclusion and exclusion of subjects clearly stated?
3. Were salient characteristics (demographic, clinical, diagnostic, etc.) of the sample of clients described in detail to permit comparisons of this sample with those used in prior (and future) studies?
4. Was a description of the nature of the informed consent process used to obtain client agreement to participate in the study provided?

INDEPENDENT AND DEPENDENT VARIABLES

1. Were the independent and dependent variables conceptually defined in an understandable manner?
2. Did the operationalization of the variables follow the conceptualization?
3. Did the instruments used in the study possess acceptable levels of reliability and validity?
4. Were the instruments clearly pertinent to the target problem?
5. Was the choice of instrument(s) supported by relevant literature?

INTERVENTION (IF APPLICABLE)

1. Was the intervention program (treatment) described in sufficient detail to permit replication? If not, did the author provide a source to obtain a treatment manual or more explicit description of the intervention(s)?
2. Were measures taken to assess practitioner compliance with intended interventions? If so, were the interventions carried out as intended?
3. If blind conditions were imposed on clients or practitioners (or both), were measures taken to assess the integrity of the blind nature of the study participants?

RESEARCH DESIGN

1. Did the authors provide a clear description of the research design employed?
2. If clients were assigned to various conditions, was the nature of this assignment process described in sufficient detail to permit replication?
3. If random assignment was employed, was the nature of the randomization process clearly described?
4. Were pretreatment measures taken of the clients' problems? If so, were the groups of clients assigned to differing experimental conditions roughly equivalent to each other pretreatment?

DATA COLLECTION AND ANALYSIS PLAN

1. Was it clear how the data was collected (where, when, how, and by whom) and recorded?

2. Was there enough information on the data collection to allow for replication?
3. Was the plan for analysis clearly presented?

RESULTS

1. Were the results obtained from the various measures consistent with one another? Was the pattern of improvement (or deterioration) clear across all measures?
2. Were the results presented in the form of graphs or tables? Is so, were the data comprehensible without recourse to the narrative text.
3. If the results were reported in the form of descriptive statistics, was each mean accompanied by a standard deviation?
4. If inferential statistics were employed, were the data shown to meet the assumptions the tests were based on (e.g., normal distribution, similar standard deviations, etc.)?
5. Did the level of measurement for the instruments used fit with the statistical tested used to analyze the data?
6. If correlational measures were employed, are the N, correlation coefficient, and alpha level reported for each such analysis?
7. If a t test or analysis of variance was used, did the report of each such test contain the degrees of freedom, t or F value, and alpha level?
8. If a statistically significant result was found, was the proportion of variance explained by this difference reported?
9. Apart from statistically significant changes, was the clinical significance of any improvements discussed?

DISCUSSION

1. Did the author clearly address alternative explanations (e.g., threats to internal validity) for the results, apart from the hypotheses that were tested?
2. Did the author report only conclusions supported by the data? Were speculations clearly described as such, rather than as facts?
3. Were the limitations of the study clearly stated?
4. Were suggestions to improve future research in this area described?
5. Were clear applications to practice derived from this study described, with special reference made to the unique aspects of social work practice?

Taken from "Guidelines for Evaluating Outcome Studies on Social Work Practice," B. A. Thyer, 1991, *Research on Social Work Practice, 1*(1), 76–91; *Handbook in Research and Evaluation*, S. Isaac & W. B. Michael, 1971, Educational and Industrial Testing Services, San Diego, CA.

CHAPTER 11

ROLE OF THEORY IN SOCIAL WORK PRACTICE

In Chapter 10, we discussed the evidence-based practice (EBP) process that integrates the client's preferences, the best available research, and the practitioner's expertise into the decision regarding an intervention for a client (Drisko & Grady, 2012). There are several critical areas for practitioner expertise: the ability to form relationships; knowledge of the population and the context of practice; and knowledge of and comfort level with different models of treatment. Another crucial area of expertise is in knowledge of different explanatory and practice theories that strongly influence the assessment and change processes. Therefore, new social workers must be aware of the important role theory has in social work practice and begin to strengthen their knowledge of and ability to apply both explanatory and change theories in their practices.

In this chapter, we hope to accomplish three primary goals. The first is to clarify and define terms related to theory that social workers will encounter in the field. The second is to explain the important role theory has both in the assessment phase and in planning for and implementing any intervention with clients. Our final goal is to help social workers strategize ways to gain more expertise in using theory to assess and inform interventions.

CLARIFYING TERMINOLOGY

Often, what creates confusion for professionals is how terms are frequently used interchangeably and often inappropriately. The terms *theory, model,* and *intervention* are often confused by social workers yet have very different definitions. While the terms are related, they each play a distinct role in social work and should be understood as separate concepts.

THEORY

According to Walsh (2013), there are several types of theories used by social workers. "*Case theories* explain the behavior of one person (for example, an individual spouse abuser"

(p. 3). It is common for social workers to develop their own theories about why their clients do what they do. A second type of theory according to Walsh is a *midrange theory*, which aims to explain "a set of cases or events" (p. 3). An example might be trying to understand the reasons for one community's spike in reports of violent crimes. Finally, Walsh identified *grand theories* that "attempt to explain all sets of events and cases (such as Freud's theory of psychosexual development or Piaget's theory of cognitive development)" (p. 3).

These theories as outlined by Walsh all represent *explanatory theories* that are designed to help us to understand and then explain to others the existence of phenomena. Social workers are often asked to explain why a client might have symptoms of depression, why a particular community is experiencing a higher rate of criminal behavior, why the morale within an organization has dropped significantly, or why family members have chosen not to speak to each other. Each of these questions requires a social worker to look at a complex picture and try to distill it down to an understandable explanation to which clients can relate.

In addition to explanatory theories, social workers use *theories of change*, sometimes referred to as *practice theories* (Walsh, 2013). These theories do exactly what they sound like they do: They provide a theory regarding how change might occur. Frank and Frank defined a practice theory as "a coherent set of ideas about human nature, including concepts of health, illness, normalcy, and deviance, which provide verifiable or established explanations for behavior and rationales for intervention" (as cited by Walsh, 2013, p. 3). These theories help to predict how change might occur or how to help to facilitate change. Rather than explain why a phenomenon exists, they serve to help us predict how a phenomenon might be altered.

All of the theories currently used by social workers were developed by someone who wanted to better understand why certain phenomena existed and how those phenomena could be altered in some way. Before a theory can be considered viable, it needs to be tested and evaluated for validity (Hutchinson, 2013). In other words, has there been research on whether the theory is accurate? Some theories are easier to test than others.

Let us take an example of an agency director who has noticed that residents from a particular neighborhood in the agency's catchment area do not come for services. She develops an explanatory theory that the reason these residents of that community do not come to the agency is because they do not have access to transportation. Using this theory, she develops a theory of change aimed at increasing participation by these residents and determines that the agency should provide buses to the neighborhood to help those individuals come to the agency. However, before moving ahead to work on an action plan to develop transportation services for this community, it is in the director's best interest to first test the theory by going out and asking the residents why they do not use the services of the agency. She finds that there is a perception in the community that the agency is biased against those individuals who live in the community, and this perception is the reason that community members do not come to the agency for help. This testing of the explanatory theory yielded a different picture of what was causing the phenomenon compared to the director's initial theory. Had the agency director moved ahead with her own theory, the agency would have spent a great deal of money on resources that would not have addressed the issue she was seeing at the agency.

Another example that is perhaps more complex is trying to understand why sexual assault occurs in our communities. There are many explanatory theories regarding why individuals commit sexual assaults, yet there is no one theory that appears to sufficiently explain this behavior among the different individuals who commit such heinous crimes (Grady, 2009). With sexual assault, there is no one theory that fits all. As such, it is difficult to develop theories of change that could then have an impact on the number of sexual assaults committed.

Although it is likely that the theories you learn in social work school have been tested and validated, it is important to evaluate the validity of the theories you learn and to place a value on the importance of testing your own ideas that you have developed about what you are seeing in your own practice settings. Social workers need to be cognizant of how their own assumptions and biases can influence their assessments with clients.

MODEL

Change theories are ideas about what might help to facilitate the intended outcome (Walsh, 2013). These ideas are then operationalized into models that help to frame how the change should occur. Models take the ideas regarding what might work and spell out how to create a desired change—step by step. For example, the Wright brothers first had an idea about how to fly before they could build a model of an airplane that they could test. In social work, models are used to operationalize an intervention approach. The model includes specific information about who meets with the social worker, what the social worker does with the clients, what kinds of questions the social worker asks, how often the social workers and clients meet, and more. Each practice model, regardless of the level of clients system for which it is designed, will provide guidance for how to organize and implement the intervention.

Some of the practice models that you learn in graduate school might include models of interventions designed to reduce depression, organize community members, or reduce violence in schools. Each of these models is based on explanatory theories, which led to theories of change, which were then operationalized into a model that provided a set of guidelines and steps to reach the desired outcome. For them to be considered empirically supported interventions (ESIs) model, they need to have met certain criteria to demonstrate that they are superior in reaching those outcomes compared to other approaches (see Chapter 10 on EBP and Drisko & Grady, 2012). While other models may be promising or perceived as helpful, a model can only be referred to as an ESI when it has met those standards. Throughout your careers, you will consistently need to evaluate different intervention models, their fit with your population, the needs of your client, as well as the research that has been used to test whether it is effective in creating change. (For a much more thorough discussion of how social workers can evaluate research as well as infuse research into their practices, see Drisko & Grady, 2012.)

INTERVENTIONS

The term *intervention* is confusing because it actually does hold different meanings. As we have already mentioned in this chapter, we have used it to talk about working with clients to create change. We are intervening or creating an intervention that is the overarching action we are taking with clients to reach an outcome. Within the intervention, we may use a particular model to help us facilitate that change.

Yet, the term *intervention* is also used to describe the specific tasks, strategies, or techniques taken within a model. A task might be to teach new skills or to provide psycho-education to a client. When referred to as a stand-alone task, they are not considered an all-encompassing model of intervention. Rather, they are a discrete action that is taken within the intervention phase of the relationship with a client or clients. Each model will often prescribe a set of tasks that is consistent with the theory of change. Walsh (2013) defined intervention strategies as the "concrete actions taken by social workers to help clients achieve their goals" (p. 4).

Let us say, for example, you have met with a client who is struggling with depression. There are numerous theories that might explain this struggle. One theory that a social worker could use is cognitive theory (CT). As an explanatory theory, CT states that the reason people feel depressed is because they have thoughts that lead them to feel sad. According to the theory, our thoughts influence how we perceive ourselves and our world (Beck, 2011). Building on this explanation, according to CT, the theory of change is that if we can change our thoughts and how we perceive ourselves and the world, we will feel better. In the cognitive model of change, the clients and practitioners meet for 12–14 sessions that are divided by phases; each session is structured in a particular format; and the practitioner takes on a particular role with the clients, often like a teacher, and teaches the clients new skills to alter the thoughts. Therefore, the specific interventions or tasks within the model are skills used to address thinking patterns to challenge or alter the thoughts that are leading to the depression.

As you can see from this example, the explanatory theory, the theory of change, the practice model, and the specific intervention strategies are all interconnected and build on each other, creating a logical sequence starting from the explanatory theory to the specific intervention strategies used to address the client's depression. According to Walsh (2013), "There should be consistency ... between a practitioner's working theory and interventions" (p. 4). Without such consistency both you and your clients can become confused about why you are doing what you are doing. The explanation for the issue should clearly link to what you and your client think you should do about it.

USE OF THEORIES IN SOCIAL WORK PRACTICE

The act of using theory to explain a phenomenon requires knowledge and several key skills. To start, social workers must have working knowledge of a range of theories that they can use to understand issues that affect different levels of client systems (micro, mezzo, and macro). Working knowledge means that they can define and explain the assumptions and key concepts of a theory.

Once there is some solid understanding of the theories, it is important for social workers to be able to apply these theories to complex situations. Understanding the ideas of a theory is different from being able to apply the knowledge. What we mean by this last statement is that being able to define the terms or concepts of a theory is a source of knowledge that is distinct from the skill of being able to use the theory to explain an issue. In other words, can you use the theory to explain what is going on with a client or client system? For example, if a family came in for help with their 10-year-old son, who was getting in fights at school, what theories could you use to help *explain* that behavior both for yourself and for the clients? Would you use an individual theory, such as CT as described previously, to explain how the thoughts or perceptions the son had about his peers led him to believe that they will hurt him if he does not show he is tough? Or, would you use a family theory to explain that, in his family for multiple generations, his family members have used violence as a way of managing uncomfortable emotions? There is no right or wrong answer as both theories help to explain the same phenomenon.

The task for the social worker is to identify which theory might be most relevant and then apply the concepts of the theory to explain the case. It is also important then to translate the language of the theory so that it is useful in understanding why the phenomenon is occurring and finally to link that explanation to the plan for action along with the EBP process. In our experience, students find that understanding the theory and its concepts is much easier than applying the knowledge to their cases and work in the field. It takes practice and a skill we encourage all readers to practice in their classes and in the field with the clients with whom they are working.

LINKING IT ALL TOGETHER

We hope you can see by now, theories play a critical role in helping to explain human behavior and social phenomena as well as planning for action. Without valid and reliable theories, social workers would simply be trying and using a smattering of ideas without having a cohesive or organized way to approach their work. We also hope that it is clear that we believe strongly that there should be a clear link between the explanation of the issue and how to intervene. For example, say you went to your doctor for help with your heel, which has been hurting. Your doctor explains the reason you have the pain is because you have been exercising in shoes that provide no support, and your heel has been strained as a result. You think, "OK, that makes sense. My shoes are really old, and my foot always hurts after I exercise." Now, imagine the doctor says to you, "So, the way to address this heel pain is for you to eat more apples." Of course, that makes no sense! The plan for intervention should match the explanation regarding the cause of the issue. A much more logical intervention plan based on the explanatory theory would be to be fitted for more supportive shoes and try to include lower-impact exercise in your routine to take the pressure off your heel. The explanation should connect to the plan.

Figure 11.1 is a visual depiction of how theories connect to the intervention process. Figure 11.1 represents the general flow of how to link your explanation to your intervention strategies.

In our experience, students and new practitioners are most anxious to know the intervention strategies. They want to know "what to do" in their work. Our response is typically, "Well, it depends on your goals, which were based on your assessment, which was driven by

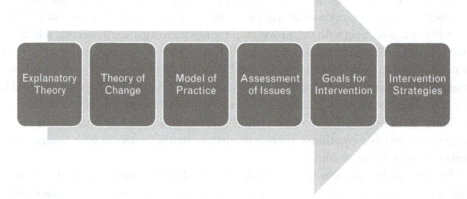

FIGURE 11.1: Connection between theory and intervention.

your model of practice, which was based on your theory of change, which was influenced by your explanatory theory." There are many intervention strategies that are used across different models of practice. However, *why* you are using it and your ability to explain that reason is connected to the explanatory theory. It is not enough just to offer clients new skills or ideas. Which ones, why those, and why now are all driven by your assessment of the issue that is grounded in the explanation.

HOW TO PICK A THEORY

If you are in school or recently graduated, you have probably discovered that you can choose from numerous social work theories. There are individual, family, group, organizational, and macro theories, all of which are useful in helping to understand clients and client systems in different ways. The summary guide at the end of this chapter provides a brief outline of some of the major theories that social workers use. It can be overwhelming for new social workers to think about learning all of the potential theories and to learn them well so that they can be applied competently to their practices.

Of course, there is no way that any one social worker can master them all. Therefore, in our teaching and supervision of social work students and practitioners, we use the following guidelines to help prioritize your learning:

- Become familiar with at least one theory for each level of social work practice: micro, mezzo, and macro.
  - Even if you think that you will always be a direct practitioner, macro and social issues influence your clients, and you must have an ability to frame larger social context issues for yourself and your clients.
  - If you are going to focus your work in one particular level of practice, you will want to learn more of those relevant theories.

- For direct practitioners specifically, learn at least one skill-based theory and model, one relational-based theory and model, and one family theory and model. You can then draw on what you need having these tools in your toolbox.
  - Skill-based theories and models are important because sometimes clients need concrete help in tackling a particular issue, especially if it is acute.
  - Relational theories and models are important because they teach you how and remind you to attend the client relationship, which research continues to show is a critical part of any form of intervention (Hubble, Duncan, Miller, & Wampold, 2010; Norcross, 2002; Wampold, 2010).
  - Family theories and models are important because they help social workers to consider systemic and multigenerational patterns that influence developmental and current patterns. Even when working individually, family theories help remind us of these influences and help us to understand their role in the current struggles faced by our clients.

Over your career, you will be introduced to multiple models of practice. We encourage you to identify ones that are most relevant to your work and to try to learn them well. "While knowledge of multiple theories may be unnecessary, it is nevertheless essential for effective psychotherapists to understand at least one theory well in order to apply it" (MacDonald & Webb, 2006, p. 3). Although MacDonald and Webb were writing about psychotherapists specifically, their ideas apply to other levels of social work practice. They also stated:

> Limited understanding of even one theory relegates psychotherapists to adding a method here and an idea there, without a systematic conceptual basis to hold those methods and ideas together; this is conceptual *syncretism*. In the worst cases, psychotherapists operate out of syncretism, wherein they unsuccessfully attempt to synthesize different, perhaps contradictory, ideas and methods, with little or no awareness of their inherent incongruities. A cogent conceptual system, though, would solve this difficulty. (p. 3)

Unfortunately, in our own careers, we have seen many practitioners, social workers as well as others from different disciplines, practice in a way that is consistent with syncretism, and these individuals are unable to article which theories they use and why. Given the multiple theories that are available, paired with the complex needs of our clients, it is easy to see why many practitioners have turned to what is often referred to as an eclectic or integrated approach (MacDonald & Webb, 2006; Prochaska & Norcross, 1999; Walsh, 2013). In fact, over several decades, practitioners were asked about their approach to working with clients, and over one third of the respondents identified eclecticism as their primary approach; this was the largest category chosen (Norcross, Hedges, & Castle, 2002). In a similar study conducted by Jensen, Bergin, and Greaves, 59% (psychiatrists) to 70% (clinical psychologists) of the groups sampled regarded themselves as eclectic (as cited by MacDonald & Webb, 2006). It is clear from these studies that many practitioners draw from multiple theories and models rather than just one. However, MacDonald and Webb cautioned that "such a strategy … is no solution for syncretism; indeed, it may increase the risk of syncretism" (p. 5).

To reduce the risk of syncretism, we advocate for an intentional or purposeful integration of theories rather than a haphazard hodgepodge of ideas that are thrown together at random. It is important for practitioners to be clear about which theories (explanatory and change) they are using and why they are using those theories and to be competent in applying them. Many models currently used combine different theoretical concepts into a new approach (e.g., mindfulness-based cognitive therapy; Segal, Williams, & Teasdale, 2012). Research consistently demonstrated that the competency of the practitioner to use theory effectively is a critical component of a successful intervention (Wampold, 2010). "Conceptual clarity is essential, though, if psychotherapy is to fulfill its claim and potential to provide scientifically based services" (MacDonald & Webb, 2006, p. 5). If, for example, an intervention approach with a client does not appear to be effective in helping the client to reach his or her goal, without a cohesive and coherent approach it would be impossible to know whether it was the approach itself, the lack of competence in carrying out the approach, the combination of ideas that have been mixed together, the absence of the parts of an approach that were dropped, or some other variable. Understanding outcomes is complex. However, by providing clients with a cohesive and well-thought-out approach will help to determine what is working and what is not.

All of this information about theories leads us to advocate for being intentional in what theories or models of practice you use and potentially combine. Think carefully about why you feel compelled to integrate different approaches and how the different theories will complement or potentially contradict each other. Plan for how you will explain these combined theories to your client and how they will ultimately connect to your intervention plan. If you feel that you need to use more than one theory to either understand or plan for change, then we encourage you to use an approach that uses "informed eclecticism" (Goin, 2005, p. 255) rather than one that resembles syncretism. Be clear about what you are doing and why so that you can articulate your approach to others. In hiring social workers for an agency in a previous capacity, I (E.D.) would ask each applicant: "What theories or models of practice guide your interventions with clients?" Applicants who could not answer that question in a thoughtful and coherent manner were not considered for the position.

WHAT ABOUT EVIDENCE-BASED PRACTICE?

In Chapter 10, we discussed EBP and its role in planning for interventions. Theory and EBP go hand in hand, but one should not trump the other. As you can see from Figure 11.1, your assessment of the issue is driven by your explanatory theory. It is important to be cognizant about which theory you tend to rely on, as this will ultimately shape how you view client issues and what you then identify as a searchable question in the EBP process. Your expertise on different theories and practice models will play a role in what you can offer to your clients as well.

At the same time, we worry about practitioners being drawn to the idea that they can do an EBP search that will identify a specific model of practice that they can just "do" with their clients without linking that intervention plan to an explanatory theory: They just get a manual and off they go. Social work is more complex than finding a manual for a standardized treatment and fitting clients into that box. As we discussed in Chapter 10, there are several limitations regarding EBP. One of these is that there is a paucity of research that will match perfectly with your clients and their needs. It is in these circumstances that your knowledge of theory is even more important. You will need to turn to your theories to help guide you when there is no relevant empirical research that might help you plan for your intervention.

The other way that theory and EBP compliment each other is when a standardized model of practice needs to be modified in some way. As previously stated, clients are complex, and they may need to have intervention plans modified to align more consistently with their cognitive, diagnostic, family, or social context needs. Your knowledge of social work theories will help to guide you regarding when and how to modify models of practice that you identify during the EBP process to best meet the needs of your clients.

SOME WORDS OF CAUTION

While we hope we have made a strong case for social workers to use theories in their work with clients, we also want to note some cautions in the use of theories. One of these is that theories are by nature reductionistic. One of the main benefits of theories is to reduce a great deal of information to a format that can be understood. One image that helps illustrate this point is the optical illusion that looks like a mess of colors and lines when you first look at it. However, once you put on special glasses (which are often colored and look funny), the image becomes clear, and the picture embedded in the mess of colors and lines stands out. This is the benefit of a theory; it is the lens through which you view a client's situation to provide clarity, understanding, and direction.

On the flip side, any theory limits the information that you use as you attempt to reduce the information to digestible portions. For example, let us return to the previous situation of the client who was depressed and how we were using CT to understand the depression. By focusing on the client's cognitions or thoughts, we have a clear theory of causation and a clear plan for intervention. However, by focusing on the thoughts, we miss the underlying poverty, racism, and community violence that are also contributing to the depression and may be the reason the person has negative thoughts about herself. When using CT, we become less interested in where these thoughts originate than in understanding their influence in the life of the client and providing new skills to alter those thoughts. The theory provides a clear path from explanation to intervention. However, it is important to remember that the path is formed by the theory's assumptions about what is important in understanding human behavior. When we choose one theory, we are therefore making a choice not to include others that could lead us down different paths with clients. The existence of multiple paths is why it is important to know multiple theories. If the theoretical path you are on leads you and the client to a dead end, you can choose another path.

Another caution is that once you learn and master a theory, you can become dependent on this theory and this theory alone. We have each had colleagues who were experts in applying a theory in their work but could not switch their perspective. They had their hammer, and everything else became a nail. So, while it is important to become competent in your theories, also remember that there are other ways to look at any one situation. The EBP process is a way to help remind us of the multiple factors that should be considered when thinking through how to work with any one client or client system.

It is also important as you learn different theories to think about why you are drawn to one theory but not to another. As we have stated previously, throughout your careers you will be exposed to multiple theories and practice models. Note which ones you embrace and which ones you reject. Be curious and critical about this process, as you may learn something about yourself during it. Just because you like it does not mean that it is a valid or reliable theory. Be cautious to embrace a theory without examining it thoroughly with a critical eye.

To that end, Hutchinson (2013) developed a set of criteria to use when learning a theory as a way to evaluate its usefulness in social work:

- **Coherence and Conceptual Clarity:** Are the concepts clearly defined and consistently used? Is the theory free of logical inconsistencies? Is it stated in the simplest possible way, without oversimplifying?
- **Testability and Empirical Support:** Can the concepts and propositions be expressed in language that makes them observable and accessible to corroboration or refutation by persons other than the theoretician? Is there evidence of empirical support for the theory?
- **Comprehensiveness:** Does the theory include multiple dimensions of persons, environment, and time? What is included, and what is excluded? What dimension(s) is (are) emphasized? Does the theory account for things that other theories have overlooked or been unable to account for?
- **Diversity and Power:** Can the theory help us understand uniqueness and diversity? How inclusive is it? Does it avoid pathologizing? Does it address power arrangements and systems of oppression? Can it be used to promote social justice?
- **Usefulness for Social Work Practice:** Does the theory assist in the understanding of person-and-environment transactions over time? Can principles of action be derived? At what levels of practice can the theory be used? Can the theory be used in practice in a way that is consistent with the NASW Code of Ethics? (p. 30)

These criteria can be helpful to review as you think about what the strengths and limitations of each theory are as well as how they fit with your own assumptions about human behavior and, most important, the clients with whom you will be working throughout your careers.

CONCLUSION

Social work theory is critical for understanding and intervening with a range of issues faced by clients and the communities in which we live. While there are limitations to their utility, they provide structure and guidance in working in complex situations, especially when there is little empirical information on which to draw. While it is tempting to integrate ideas from multiple theories to help address the complexities of practice, social workers should be intentional in their blending of theories to ensure that their approach remains purposeful and cohesive. We strive to be versatile in our use of theory in an effort to prevent becoming stuck in one way of working that is likely not to be beneficial for all clients. Theory provides social workers with the language to articulate to clients and others why we are doing this particular act with this particular client at this particular time.

CHAPTER 11 RESOURCE GUIDE

This chart provides a brief overview of some of the major theories social workers use in practice.

Name of Theory	Theory Focus	Explanatory Concepts	Intervention Concepts	Specific Techniques Used	Influential Theorists/ Clinicians
Psychodynamic Theories (with attention to Attachment Theory)	How internal and external forces interact to shape and influence emotional development and social functioning	• The mind consists of an unconscious and conscious. • Defense mechanisms protect humans from anxiety and unacceptable impulses. • Humans adapt to their environment. • Humans have inborn needs to attach to others and internalize relational experiences, forming views of self and others. • Infant–caregiver relationships set developmental trajectories, influencing how the past persists into the present. • Humans need a responsive environment to develop a sense of trust in the world, but when early developmental needs are not met, individuals develop unhealthy patterns of functioning and relating.	• Change comes through provision of a "secure base" for relationships to develop, leading to a corrective emotional experience. • SW [social workers] and others must be careful not to reenact past negative relationship patterns. • Through increasing recognition of interpersonal patterns and understanding of the origins of these patterns, clients are able to consciously make different choices, develop more positive relationships, and have increased functioning.	• Attention to affects, emotions, and developmental processes • Empathy • Clarification • Exploration • Education • Support of adaptive functioning • Interpretation • Provision of a secure, holding environment for client to explore experiences, thoughts, feelings, relationships • Use of therapeutic relationship as reflective of client's experience	Sigmund Freud Anna Freud Hartmann Erikson Klein Mahler Winnicott Kohut Bowlby Ainsworth

| Behavior Theory and Cognitive Theory (with attention to Cognitive Behavioral Practice Theory) | Seeks to understand how overt behaviors (actions) and covert behaviors (thoughts or emotions) can be understood through examining unhelpful thinking and/or behavioral patterns that have been learned over time | • Cognitive: Activating Event-Belief-Consequences:
  • The person's thoughts influence their feelings and behaviors.
  • Unhelpful thoughts create unhelpful consequences.
• Behavioral: Antecedents-Behavior-Consequences:
  • Respondent: pairing two stimuli together will create an association.
  • Operant: the consequences following a behavior will either increase or decrease the likelihood of the behavior continuing.
• Social Learning Theory: Modeling
  • Behavior is learned through individual experiences.
  • Behavior is maintained through its antecedents and consequences. | • Cognitive: Therapists help individuals to recognize their unhelpful thought patterns and teach new skills to challenge and alter those thoughts so that the subsequent consequences will be different.
• Behavior: Change is focused on either altering the antecedents (respondent conditioning) or the consequences (operant) or a behavior.
• CBT [cognitive behavioral therapy] is a practice model that combines both into one intervention approach with the assumption that thoughts, behaviors, and emotions are all connected, and changes in one of those domains changes the others. | • Cognitive restructuring techniques: e.g., Socratic questions; evidence for & evidence against
• Cognitive coping: e.g. "I" statements, coping cards
• Exposure therapy or systematic desensitization (based on classical conditioning)
• Operant conditioning with positive or negative reinforcements, such as Reward charts
• Mindfulness—connecting mind and body
• Increasing emotional vocabulary | Bandura
Pavlov
Skinner
Watson
Albert Ellis
Aaron Beck
Judith Beck |

(continued)

Name of Theory	Theory Focus	Explanatory Concepts	Intervention Concepts	Specific Techniques Used	Influential Theorists/Clinicians
General Systems Theory (with attention to Family Emotional & Structural Family Systems Theories)	How persons interact with their environment; how the family system affects functioning across the life span	• Persons are in continual transaction with their environment. • Systems are interrelated parts or subsystems constituting an ordered whole. • Each subsystem impacts all other parts and the whole system. • Systems can have closed or open boundaries. • Systems tend toward equilibrium. • Individual functioning shapes family functioning, and family functioning can create pathology within the individual. • Boundaries regulate the flow of inputs (energy, information, resources) entering and leaving the system. • Open dynamic systems are both self-maintaining and self-transforming.	• Behavior is related to structure of one's family system, and problems in functioning stem from problematic family structures. • Changing one part of the system (e.g., the family system) can have an effect on the system as a whole. • Targeting the whole system can address issues of any one individual. • By changing the system, each individual may function better. • Change occurs by taking in energy/information/resource and then expelling energy/information/products that are different from the inputs.	• Attention to interconnections between person and the environment • Use of ecomaps and genograms to understand system dynamics • Focus on improving verbal and nonverbal communication among subsystems • Assessment of family development and life-cycle transitions • Use of family and parent coaching • Use of joining techniques, disequilibrium techniques, and psychoeducation	Durkheim Parsons Weber Merton Bertalanffy Germain Gitterman Bowen Minuchin

| Organizational Theories (with attention to Contingency Theory) | How individuals and groups in organizations gain power, access to resources, and control over their lives, often through collective action | • Groups are open, dynamic systems with both change and conflict present.
• Groups are stratified, with different and unequal levels of power and control.
• Oppression occurs when upward mobility is systematically denied.
• The structure of organizations influences the success of staff and the outcomes for clients.
• There is no one best way to manage organizations; it depends on the nature of the environment.
• Organizations and the social context must be critiqued and deconstructed.
• Assessment of internal and external resources leads to structural and process decisions within organizations.
• There needs to be a good "fit" between internal organization features and environmental demands. | • Explain and map the direction and role of collective action
• Assess power blocks
• Build individual and community strengths
• Support upward mobility of oppressed groups
• Assess the fit between internal and external resources; stated and real goals | Weber
Taylor
Mayo
Bertalanffy
Lawrence
Lorsch
March |

(continued)

Name of Theory	Theory Focus	Explanatory Concepts	Intervention Concepts	Specific Techniques Used	Influential Theorists/ Clinicians
Conflict/Critical Theory (with attention to Empowerment Theory)	How power structures and power disparities impact people's lives, both individually and as a society	• All societies perpetuate some forms of oppression, injustice, and structural inequity. • Power is the ability to influence the course of one's life. • Power is unequally divided, and some groups inevitably dominate others. • Social order is based on manipulation and control by dominant groups. • Social change is driven by conflict, with periods of change interrupting periods of stability. • Life is characterized by conflict, not consensus. • Structural barriers prevent people from accessing resources necessary for health and well-being and reaching full potential.	• Understanding conflict between persons, ideas, groups, classes, and larger social structures is useful for macro-level practice and policy analysis. • Formulating assessments of client vulnerability and oppression may lead to client organization and an increased sense of power. • Increasing personal, interpersonal, or political power enables individuals, families, and communities to take action to achieve personal and collective goals.	• Attend to evidence of oppression within individuals, groups, and communities • Attend to the role of conflict leading to client vulnerability • Recognize the dominant and subordinate groups that compete for resources • Focus on individual self-efficacy and consciousness-raising • Empower oppressed and vulnerable populations by organizing to alter power relationships	Marx Manniheim Lukacs Marcuse Mills Dahrendorf Freire Solomon Gutierrez Rose

Used with permission from Susanne Bennett, PhD, associate professor at the Catholic University's National Catholic School of Social Service.

CHAPTER 12

THE MIDDLE PHASE
OF TREATMENT

The middle phase of treatment is often the one that students and new clinicians are most eager to learn and often remains the most challenging part of working with clients. It is the part where students say, "OK. I have figured out how to form a relationship with my clients. I have gathered all sorts of information about their struggles, challenges, as well as their strengths and protective factors. This chapter addresses the phase that comes next with clients. It is often referred to as the middle phase of practice because it comes after the assessment and before the termination or ending phase. However, in reality, these three phases often blend into each other because the minute you meet your client, the work begins. In addition, in the very first session there should be a conversation about the end, often referred to as termination, which is then referenced during the entirety of the work with clients. Therefore, while this chapter addresses a middle phase of the work, your "intervention phase" with clients begins as soon as they make contact with you or your agency.

THE INFLUENCES OF THEORIES
AND MODELS ON THE MIDDLE PHASE

The type or the specifics of the work that takes place during this phase of intervention greatly depend on the explanatory and change theories used (see Chapter 11) as well as the distinct model of practice that has been chosen during the evidence-based practice (EBP) process (see Chapter 10) and treatment-planning processes (see Chapter 13). The types of tasks that are described in the treatment plan are generally created based on the chosen approach to addressing the problem. For example, if the client and social worker have chosen to use cognitive behavioral therapy (CBT; Beck, 2011) to address the issues, then the tasks and focus of the intervention will be on addressing cognitive and behavioral patterns.

If the client and social worker have chosen a family therapy approach, such as Structural Family Therapy (Walsh, 2013), then the focus in the intervention phase will be on addressing role and communication patterns within the family, among others. If the chosen form of intervention is the use of case management (Greene et al., 2006), then the focus will be to increase social supports based on patterns of isolation or social needs. A final example is if the client and social worker have chosen to use a relational approach, such as Child-Parent Relationship Therapy (Bratton, Landreth, Kellam, & Blackard, 2006), then focus is on interpersonal or relational patterns.

In all of these scenarios the key word is *patterns*. Regardless of the type of intervention that a social worker in partnership with a client chooses to take, the focus is on recognizing the patterns that are creating the distress or contributing to the presenting issue. Based on these patterns, practitioners then offer new skills, experiences, or resources to disrupt or alter the unhelpful patterns to create new, more adaptive or helpful patterns. The social workers role, then, regardless of the model of intervention, is to help clients recognize how these patterns contribute to their current struggles, to link the pattern to the presenting concern, and then to help the client to develop new patterns.

The explanatory theory that you have chosen to use is a critical tool during this process. It is helpful for clients to understand *how* these thinking patterns or relational patterns are connected to their current struggles. The explanation provided by the social worker helps clients to make the link between the why and the "what next." The what next or the intervention will then involve asking clients to do things differently, which can be scary. Yet, there are many paths to take, and an open and collaborative approach with clients will help ensure that they are engaged in and understand the chosen plan. The pathway that is chosen for these tasks will vary depending on the selected intervention approach.

It is beyond the scope of this book to describe every approach to addressing patterns. There are some excellent resources provided in the summary guide to help social workers dive more deeply into the particulars of the different approaches. Books that offer chapters on different models of intervention are wonderful resources to understand how various approaches help you execute the intervention phase. However, in this chapter, we provide some commonly used tools that can help social workers in this middle phase of intervention to begin pattern recognition and alteration.

We find it useful to organize this phase of treatment into four main steps. We encourage our students to be explicit and transparent with their clients, as we are with our own clients, about these steps so that the clients themselves are aware of the process and can be partners in it. Different change approaches will emphasize some of these steps more than others, yet in our experience of studying, teaching, and using different models of intervention, they all adhere to this general structure.

1. Identify the patterns
2. Link the patterns to the presenting problem/issue/concern
3. Explain how the pattern may have developed and its purpose
4. Develop new patterns

We believe that these steps capture the essence of the intervention phase of working with clients in practice.

1. PATTERN IDENTIFICATION

As stated previously, the first phase of the intervention process is to identify the problematic patterns. What is challenging about this phase is that the clients may not be aware of the patterns that are creating their distress, may not be interested in addressing these patterns as they may be mandated clients, or may be aware of patterns that are challenges for them but may not recognize the role they play in their distress. It is therefore important for the social worker to help clients identify patterns using a client-friendly and nonthreatening method. In this chapter, we cover two main formats for identifying patterns: charts and journaling. Different models may use other methods or slight variations of the two that we present here. These examples give you an overview and understanding of the main methods for gathering the information you are seeking.

CHARTS

The most common way of identifying patterns is to chart them. Charts are used in multiple formats and can be easily individualized to help clients identify different information about the patterns. The main information that is captured in a chart includes

- **When** the pattern occurs (e.g., time of day, location, with certain people, under what circumstances), which helps to identify specific triggers;
- **What** occurs within the pattern (e.g., descriptions of thoughts, emotions, physiological responses, behaviors);
- **How** often the pattern occurs (e.g., daily, weekly, hourly counts);
- **Intensity** of the experiences identified in the "what" step (e.g., defined on a standardized scale or a 0–10 well-defined scale); and
- **Duration** or how long the pattern lasts (could be within a day or over longer periods of time).

The information regarding the pattern that is captured on the chart could be tracking anything from internal experiences, such as a mood or physical sensation, to external experiences, such as getting into a fight or losing a job. What you are trying to elicit will often be led by the theory you are using to guide your practice (i.e., behaviors, thoughts, relationship patterns, communication, symptoms).

There are multiple benefits to charting patterns, including

- Identifying triggers (i.e., people, places, things)
- Increasing self-awareness
- Empowering client to have a role in the process
- Conveying the value of the client's knowledge and insights about the problem
- Organizing complex information
- Creating a format to focus the targeted information being sought

While there are many benefits, it is important to recognize that while charting can seem easy on the surface, it can be difficult for clients to complete for many reasons, including the following:

- Disorganization (i.e., losing the paper or forgetting to write information down)
- Embarrassment about what it reveals about their thoughts or behaviors
- Lack of motivation (i.e., they may see the issues as others' fault; however, those can also be charted)
- Challenges due to learning disabilities, cognitive disabilities, or reading and writing limitations
- Lack of resources or proper environment (i.e., no writing supplies, living space that does not provide privacy or space to think)
- Fear (i.e., concerns about others around them accessing the information)
- Fear of placing a burden on others (e.g., a teacher who is being asked to track the details of multiple behaviors of a student in a class of 30 others)
- A feeling that charting is too much like homework for those who have had negative academic experiences
- Need for time to capture information
- Lack of a chart at the time of the event
- A burdensome feeling to the client or whomever is completing the chart

Due to these reasons, it is imperative that social workers and the clients work together to develop a realistic charting system that will work for them. It may seem that there are more costs to charting than benefits. However, in our experiences, the benefits often outweigh the costs, and we have also found that many of the concerns about charting can be managed or addressed in open discussions about why they are used and what benefits the client can expect from their work.

The structure of the chart can be whatever the social worker and the client feel captures the information in a useful way. Most of the time, the information that is being sought is placed across the top of the sheet with a separate column for each piece of information; each individual event that is tracked is on the left-hand side of the paper. Please see Tables 12.1 and 12.2 for examples of charts.

TABLE 12.1: Chart Example 1

Date/Time	Event	Thoughts	Feelings	Behaviors

TABLE 12.2:	Chart Example 2			
Date/Time	Event	Behavior	Intensity	Duration

JOURNALING

Journaling is another method often used to capture information, and for some clients it is the preferred method. Rather than dissecting each aspect of any pattern, journaling allows clients' entries to be less formatted and more descriptive about their patterns in their own voice and style. Some clients prefer a more open approach to capturing their experiences, and journaling allows them to express their experiences in a narrative form.

Journaling can take many forms, but generally it simply involves clients writing in a book or on a pad of paper about what they notice, attempting to record the same information that a chart would capture. The information sought is the same. Only the format used to capture the information is different. Clients can then write about their experiences in whatever format they find to be most useful in describing their experiences of the pattern. Some of the benefits include the following:

- There is flexibility in describing information.
- It can be less confusing than figuring out what information goes where on a chart.
- Additional information may be captured beyond the standard information (i.e., their own insights or "aha moments").
- It encourages self-reflection.
- Clients are empowered to find their own "voice" through their writing.
- Writing is another medium for those who are not verbal processors to express their ideas.

However, as with charting, there are downsides to journaling. Many of these are the same as for charting. In addition to those already listed, journaling can raise anxiety levels in some clients as they struggle to capture their thoughts in what they perceive is a "right way." They may worry about what you will think when you read the journal or fear it being found and read by others. For many clients who struggle with spelling or writing, journaling may feel burdensome and intimidating. Therefore, as with all tasks suggested to clients, it is important to assess your clients' willingness, motivation, and capacity to carry out any task asked of them.

For clients who struggle with writing or have other challenges with written expression, there are several other options that they can use to capture the same information that might be captured in a chart or in a journal. One option is for them to use pictures. These pictures can be drawings or stickers. Another option is for the practitioner to provide the client with a premade chart that has either pictures or words that might capture an experience or feeling. Instead of writing out the experience, the client can circle already-printed words on a chart or other form. In addition, many clients now have smartphones that have apps for tracking a wide variety of information, including feelings and behaviors. Practitioners can work with clients to identify free apps that are helpful in tallying whatever information might be useful in their process. One final option, also using a smartphone, is to make an audio recording, with the client verbally describing the information you are trying to capture. This option may be helpful for individuals with learning disabilities or for younger children who struggle to translate thoughts into written words.

Regardless of the format used to record the information about the pattern, the main goal of this first step is to help you and your client identify in detail the patterns with which the client is struggling. Once this information has been captured, it is much easier for you to help your client connect those patterns to the presenting problem or concern for which they are seeking some support.

2. LINKING THE PATTERN TO THE PRESENTING CONCERN

Now that you have helped the client identify the patterns, the next step is to link this pattern to their presenting problem. This step in the process and the following one are both linked closely to your use of an explanatory theory. What we mean is that here your job is to help your clients understand how the patterns that they have identified are no longer helpful to them although they may have been during different phases of their lives (we expand this point in Step 3). Your explanatory theory is the key to helping them to make this connection.

For example, imagine you are working with a 25-year-old woman named Jackie who has been attempting to secure employment. However, each time she gets to the interview stage that her vocational counselor has arranged, she is rejected immediately after the interview. Her vocational counselor feels qualified to help her connect to positions that are a good fit based on her job skills, but the social worker does not feel qualified to help her address some of the "issues that keep getting in the way" of her being hired for a job. She has been referred to you to ultimately help her to secure and maintain employment.

During the assessment phase, you ask Jackie to complete a chart that describes her last three job interviews, including her thoughts, her physical reactions, her feelings during the interviews, and what she said to the interviewer. See Table 12.3 for her completed chart.

TABLE 12.3: Completed Chart for Jackie Using CBT

Date/Time	Interview Number	Thoughts	Physical Reactions	Feelings	What Said/Did
March 21 10:00 a.m.	1	They will never hire me.	Tired	Hopeless	Nothing; tried to respond to questions
March 30 9:30 a.m.	2	She thinks I am an idiot.	Butterflies in stomach	Scared	Just sad and hoped it would end soon
April 4 1:00 p.m.	3	I do not know what they want.	Sweaty palms	Nervous	Waited to see what they wanted me to say

What emerges in the chart is that each time Jackie entered into a dialog with an interviewer, she had thoughts such as "They will never hire me" and "She thinks I am an idiot." When she had those thoughts, she felt hopeless, and then she reported that she stopped talking and just nodded her head rather than share her skills and competencies. As a result, the interviewer did not have the opportunity to learn what Jackie had to offer to the position, and ultimately she did not get hired. This result only confirms her belief that she will not get hired. She then carries this strengthened thought with her to the next interview, leading to the same cycle.

What may seem obvious to you (i.e., that these self-defeating thoughts ultimately led her to not get hired for a job) may not be so obvious to Jackie. Therefore, your task here is to help her see how these thoughts led to her negative feelings, which led to her behavioral response of shutting down during the interview, which eventually led to her not getting the job. It is only after she has recognized the patterns identified in association to the main event (the interview) will you be able to help her with this connection. This example used a cognitive behavioral framework. As such, the information that was gathered on the chart focused on thoughts, feelings, and behaviors—all hallmarks of CBT.

Another approach would have been to gather information regarding interpersonal styles. Table 12.4 reflects a chart that captures interpersonal patterns.

Using a relational framework that might be seen in numerous models, such as mentalization (Bateman & Fonagy, 2011) or Child–Parent Psychotherapy (Bratton et al., 2006), the focus in Table 12.4 is on Jackie's interpersonal patterns and how those patterns relate to the presenting issue. This chart demonstrates that if she is around an authority figure, Jackie withdraws. In conversations with her, you find that this pattern has existed for as long as she can remember, including in school with teachers, her friends' parents, and any other adult figure. In these situations, the pattern is the same; she perceives the adult to be in a position of authority, and her style of engaging with adults is to withdraw and to be overly deferential, and in the job search ultimately leading to the same outcome—she does not share the information she has about herself with the interviewer, so she does not get the job.

TABLE 12.4: Interpersonal Chart for Jackie

Date/Time	Interview Number	Description of Person	What I think of That Person	What I Think That Person Thinks of Me	What Said/Did
March 21 10:00 a.m.	1	Older female— maybe 50 years old	She seems scary.	That I am stupid and talking too much	Nothing; tried to respond to questions
March 30 9:30 a.m.	2	Older female— 60 years old	She looked like she gets annoyed easily.	That I should stop talking	Just sad and hoped it would end soon
April 4 1:00 p.m.	3	Older male— 50 years old	He seemed impatient.	That I should only answer the questions he wants and no more	Waited to see what they wanted me to say

As stated previously, the social worker's job in the second step is to help the client to recognize this pattern and how it is not helping her to achieve her goal. The explanatory theory used by the social worker will often shape the *type* of information that is captured during the pattern identification, but it does not need to be exclusive. Theories reduce information as a way to focus the work, but at the beginning, the social worker may use several theories to gather the information necessary to help the client. Once the pattern has been identified and linked to the presenting problem, the explanatory theory is used to explain how this pattern emerged.

3. EXPLAIN BOTH HOW THE PATTERN MAY HAVE DEVELOPED AND ITS PURPOSE

The third step involves helping clients to understand the *whys* behind the pattern: Why did it develop in the first place? The amount of emphasis placed on this step varies depending on the explanatory theory used. For some theories, like behavioral theory, the why behind the pattern is less important than theories for that have derived from a psychodynamic base. The reason for these differences lies in the assumptions of the theory: Does the theory assume that gaining insight into the origins of behavior is important in creating change? If the answer is yes, then more time is spent on this step. If the answer is no, then less time is spent here.

Regardless of the amount of emphasis placed on this step, we have found that clients are relieved to understand that the pattern developed *for a reason*, and that it served an important function in their lives at some point. They often feel relief or have an aha moment when they realize that the behavior came from somewhere and when put into that context actually makes sense. For some of our clients, understanding why this pattern was useful to them is one of the most valuable aspects of the work.

Returning to the case of Jackie, her history involved being raised by her paternal grandmother, who was unhappy about having to raise another child after her own children were grown. Jackie began living with her after her mother lost custody of Jackie after a teacher at school became concerned about bruises she saw on Jackie's arms and legs. Her mother was addicted to drugs, and Child Protective Services determined that she was also physically abusing Jackie. Although she came to live with her paternal grandmother, no one knew where her father was because he had never been active in Jackie's life. The state approached her grandmother, stating that she was the only suitable relative, and if she did not take Jackie, the child would be sent to foster care. Jackie was 11 at the time, and her grandmother immediately told her she was to "be seen and not heard," as well as not give her grandmother "any trouble" because if she did Jackie would be "sent off to a foster home where you [she] would surely get abused." So, while her grandmother provided her with a home, food, and other basic needs, Jackie was isolated and learned quickly that if she asked her grandmother for anything beyond the most basic of needs, she was "too much." Jackie learned not to ask much of her grandmother and quickly withdrew from engaging with her.

Her grandmother did not encourage Jackie to bring over friends or encourage her to play with other children outside the home. As a result, she was an isolated child; she had no other siblings and lived in a rural community away from many neighbors. Even prior to living with her grandmother, Jackie's mother's long history of drug use left her alone often. Jackie also reported that if she asked her mother for food or made other requests, she was hit and told that she should "appreciate what you have."

In the discussions of the previous intervention steps, we demonstrated how different theories explain the current pattern and guide the information gathered. These theories also explain why the pattern exists and the purposes it served. Using the case of Jackie, we have discussed what information would be captured with both a CBT and a relational approach in the previous steps. In Step 3, the theory also plays a significant role in helping to explain the origins and purpose of the patterns.

CBT Approach. The CBT approach would explain Jackie's pattern of withdrawing as stemming from her core belief (or the main, raw, and unfiltered view she has of herself) that she is unworthy. This core belief developed as a result of her experiences with her mother, grandmother, and father, who all communicated to her that she did not deserve to have her needs met and that no one really wanted her around. These experiences influenced the development of schemata or thought structures. These schemata formed the lenses through which she interprets and filters the information about herself, others, and the world. Her core belief leads her to have automatic thoughts of "they will reject me" and "I am not good enough." When she thinks these thoughts, she feels hopeless and dejected, and the way she has learned to cope with these feelings is to withdraw and further isolate herself, like she does in the job interviews. Her family, who explicitly stated that she should not assert herself, also reinforced this pattern of withdrawal.

Relational Approach. The relational approach would explain this pattern by looking at her current behaviors and how those were learned in her childhood. It is clear from Jackie's relationship history that it was protective for her to withdraw from others in authority. Her early relationships included one with her mother, who abused her when she asked for her needs to be met. Through this experience, she learned to suppress her needs within relationships and wait for adults to provide for her. Moving to her grandmother's house only solidified this pattern. She was again told that her needs were not valued, and that she would be accepted and safe only if she remained withdrawn and without needs. Through these experiences, she developed an interpersonal pattern of deferring to and withdrawing from adults, as well as suppressing her own needs. This pattern served her well as a child because by doing so she was not hit when she was with her mother and while with her grandmother she was not sent to foster care where her grandmother told her she would go. In her past, it was helpful for her to withdraw and not be seen. Although she now is an adult and is not sitting with her grandmother or her mother, she transfers these same experiences she had as a child to current interactions and withdraws again.

In both of these explanations, although quite different, Jackie's pattern makes sense. It is hoped that it is obvious that, given her childhood, these patterns helped her survive in the context in which she was raised; the pattern of withdrawing was an effective survival strategy. However, what we also hope is becoming clearer is that while this pattern was helpful to her then, it is no longer useful to her. In fact, that same pattern that was so important for her survival then is now causing her stress and challenges in finding employment. Communicating this message is the key aspect of this step in the intervention phase. What worked for the client in the past is no longer working or helpful to her in the present. To reach their identified goal, the key is to change the identified pattern, which will lead to the final stage of the intervention phase.

4. DEVELOP NEW PATTERNS

The final step of developing new patterns is in some ways self-explanatory, but of course challenging as it requires clients to do something different. Some clients are eager to change, yet still struggle to do so. Some of the challenges to adopting new patterns stem from fear, a lack of support in their network, or other barriers. For those who are not interested in changing, this stage can be even more challenging for those invested in helping them address their issues because these clients lack the motivation to put the time, effort, and energy into making changes in their lives. We, along with every other instructor and clinician, wish we had the magical solution for those clients who are unmotivated to change. As we noted previously, in those situations it is important to find some common ground that can be helpful in engaging them in the work. Many clinicians have found that using an approach like Motivational Interviewing (Miller & Rollnick, 2013) can be helpful in these cases. It would be impossible to try to anticipate all of the various challenges that social workers may have in this fourth step. Therefore, we identify the key aspects of this step in the intervention phase in hopes that it guides your work with clients.

The key to this phase is working with clients to do something different; even small incremental changes can be powerful in changing the pattern. The tasks used to change those patterns are often driven by the explanatory and change theories that you are using. As discussed in Chapter 11, these two theories often go hand in hand. Your explanatory theory should be connected in a logical way to your change theory so that the link between why you think the issue exists is connected to the pathway to alter it. It is during this step of the intervention phase that learning different approaches to intervention can be especially helpful. Each model will provide a different set of tasks that can be done to shift patterns.

For example, we have used two different approaches to identify, link, and explain the pattern that informed Jackie's presenting problem. If we were using CBT to change the pattern, our tasks would involve skills and strategies to change her thoughts and behaviors, as these are areas that we assessed to be problematic for her previously. Therefore, by changing the thoughts, Jackie's feelings will change, which will result in a different behavior. If we were using a relational approach, we would focus on shifting Jackie's relationship patterns through her experiences of different relationships, including your relationship with her. In the professional relationship, you would provide her with a new or corrective relational experience by which she could assert herself and be accepted. You would also teach her assertiveness skills and have her practice these with individuals with whom she was ensured a positive response, such as her vocational education counselor.

There are many different approaches to addressing client issues, and readers are encouraged to explore those further in coursework, continuing education, independent learning, and supervision. Identifying an approach that is most appropriate for clients is trial and error, but using the EBP process (see Chapter 10) is an excellent way to incorporate the client's unique needs, your expertise, and the best available research as you and your client decide on the approach. The specific strategies within the approach are the tasks that you identify within your treatment plan (see Chapter 13).

Once you and your client have agreed on an approach, it is important to remember that how you deliver the approach is a combination of the art and science of social work. Through the use of EBP or other methods to infuse research into your approach, the art is up to you. *How* you engage your clients in the phase, *how* you work with them to make changes both during your time together and outside it, *how* you introduce and help them master new skills, and much more are part of the art of social work.

This step can be frightening to clients. You may be asking them to do activities that are frightening or disorienting. Even clients who are strongly motivated to change will at some point have ambivalence about it. There is always some gain to the status quo and some loss involved in changing. For example, when Jackie is able to get a job, she will lose the supportive relationship with her vocational counselor and even need to terminate with you. She knows what it is like to be unemployed and stressed about finding work, but can she see herself being successful in a job and able to keep it long term?

Many clients speak to this ambivalence about change and fear of the unknown as the phenomenon of "the devil you know is better than the one you don't." If you empathize with this ambivalence, and not label the client as "resistant," you are likely to help the client reach his or her goals. It is important to "honor the resistance," as it will help you to better understand the origins of the ambivalence and be more effective in addressing it (Teyber & McClure, 2011, p. 95). It will be especially important at this time for you to remember that the relationship that you have with your clients is a critical factor in the success of whatever approach you take (Wampold, 2010). Research has continued to show that the relationship between the worker and the client is a critical component of a successful intervention (Norcross, 2002). Through your support and by remaining attuned to the pace, their needs, and the subtle changes in the work, clients will gain more confidence in their ability to learn and master new skills and ultimately change their unhelpful patterns to more helpful and adaptive ones.

CONCLUSION

This chapter discussed the middle phase of working with clients, often referred to as the intervention phase. While there are many different approaches social workers can take to work with clients to reach their goals, most of these approaches follow four steps: identify the patterns; link the patterns to the presenting problem, issue, or concern; explain how the pattern may have developed and its purpose; and develop new patterns. Each of these are driven by the social workers' explanatory and change theories and models (e.g., interpersonal, behavioral, cognitive) and as a result will involve different tasks to ultimately help clients alter the patterns that are unhelpful to them in reaching their goals. Social workers should work closely with clients to address any potential barriers to changing their patterns, always in the context of a supportive relationship that balances the art and science of social work practice.

CHAPTER 12 RESOURCE GUIDE

RESOURCES

Dewan, M. J., Steenbarger, B. N., & Greenberg, R. P. (Eds.). (2004). *The art and science of brief psychotherapies: A practitioner's guide*. Washington, DC: American Psychiatric Press.

Frew, J., & Spiegler, M. D. (2013). *Contemporary psychotherapies for a diverse world*. New York, NY: Routledge.

Gabbard, G. O. (2009). *Textbook of psychotherapeutic treatments*. Washington, DC: American Psychiatric Press.

Gabbard, G. O., Beck, J. S., & Homes, J. (Eds.). (2005). *Oxford textbook of psychotherapy*. New York, NY: Oxford University Press.

Messer, S. B., & Gurman, A. S. (2011). *Essential psychotherapies: Theory and practice* (3rd ed.). New York, NY: Guilford Press.

Turner, F. J. (Ed.). (2011). *Social work treatment approaches: Interlocking theoretical approaches* (5th ed.). New York, NY: Oxford University Press.

Walsh, J. (2013). *Theories of direct social work practice* (3rd ed.). Stamford, CT: Cengage.

CHAPTER 13

PLANNING FOR CHANGE AND SETTING GOALS

In our conversations with many practitioners, we have found that they rarely establish a treatment plan that includes setting clear and measurable goals with clients. We find this information remarkable and a bit disturbing for a number of reasons. Without a plan, how will you and your client know how you will address the presenting concerns together? Without a plan, how will you and the client know whether your strategy is working or not? Without a plan, how will your client, you, and others know what is expected of everyone? Without a plan, how will you and your client even know where you are headed in the intervention process or when it is time to end the work?

Imagine going to see your physician, a financial planner, or another type of service provider. Imagine yourself walking in the door to his or her office and asking for help with an issue, such as a health issue or assistance with budgeting. Now, imagine if this person listened well to your wishes and concerns and then simply said, "Why don't you come back next week, and we can continue talking about this issue?" Many of you would most likely find this response frustrating. Your frustration may stem from wanting to have answers to a variety of questions, such as, "What are the next steps?" "What should I be doing to address this issue?" "What is the provider going to be doing to address the issue?" "Why can't you do something to help me today?" Clients are coming to you for help with a specific issue and, rightfully so, want to know what action steps will be taken to address the issue. They are most likely coming in now because they feel ready for change or have been told they need to change *now*. Planning for change and goal setting is a critical stage of the work with clients. This stage clarifies for everyone involved what the plan is for helping the client resolve the presenting issue. Therefore, we encourage all of you to incorporate such planning into your work with clients.

This stage of working with clients is often referred to as treatment planning. However, many of you will not be working with clients in a treatment setting, meaning you will not be providing psychotherapy services to your client. Whether you are working in a clinical or macro setting, the phase that we are calling planning for change is the same across settings. We were concerned that by referring to this phase as treatment planning many readers might assume that these ideas only apply to those social workers who are working with clients in a traditional therapy context. We believe that generalist social work practice can be transformative regardless of the setting or type of service offered. Therefore, we want to ensure that, regardless of the context, social workers include thoughtful planning in their work with their clients.

BEFORE YOU START

There are a few important questions to ask yourself before you begin the planning phase. These questions are listed next and should help provide a guide for when you are ready to begin this phase of your work with clients.

- Are you clear about what types of services you and your agency can offer *and* what you cannot?
- Have you thought through what potential triggers might emerge for you with this client (i.e., what issues or topics could be discussed that might create strong reactions in you)?
- Have you conducted a thorough assessment so that you are clear about what the issues might be?
- Have you completed the evidence-based practice (EBP) process so that you and your client are clear about what types of interventions might be worth exploring to help the client with his or her presenting concern?

Once you feel confident in your readiness to embark on the change process, you can begin thinking about creating goals for your work together.

One important piece to remember during this phase, as with all other phases of work, is to assess for and build on the clients' strengths. As you are working toward helping clients to address their presenting issues, it is essential that their existing coping strategies and their capacities for success be considered. Asking clients about how they have addressed these issues so far is a good place to start. You can also explore other changes they have made and how they accomplished them. These strengths should be incorporated into the planning stage as much as possible. Not only does including strengths provide the social worker with a clearer baseline of where the client is, but also it is a way to build confidence and momentum as clients feel more confident in their capacities to take on this new challenge.

In addition to ensuring that strengths are remembered in treatment planning, it is important to remember that this planning for a change process is a *mutual undertaking*. Helping professionals should make every effort possible to have this stage be a collaborative process that is *driven by the clients and their needs*. For some situations, this goal of inclusion is a challenge. These situations include working with mandated or court-ordered clients or minors who are referred by a third party. When clients have not self-referred, they may be less invested in planning for the change process, as they may not believe that there is a need for any change. In such cases, we wish we could offer a magical solution to increase their motivation. However, we cannot. There is some research that indicated that techniques such as motivational interviewing (MI; Miller & Rollnick, 2012) are effective with involuntary clients in engaging them with the helping process. Whether you are using MI or another approach, it is important to find a way to connect with clients concerning what *they* want out of the process.

For example, imagine you are working at a social service agency with a parent named Ms. K who has been mandated to receive parent education services because of inappropriate discipline strategies. Ms. K does not believe that she was inappropriately rough and is angry because she has to participate in this service. The agency has identified specific outcomes that they want Ms. K to achieve before they are willing to stop services. If she does not comply, the agency has threatened that it will remove her children from the home. Ms. K expresses a great deal of anger and does not feel she needs to work on any of the mandated goals. Given this perspective, it will be difficult for her to plan for change because she does not feel she needs to. One way to approach this type of situation is to join with her concerning that she wants the agency to be out of her life. If this is *her* goal, what can you help her with in the process toward achieving the goal of getting the agency out of her life? Sometimes by joining with her concerning such a goal, there is a middle ground that can be found and a plan of action can be established.

In essence, you want to acknowledge for the individual who is mandated that this person does not want to be there. Yet, simultaneously, you also want to continue to work toward his or her goals. Whether you are working with a teenager, child, or adult, the message can be that you understand his or her ambivalence about being there, but there may be some ways that the two of you can still find a goal or focus that might be useful to that individual. A useful way to engage in this process is to say something such as, "Since you have to be here, how do you want to spend this time in a way that benefits you? We have to address xyz, but is there something you want to do with our time that you would find valuable?"

SMART FORMAT

As you begin to think about planning for change-oriented work with clients, it is important to keep in mind several important components of the plans you will be writing together. As you articulate the plan, it is important for the plan to be **s**pecific, **m**easurable, **a**chievable, **r**elevant, and to have a **t**ime frame, also referred to as SMART (Doran, 1981). The SMART format in direct practice has been borrowed from macro practice focused on project management as a way to ensure that projects are clearly articulated and manageable (Doran, 1981; Meyer, 2003). The acronym remains the same as first articulated by Doran over 30 years ago:

- **Specific**—clearly articulate what will be accomplished. The goals, objectives, and tasks should answer the questions of what, when, where, and how. They should also specifically address who will do what.

- **Measurable**—The process will quantify in some way how progress or achievement will be assessed.
- **Achievable**—The goals are attainable and appropriate given the client's context, capacities, motivation, history, and any other relevant factors that should be considered.
- **Relevant**—Do the goals link to the issue of the client? In addition, are they realistic, and do they resonate with the client's wishes?
- **Time frame/time bound**—There needs to be a time frame established for when the plan will be achieved, with specific time frames for each stage of the process.

Since Doran (1981), others have added an R at the end to create SMARTR goals, with the R representing **r**eevaluate to emphasize creating and working toward goal attainment as a dynamic process (Yemm, 2012). The SMART or SMARTR format should be applied to all parts of the final document that represents the plan for the work together, including the goals, objectives, and tasks outlined in the document.

GOALS, OBJECTIVES, AND TASKS, OH MY!

In our work with students, we have found that clarifying the differences between goals, objectives, and tasks is a constant challenge. These three components of an intervention plan seem to become muddled and confused by practitioners, yet they represent distinct components of a plan for change. We hope that by the end of this chapter we have clarified these important and distinct entities of a plan.

GOALS

Simply put, goals are where the client wants to be at the end of the process. We often refer to a goal as similar to the destination you might put in your GPS. For example, if you are in Washington, D.C., there are lots of places you could go from that location. Getting in your car and starting down a road might be an interesting adventure, but without a goal or destination, it will be a meandering experience. Therefore, it is important that we help clients be clear about where they would like to be by the time the work together ends.

While it may sound easy in theory to establish goals with clients, it is actually harder than it appears. Clients often focus on what is not working; therefore, it can be difficult to have them shift to what they want or what would be better. Sometimes, it is hard to imagine what they want as they and everyone else has spent so much time focused on what they do not want. It can be difficult to articulate those hopes in a way that is meaningful and realistic given all of the contextual factors in their lives. Therefore, clients may need your help to articulate their goals in a clear fashion. However, as stated previously, it is important to ensure that this process is collaborative. While clients may need help articulating their goals, the goals you establish should not be yours. Every effort should be made to have the client take ownership of the goals rather than have the goals comprise your wishes for them. To help with this process, we have the following guidelines that we hope will help you in your goal creation process with clients:

Goals should be linked to the target concerns: Goals should connect directly to the client's presenting issue or, in the case of mandated or involuntary clients, those goals that are stated by the mandate or court order (Hepworth, Rooney, Dewberry-Rooney, & Strom-Gottfried, 2013). There should be a clear link between the target issue and the goal that you are creating with the client. In addition, goals should be consistent with the client's wishes as much as possible rather than yours or anyone else's. For example, if an individual is struggling with test anxiety and was sent to you, the school social worker, for help with this issue, the goal should be related to managing test anxiety and pressures at school, not something outside academic issues, such as managing friendship dynamics.

Goals should be written in the positive: Goals should be about what people want rather than what they do not want. As stated previously, clients have often spent so much time focused on what is not working it can be difficult for them to imagine what they want instead. This struggle is where you can help. They may need help in focusing what they want *instead* of what is currently happening. The distinction is subtle, but important.

Another way to make this distinction is through an expression that is used in the field called "the Dead Person Rule" (Spiegler & Guevremont, 2010, p. 57). If a dead person can do it, then it is not an appropriate goal. For example, a dead person can stop drinking but cannot increase coping capacities to manage sobriety. A dead person can stop cutting or self-harming behaviors but cannot learn to regulate his or her affect. A dead person can stop fighting but cannot learn how to use "I statements" to increase positive communication. Therefore, you may need to help your clients find ways to express their goals in positive and active language that will help them articulate what they want to see at the end of your work together.

Goals should be future oriented: While this guideline may sound obvious, you may find that some clients are heavily focused on the past and wish to change parts of the past. They may need to help refocus their attention on the future and where they hope to be rather than where they wish they were. For clients who struggle with loss or depression, this aspect of creating goals can be especially challenging. Yet, creating goals is about looking ahead and articulating where you want to be in the future, so it should be focused on looking ahead rather than looking back. For example, if you are working with a survivor of sexual violence, the client may set a goal of returning to a normal life like before the assault. Turning this goal to be future-oriented would mean that the client would work on integrating the traumatic experience into his life so that it did not define him or his behaviors moving forward.

Goals should be time limited: Goals should be given a time frame. Not only does this help you and your client stay focused, but more often than not, third-party payers (i.e., insurance companies and Medicaid) require that the work we do with clients be time limited. Time limited does not need to translate as brief, although it can. What we mean here is that you and your client should set a realistic time frame for when you anticipate the goal to be achieved. Ideally, the issue and the client's capacities and motivation to address that issue would determine the date. However, it is more often the case that dates are chosen because of external pressures, such as the end of the academic school year (either for the social work intern or the clients), or by the policies of the third-party payer that limit the amount of time for the intervention. In the best case, you would set a time limit on a goal based on what is realistic for the client. A goal statement with a goal would then include the goal along with the time frame, such as increasing the client's capacity to take her medications regularly by December 31.

Table 13.1 provides you more examples of goals. As you will see from the examples, goals can be and should be simple. The more specific you can be and the simpler you can be in the language, the easier it will be to remain focused and not become distracted by trying to do too much.

OBJECTIVES

Objectives are the part of the plan for change that operationalizes the goals. They serve as concrete, measurable, and objective markers that you will use to identify whether you are moving in the right direction. Objectives can be short or long term, but in either case, they should be clear about how the outcome of the intervention will be measured. Goals are often seen as the conceptual or big-picture view of where you want to go, while objectives are the milestones used to determine whether you have achieved those goals.

Going back to the GPS metaphor with you in Washington, D.C., let us say you have identified your goal as wanting to get to the Brooklyn Bridge in New York City. It is clear where you want to go, and everyone has agreed that this location is the final destination. As you start your journey to the Brooklyn Bridge, there are lots of ways that you can get there, but how will you know if you are heading in the right direction? Well, you could look at your GPS and see whether it visually shows if you are on the right track. You could use a compass and check it regularly to see if you are still heading in a northeastern direction. You could look for signs along the interstate to see if the signs are for New York, as well as other approaches. Each of these helps you determine whether you are getting any closer to your goal.

Objectives in social work serve the same purpose. They are used to provide real-time evaluations of where you are in relation to the goal. If, for example, the client's goal is to increase her coping capacities to more effectively manage angry and violent outbursts, how would you and she know if what you are doing together is working? A possible objective might be to count how many fights she gets in over a period of time and compare that rate to a baseline rate. Another option might be to have her use an objective measure to self-assess the number of skills she uses in her day-to-day life with regard to her emotional regulation. The chapter on endings provides a more thorough discussion of ways to measure the outcomes, which are often similar to the objectives used in the treatment plans. The tools described in that chapter provide you and the client with concrete measures of progress.

Objectives are often used in conjunction with the phrase "as evidenced by" (AEB). This phrase is commonly used in plans for change to demonstrate how the attainment of the goal will be identified. Social workers should ask their supervisors whether this phrase is used within the agency. It is essentially saying that you will know that the person has reached her goal AEB a particular outcome or milestone, which is then listed in the plan as the objective.

As a guiding principle, most plans include at least two objectives for each goal to ensure that there are multiple markers for measuring the goal. While it is easy to ask the client if he or she believes that the treatment is working, this is often not the best measure of progress for a variety of reasons. The chapter on endings provides a thorough discussion about self-report options, and readers are encouraged to review that section if planning to use self-report indicators.

Regardless of what types of objectives are used in plans, the key is to make sure that they are accurate indicators of progress. Including an objective that does not actually assess for progress toward the goal is not helpful. Using our trip to the Brooklyn Bridge, asking ourselves whether we are having a good time on our journey will not provide us with information about whether we are moving closer to the Brooklyn Bridge. Also, asking us whether we *think* we are heading in the right direction based on our internal compass is also not an objective way of measuring progress. Therefore, when choosing objectives, it is important to consider whether they are objective (versus a subjective measure) and a relevant outcome related to the goal. See Table 13.1 for how the objectives are phrased and aligned with the goals identified.

MODALITY

The modality of intervention is sometimes included in treatment plans, but often not. We have chosen to include it here as we believe it is another way for social workers to be transparent with clients and their caregivers about what will be happening in the work together with the client. What we mean by modality is the approach that you will be using when working with a client. Sometimes, modality is referred to as the broad category of intervention that will be used, such as individual, group, or family levels of intervention. Other times, the modality of treatment is referred to as the specific practice model that will be used in the work with the client, such as psychodynamic therapy, cognitive therapy, or case management. Social workers should discuss with their supervisors regarding what should be reported on the plans for change.

Regardless of which definition is used, the modality of intervention outlines which approach will be used to reach the client's goal. Returning to the goal of reaching the Brooklyn Bridge from Washington, D.C., there are many modalities that you could use to get there. You could drive, take a plane, walk, bike, take the train, or even arrive by horseback! For many clients, knowing how you will get there is comforting.

Regardless of which modality you use, the objectives and goals remain the same. You still want to know if you are moving in the right direction and getting closer to your goal. If the client's goal is to increase his or her coping capacities to more effectively manage angry and violent outbursts, you can achieve that goal through group therapy that utilizes psychodrama, individual therapy that uses cognitive behavioral therapy (CBT), or a family approach that looks at the issue from a systemic lens. Which approach you use will be determined by the EBP process that incorporates relevant client factors; your expertise, which includes your knowledge of theories and practice models; the best available evidence; and the contextual factors that are relevant to this client's life (see the chapter on EBP for a more thorough review).

Once you have determined your modality, the tasks that you will use often fall into place. Different practice models will often provide tasks that are linked to the theory of change. These tasks or intervention strategies are then used to create the desired changes or goals that have been set. For example, in a CBT approach, some of the tasks would include identifying cognitive patterns and then learning new skills to change those patterns. The timelines for completing these tasks and the specific instructions for these tasks are what is placed in the tasks section of the plan for change. The social worker, based on his or her assessment, will determine which tasks have the potential to be most relevant in helping the client to achieve his or her goal. Ultimately, these tasks should link back to the client's goals that were based on the assessment using a specific practice model, which is based on a theory of change that is linked to an explanatory theory. This last statement should sound familiar as it comes from the previous chapter on the use of theory.

To close our metaphor with trying to reach the Brooklyn Bridge from Washington, D.C., the specific tasks we would need to undertake to get there are based largely on the modality we have chosen. If we decide we want to arrive by plane, then we need to purchase tickets that will get us there by the date of our goal. Another task would be to figure out how we will get from the airport to the bridge. If we decide that our modality will be by bike, then we have an entirely different set of tasks, which involve food storage, equipment, identification of safe bike routes, assessment of fitness levels, and much more. We will let you play out the tasks that would be necessary for the horse-back option.

Please refer to Table 13.1 for examples of potential tasks. The ones listed are just examples and are not meant to be comprehensive of what might be included in a plan for change. They are simply to give examples of potential tasks that might be included. There are often many more tasks than just two for each goal. You may also note in some of the examples that the social worker is named as someone who will be completing tasks. The social worker, family members, physicians, and others may all be listed as individuals who have a role to play in the plan and should be included when appropriate.

TYING IT ALL TOGETHER

As you can see, there are numerous potential tasks that could be used to achieve the same goal. These tasks are determined by the modality that has been chosen, ideally through the EBP process. Regardless of which path is chosen, the clients and social workers need to identify objectives that will provide markers for their progress toward reaching the goals set by the clients. For each of these aspects of the plan, the SMART format should be used throughout. The SMART or SMARTR format can be used to ensure that, for each of the sections of the plan, you have been specific; provided measurable goals, objectives, and tasks that are achievable and relevant; as well as have a time frame for each.

TABLE 13.1: Examples of Goals, Objectives, and Tasks With Modality Identified

Example 1 Goal: Client will increase her support networks by 50% the end of 6 weeks.

    Objective 1: By the end of 1 month, the client's list of individuals and community resources that she considers a support will be 30% higher than at baseline.

    Objective 2: Client's family will report a decrease in phone calls by at least 50% compared to baseline by the end of 1 month.

    Modality: Individual case management

        Task 1: Within the first week, client will compile a list of her current supports, either individual or community agency support.

        Task 2: In the second week, the client will identify at least three individuals or organizations that she will contact that she believes could serve as a social support.

Example 2 Goal: Client will increase his social skills to more effectively manage conflict with peers in school by the end of 6 months.

    Objective 1: Teachers will report a decrease in peer conflicts at school by 50% by the end of the first quarter.

    Objective 2: Parents will report a decrease in peer conflicts in the community by 75% by the end of 4 months.

    Modality: Structural family therapy

        Task 1: Within the first week, the family will identify the rules and consequences at home for both desired and undesired behavior.

        Task 2: Within the first month, the parents will chart the number of conflicts with peers in their community and family, their responses to those behaviors, and how the client responded to those responses.

Example 3 Goal: Client will secure stable housing by the end of 6 months.

    Objective 1: Client and social worker will have a list of possible housing options by the end of 1 month.

    Objective 2: Client will have made at least four phone calls to explore different housing options by the end of 2 months.

    Modality: Individual case management

        Task 1: Within the first week, client will compile a list of supports and barriers to finding secure housing.

        Task 2: In the second week, the client will brainstorm with the social worker ideas for how to address the identified barriers.

Example 4 Goal: Client will increase her capacity to manage symptoms of anxiety at the end of 9 months.

    Objective 1: Client will show a decrease by at least 10% on the XX Anxiety Rating Scale by the end of 2 months.

    Objective 2: Client will report a decrease in panic attacks from her baseline by at least 50% by the end of 6 months.

    Modality: Individual therapy using cognitive behavioral therapy

        Task 1: Within the first week, social worker will provide psychoeducation concerning anxiety, panic attacks, and the CBT model.

        Task 2: Starting in the first week and for the next 2 weeks, the client will complete a thought record to record at least three times/week periods of anxiety. The chart should include the time/day and the thoughts, feelings, and behaviors that the client noted at the time.

A FINAL CONSIDERATION

We recognize that we have provided a description of the ideal scenario of treatment planning. There are many situations, such as in a crisis, for which you may not be able to walk clients through such a clear process. There are also other limitations, like a client's severe mental illness or cognitive limitations, for which you might need to modify the planning process. There are some models of intervention, like the Recovery Model (Deegan, 1988), that specialize in having you think about how to modify and challenge our ideas of "intervention" when working with unique populations. While we want to emphasize the importance of finding ways to follow the process we have described, it is also important to be client centered and flexible when working with clients in assisting them to reach their goals.

CONCLUSION

A comprehensive and well-thought-out plan for change is the foundation for being able to then evaluate the effectiveness of the approach you and your client have chosen to take. Much of the work needed to do the final stage of the SMARTR format involving reevaluating is already done. In Chapter 15 on evaluating practice, we provide a more thorough discussion of how to evaluate both the progress your clients are making toward their goals and how to determine if they are ready to end the work you have been doing together. The time invested in drafting a useful plan will serve social workers well as they then move to the intervention phase of the work, which requires continuous monitoring and evaluation to be consistent with our own profession's code of ethics.

PART III
ENDING WITH CLIENTS

CHAPTER 14

ENDINGS

There is a funny mock exchange between a therapist and a client in an article called the "The Last Session" (Kenny, 2008) that was published in *The New Yorker* (http://www.newyorker.com/magazine/2008/01/28/last-session). It is written as a dialog from a session when the client comes in to discuss ending with therapist. The therapist displays a host of inappropriate behaviors throughout the session while simultaneously managing to completely avoid talking about ending the relationship. In the end, after many examples of avoidance and unhelpful exchanges, the therapist states, "We have to stop. Let's pick up here next week." The exchange in the scenario is disconcerting for many reasons and underscores many of issues we addressed in the previous chapters (i.e., boundaries, self-disclosure, use of self). The piece is obviously meant to be humorous as it highlights some of the stereotypes that are held about therapists. However, these stereotypes are not limited only to social service providers practicing psychotherapy. Even with the best intentions, all social workers, regardless of the type of social work service we are providing, could fall prey to some of these behaviors in our work with clients. Some of the most egregious stereotypical behaviors illustrated involved the portrayal of a therapist who had no plan for ending with a client, had no methods to determine whether the work with the client was having a measurable impact, and was unable to have a conversation about whether the client had met any concrete goals through their work together.

This chapter is designed to ensure that your work with clients will not follow the same path as the therapist portrayed in that scenario. Although we recognize that every situation is unique, in this chapter we provide some concrete guidelines to help direct your termination process with your clients. While we have separated the chapters on termination and evaluating one's own practice, the two chapters go hand in hand. Therefore, we encourage readers to consider the chapters as two sides of the same coin as it is impossible to extract one from the other.

THE WORD *TERMINATION*

Take a minute and think about what associations you have with the word *termination*. Are these associations pleasant? Negative? What images come to mind? For many people, the word *termination* conjures up images of being fired, eliminated, cut off, and removed with a sense of finality. If these images are consistent with what you identified, keep in mind that they may be similar for your clients as well. Given these associations, it is essential that social workers thoughtfully approach termination with clients. We want to ensure that this ending is different from other endings so that clients are not left feeling rejected and abandoned. Although the word *termination* is used in the literature, we often prefer to use the word ending. We use termination here to stay consistent with the literature, but we encourage you to think of your own phrase or use ours to communicate the ending of the work while finding ways to remove some of the harshness from the language.

In addition to attending to your clients' associations with the word *termination*, it is important to pay attention to your own associations, such as the images you identified previously. How do you "do" endings? Are you typically able to talk through these experiences in your personal life, or do you avoid them at all costs? The ending of a helping relationship is unique. We do not typically end relationships that are working well for us or that we feel good about. How often have you called up a friend and said, "This friendship has been really great for me. You've been supportive and really fun, and I've enjoyed spending time with you. However, at this point I feel I have done all the work as a friend I can do with you, and it is time to terminate our relationship." No one does that! It is an experience not found outside the working relationship between client and practitioner.

How *you* feel about endings has the potential to influence how you end relationships. It may be that you avoid talking about termination because of your own discomfort with endings in general. It could be that you eagerly bring up termination because of the feelings you have about a particular client. How social workers manage the endings of relationships with clients is a combination of both their own feelings about endings *and* their feelings about particular clients. Therefore, it is critical that you use your self-awareness to recognize how this combination can directly influence the work with clients.

WHEN TO START THE TERMINATION PROCESS

In reality, the termination process begins during the first meeting with your clients or as soon as you have created a contract for whatever service you are providing. We discussed in Chapter 12 how creating concrete and measurable goals using the SMART (**s**pecific, **m**easurable, **a**chievable, **r**elevant, and with a **t**ime frame) format is an important step in the process. In creating such goals, you and your client have already identified the path you will take to reach the client's goals. The objectives you and your client developed established concrete outcomes that will identify whether the goals of the work have been met. Therefore, the time invested in creating such concrete objectives at the beginning stages of the work with clients has a direct impact on the termination process.

Unlike "The Last Session" (Kenny, 2008) scenario in which the therapist and client have been meeting for 20 years, the vast majority of you will never see clients for that length of time. This stereotype of the work that social workers do with clients is just that, a stereotype. In reality, most often you will be working with clients for a shorter, more specified length of time. This time frame may be determined by a number of factors, including their insurance plans, which could be private, Medicaid, Medicare, or some other third-party payer. Other factors may be the realities of their lives. Many clients do not have the time or the money to see a social worker for years. Clients have jobs, child-care responsibilities, and other obligations that make it impossible for them to have this type of service for such a long time.

Now, although we have just explained that this length of time is a stereotype, we do not want to imply that some clients do not need to have services on a long-term basis. There are many clients who can benefit from services for many years. However, the key phrase here is that they continue to benefit from services. Our Code of Ethics (National Association of Social Workers; NASW, 2008) states that we must provide services that are effective (Section 4.01). Yet, there are many examples that we have seen in our years of practice of clients continuing to receive services, yet it is unclear what they are gaining from those services. Part of our responsibility as professional social workers is to regularly discuss the progress the clients are making toward their goals. In these discussions, we need to recognize that goals shift and the treatment contract may need to be adjusted, which may alter the course of the intervention. Our Code of Ethics also states that if clients are no longer benefiting from services, we must terminate services or transfer to another service or provider (Section 1.16). Therefore, we support clients receiving services on a long-term basis as long as it is clear that the client is still benefiting from those services. We do not want to create a working relationship in which the client is dependent on the practitioner. As stated previously, evaluating one's practice is a critical aspect of termination. To that end, we discuss how to evaluate whether the provided services are effective in Chapter 15.

TYPES OF TERMINATION

As stated previously, the termination process should begin as soon as the contract is created. In an ideal world, the client and the worker have identified a time frame for the work and the specific objectives that will be reached by the end of that time. When the client has met those goals and objectives, the work together ends. In some cases, you and the client might end before the set date once the client is confident that he or she is able to reach the stated goals independent of the social worker. These examples, albeit ideal, are of one type of termination referred to as a *planned termination* (Gambrill, 2013). The worker and the client have planned together for when the work will end. Together, they have planned for the ending using the predetermined date in the treatment contract or based on the agreed-on outcome. In a planned termination, everyone is clear regarding when or under what circumstances the termination will occur.

Other types of planned terminations include endings that are based on external factors that may be unrelated to reaching the agreed-on goals. Such factors might include the worker leaving the agency (i.e., an internship is ending or the worker is leaving the area), the client moving, or the insurance company setting a number of predetermined sessions. While these scenarios may not be ideal as they are not based on the client's needs, these still qualify as planned terminations because the worker and the client both know that an end date is approaching and can plan ahead for that date.

For planned terminations, we created the guidelines shown in Table 14.1 to help you create a plan with the client. However, these are meant as guidelines and, as with all of the guidelines in this book, should be used in consultation with your supervisors. In addition, all guidelines should always be considered in the context of your specific client and his or her circumstances, as well as the mission and standard of care for the agency.

The other type of terminations that occur more often than we would like are referred to as *unplanned terminations* (Gambrill, 2013). These are exactly as they sound, unplanned, and can often leave both the worker and the client feeling like the work is undone. Unplanned terminations can occur for a number of reasons. Some examples include situations when the client just stops showing up for any number of reasons or the worker has an unexpected personal emergency, such as an illness. With unplanned terminations, there are no opportunities to reflect on the work together or plan for how to say good-bye. The lack of ritual or reflection can often leave the worker feeling a range of different emotions, including anger, relief, guilt due to feeling "I should have done more," sadness, and self-doubt, among others. When I (E.D.) was supervising student interns at a local nonprofit agency providing counseling for trauma survivors, it was common for students to express a lot of self-doubt when clients would just stop coming without explanation. The student would often discuss these reactions in supervision; many would ask questions like the following:

- "Did she just not like me?"
- "Did I say something wrong?"
- "Am I just no good at this?"
- "Will I ever be able to keep a client engaged in the work?"

TABLE 14.1: **Planned Termination Guidelines**

Guidelines to Follow for Planned Termination in Consultation With Your Supervisor

- Identify at the contract phase what the objectives are that you and the client will use to measure goal attainment (see Chapter 12 on creating goals).
- If there is a predetermined date for termination, remind clients at regular intervals regarding this date and the remaining time.
- If there is no predetermined date for termination and the treatment is based on goal attainment, identify tools to measure outcomes and time frames for their use.
- Discuss the client's confidence in his or her ability to continue to reach his or her goals without the social work service.
- Depending on the time frame, approximately 1 month from the end of the service, discuss with the client potential rituals or ways he or she would like to say good-bye.
- Depending on the time frame, if additional services are needed, begin planning at least 1 month in advance to prepare a "warm handoff" to the next provider.
- Process rituals, plan for the ending, and your own feelings with your supervisor.
- Anticipate with your client what feelings, behaviors, concerns, or patterns they might have as the final session approaches (i.e., cancel last sessions, feel angry).
- Normalize these feelings with your client. Even when the termination is planned far in advance, it is normal to have feelings about the ending that can be complex.
- Document every step of the process, especially the plan for after the final session, whether they will be working with another provider, or if they have been given contact information for how to connect to another service provider.

We, along with many other highly seasoned practitioners, have experienced unplanned terminations. These endings may in fact have to do with something that the practitioner did or did not do. However, there are many circumstances that may contribute to the premature end of the work and that have nothing to do with the skills or the "likability" of the social worker.

It is important for social workers, especially interns and new workers, to consult with their supervisors or other senior colleagues within the agency to create a plan for how to respond to an unplanned termination. These terminations could also include mini-terminations that stem from something in the practitioner's life, such as a long vacation, maternity/paternity leave, or a leave of absence due to an illness. It is possible that the feelings you have about termination listed previously may influence your own judgment about how to best respond to the situation. In addition, there may be safety issues or other situations that may influence how much more outreach the social worker or the agency feels compelled ethically or legally to provide to the client. Regardless of the plan of action that has been developed, it is essential that the decisions made by you, your supervisor, or your agency be documented clearly in the client's file, including any follow-up communication between any individual from the agency and the client. The key message for you to remember is to document every decision and any communication between the agency and the client; each phone call, e-mail message, or other written communication should be documented and dated and placed in the client's file. Table 14.2 provides guidelines for unplanned terminations.

TABLE 14.2: Unplanned Termination Guidelines

Guidelines to Follow for Unplanned Termination in Consultation With Supervisor

- If a client stops coming to meetings:
  - Consult with a supervisor regarding the policy on contacting clients (i.e., letters versus e-mails versus phone calls).
  - Discuss with your supervisor how often and the appropriate number of times the client should be contacted.
  - Inform your supervisor of any safety concerns, such as suicidal or homicidal ideations, potential for physical abuse (either as a victim or as a perpetrator), risk of alcohol or drug relapse, or other safety concerns.
  - Document every attempt at communicating with the client.
  - Document every discussion/consultation with senior colleagues regarding how each decision was made about communicating with clients or ceasing communication.
- If the social worker has a personal issue that results in an unplanned ending,
  - At the start of your internship or employment, discuss with your supervisor the emergency coverage policy for the agency.
  - Become familiar with this policy and inform in writing each of your clients so that they know who to contact if you are unavailable.
  - If you are able to contact clients, remind them of this policy and provide them with the name of the appropriate contact person who will help them when you are unavailable.
  - If you will not be returning to the agency, discuss with your supervisor how to contact the clients and what should be shared with them regarding why you are not coming back to the agency.

PROCESS OF TERMINATION

In addition to the timing of the termination, it is important to think about the termination process itself (Bogo, 2006). While there are many aspects to consider in the process of saying good-bye, there are four main tasks to consider: (a) review the process of the work together; (b) consolidate gains; (c) plan for next steps; and (d) process the emotional bond (adapted from Bogo, 2006). The opportunity to consider the process in termination occurs when there is planned termination, and we encourage all readers to process each of these aspects with other colleagues or supervisors before doing so with a client. (The following discussion is adapted from Bogo's 2006 steps.)

REVIEW PROCESS OF THE WORK

As we stated previously, much of the work for knowing when the client has reached his or her goals is done at the beginning stage of the work together. We discuss in the next chapter more specific methods on how to evaluate whether the goals have been met. While identifying whether goals have been met is important, it is also important to remember that there is more to this phase of the termination process. Reviewing the process of the work you and clients have done together also means you need to take time to consider what specifically has changed. What have your clients noticed? What is different? In addition to noting the changes, it is important to note to what they attribute the change. What changes have they made that they believe have had the greatest influence on their ability to reach their goals? In other words, what have they taken from this experience that they feel is especially useful to them?

Another piece of this stage of termination is to help the client identify areas that remain a challenge. It is important to note these areas for a couple of different reasons. First, it is helpful to normalize the reality that not everything is "perfect," and while the work the client has done at this stage has been helpful, not every issue has been resolved. Second, this discussion leaves the door open for clients to return to you, the agency, or another service provider to work with them in the future should they need additional assistance with the same issue or a different one. Finally, a third reason is to help them anticipate and then plan for potential setbacks. In many fields of practice, clients work on relapse prevention plans (Beck, 2011; Steen, 2001) with their social worker as they move closer to the planned termination date. These plans are concrete tools with which clients can document potential challenges *and* what they will do to address those in the future, which could include using a particular skill or contacting a support person.

Ideally, the relapse prevention plan and the review process highlight and celebrate the client's strengths. Social work is a strengths-based profession (Corcoran, 2011; Miley, O'Melia, & DuBois, 2013; Shulman, 2012); yet, it can be easy at every stage of the work with clients to remain problem focused. It is our job therefore to remain our clients' biggest cheerleader and celebrant of their strengths and their numerous capacities. Noting even small changes can encourage clients to feel empowered to continue the work they have done with the worker beyond the termination phase.

CONSOLIDATE GAINS

Consolidating gains means helping the client develop a narrative of what the client learned, gained, and achieved in your work together. Ideally, the client would be able to identify what has changed and be able to compare where they are now to where they were at the start of your work together. As you highlight and celebrate their strengths and achievements, it is also important to help the client take ownership for the work that they have done with you (Bogo, 2006). Some clients, due to their cultural or social background, may give the majority of the credit to the worker. While it is important to acknowledge your role, we see the practitioner's role as a facilitator and a partner in the process. The work that clients have done is theirs, not ours. We are privileged to have been part of their process. In your own way, you can convey this message to the clients as you process the end of your work together. It can also be helpful to share what you have learned from them or how working with them has been a positive experience for you.

PLAN FOR NEXT STEPS

For some clients, ending the work with the social worker may mark the end of services. If this is the case, it is important to discuss with the client what to do should he or she feel the need for additional support in the future. Can the client return to the same agency? If so, what are the actions he or she should take? If either of you anticipate that the client might need crisis services, the appropriate information about these services should be provided at this time. It is imperative that the worker create a balance of conveying to clients that he or she has confidence in the clients' capacities to manage on their own, while also preparing for any future challenges and identifying appropriate supports before they leave.

Other clients will need additional or ongoing services beyond the work that you have done with them. In that case, it is essential to anticipate these needs well in advance of the final meeting with you. Careful planning with your client or the client's caregivers will reduce the client's anxiety and be helpful in preventing potential gaps in services or crises. We next provide a list of what to consider when planning for ongoing care. We have not given any time frames for these tasks as they will depend greatly on the context of the work you are doing with your clients. It should be assumed that the more time you can allow for each task, the better the transition will be. With each step, the social worker should document in the client's chart every action taken.

- Create a list of needs the client will have at the end of the work.
- Obtain signed authorizations to release any relevant information to future providers.
- Contact any other providers, caregivers, or individuals who are involved with the client (i.e., physicians, teachers, juvenile justice providers) and discuss with them the plans for termination and continuation of care.
- If the client is under a physician's care for medication, discuss with the client and the physician any potential needs, such as prescription refills or follow-up appointments.

- Identify any impact a change in services may have on the client's finances, either a change in cost, including a copay change, or if their insurance (including Medicaid or Medicare) pays for the services in a similar fashion. **Any potential change in cost should be discussed clearly and explicitly with the client and/or caregivers.**
- If the client will be continuing his or her care with a new provider, the social worker should facilitate a dialogue regarding how to create a smooth transition. In some cases, it might be helpful to have the client meet the new provider prior to the final meeting, while in other cases, it may be more appropriate to wait until the work with the first social worker has been completed. Each client's needs should be considered on an individual basis.

PROCESS THE EMOTIONAL BOND

Depending on the work you are doing with clients, this final task of processing the emotional bond (Bogo, 2006) may seem strange or only reserved for situations for which you are providing psychotherapy. Yet, we argue that social workers should not underestimate the impact that we can have on the lives of clients, even in brief relationships that involve what appear to be "only" concrete services. Imagine if you have been hospitalized for a physical illness that emerged suddenly. It is easy to envision that you might feel scared, overwhelmed, worried, and anxious about what the future could hold for you. Then, imagine if a social worker came to you and helped normalize your feelings, helped you identify your needs, used their knowledge to assist you with planning for those needs, and provided you with information about what to expect socially, emotionally, physically, and relationally. It is easy to see how having such an exchange with a social worker, even if over a short amount of time, could create a sense of relief, comfort, and gratitude and even an emotional bond. Therefore, while it is easy to see how a bond can be formed when working with a client over a longer period of time, it is important that we do not dismiss the possibility that a bond can be formed quickly between a client and a social worker. A key ingredient in the work we do with clients is the relationship we form with them (Bogo, 2006; Cameron & Keenan, 2013; Norcross, 2002; Wampold, 2010). As such, to ignore this aspect of our work is to ignore a critical tool in the work we do with our clients.

The processing of the bond can be emotional for both you and your client. As stated previously in this chapter, termination can bring up a number of emotions for all parties involved. Discussing the connection that was formed between you and your clients may be difficult, for each of you, depending on your respective comfort levels with emotions. It is important to keep in mind that the reactions of your clients to processing the emotional bond are influenced by many factors, including their culture (Conner & Grote, 2008; Fontes & Plummer, 2010; Zayas, Torres, & Cabassa, 2009), as well as the power differential that exists between you and your clients (Ow & Katz, 1999; Xiong, Tuicomepee, LaBlanc, & Rainey, 2006). The emotions they experience may also be connected to their past losses.

You may also have strong feelings about your client, positive or negative. These feelings should first be processed with your supervisor, and together you can decide on what is appropriate to share with your client *and* what is not. Remember that the work you do with your clients is *always* in the service of your client, not you. While it is important to be authentic with your clients, your needs are not to be met here and should be addressed outside the work with the clients.

BOUNDARIES AND TERMINATION

It is at the boundary and termination times when there is the potential for social workers to cross boundaries or violate one of our professions ethics. These violations are almost always unplanned and started with the best intentions, most often due to not wanting to abandon the client or wanting the client feel that the worker still cares. These intentions can turn into dual relationships or promises made that are outside the scope of the relationship. Workers might also at this time feel that sharing personal information, such as a social media or e-mail account, a cell phone number, or some other personal information, is a way to "stay in touch." We caution you strongly to avoid this temptation. Ask yourself, "Whose needs am I meeting by providing such information?" Discuss each of these potential decisions with a senior colleague or your supervisor before offering any such information. Your job is to protect the client, and it is essential that you use your self-awareness and supervision to ensure that every decision you make is consistent with that responsibility.

There is often debate about how long a former client is to be considered a client. How long after ending a professional working relationship is it okay to transition to a different kind of relationship? Our Code of Ethics does not concretely answer this question, so it is up to you to think about agency policy and your own boundaries to make a determination about this. Think carefully about how to handle requests years down the road.

We take a blanket stance on this issue, with the feeling of "once a client, always a client." This comes from many years of working in the same agency and then the same city providing counseling services in the community. I (E.D.) recall a time when a former client contacted me to let me know she had graduated from her professional school. Working on her own self-doubt and barriers to success in school had been part of what she explored in our work. She was proud and wanted to share this news with me. After a brief chat in which I congratulated her on this tremendous achievement, she asked if we could get together for coffee. I let her know that I could not do that. I explained that I believe it is important to always remain in our professional roles in the event that she ever needs services from me at some point in the future. When I asked how she felt about that, she said she was disappointed, but understood. A few months later, I heard from her again; this time she was asking to come back for counseling. In our meeting, she said she realized that what she really wanted was to come back for more services, but did not want to admit to me, or herself, that she still had more work to do. Each practitioner needs to come to his or her own position on this, but it should be consistent across clients and over time.

RITUALS/CELEBRATIONS

There are many ways to celebrate the ending of the work you and your client have done. Some rituals are built in to a program, such as a graduation from a school or group home.

These rituals can be done on an individual basis, or they can be conducted for an entire cohort that may have started and have ended together.

If there is not a built-in form of celebration, many social workers have found that using rituals is a powerful and meaningful way to end the service with a client (Hepworth, Rooney, Dewberry-Rooney, & Strom-Gottfried, 2013; Miley et al., 2013). As with all aspects we have discussed so far, it is essential to discuss ideas with supervisors regarding the appropriateness of any celebration. The ritual on which you and your client agree must be consistent with the culture and mission of your agency. In addition, it is important to ask your clients how they would like to mark the ending of the work. It may be that they would not like to do anything, and those wishes should be respected.

Celebrating the ending of your work with clients can be a time to be creative but should always be based on the needs and wishes of the client. You can also use activities or certain tasks to help clients keep the date of your final meeting in mind. The following is a list of the rituals that we have used in our own clinical work:

- Calendars—These can be photocopied or downloaded. On the calendar, the dates of each meeting can be marked to keep track of the remaining meetings.
- Braid or rope—Children especially can have a difficult time with time. Rather than a calendar, which might be too abstract, you and your client can create a braid or rope and tie knots in the rope that represent the remaining number of meetings. At the end of each meeting, the knots can be cut off and placed in a container of some sort.
- Transitional object—Psychodynamic theory discusses the idea of a transitional object (see Applegate & Bonovitz, 1995, for more information on this concept). The idea of a transitional object is that it is an item that helps the individual remember the person who is associated with comfort even when that person is not physically present. Clients can take a transitional object with them from the end of the work together. It can be a termination letter you write them summarizing their accomplishments, a business card in case they have questions after the end of the work, or some other object from your office. I (E.D.) used to have a Zen garden in my office that clients could use. I would put stones and seashells in the sand. At termination, I would allow clients to take an item from the Zen garden with them if they wished. I (M.D.G.) have had clients take with them an item from my sand tray collection that represented a particular part of the work together to remember the work that they did with me. Clients may also choose to leave a transitional object with you, such as a handmade card of thanks or other object that has meaning. Transitional objects can often fall under the category of gifts, which we discuss more fully in the next section.
- Discharge summary—It can often be difficult for clients to internalize or remember all of the feedback or sharing that takes place during the last few meetings. One option is to write and give the client his or her own "discharge summary" that provides an overview of where they were at the start of your work together and all that he or she had accomplished. It can also serve as a platform to highlight and emphasize the client's strengths, as well as record any relapse

prevention actions or follow-up supports that you have discussed. It is a document that the client can take and review as many times as desired.

GIFTS

Often associated with endings and celebrations or graduations are gifts. We have discussed gifts previously; however, it is worth repeating that it is important to ask your supervisor about the agency's gift policy and to be prepared to respond if a client gives you a gift so that you can act consistently with the agency's policy. It can be helpful to think this through in supervision and even role-play what you want to say. We do not believe that there is a right or a wrong answer to the idea of giving or receiving gifts. These decisions should be based on the individuals with whom you are working and in consideration of the agency's culture and policies. As with sharing information, if you wish to give a gift to a client, it is important to discuss this wish with your supervisor and the appropriateness of such a gift, regardless of how small or inconsequential you believe such a gift might be.

KEY POINTS TO REMEMBER FOR TERMINATION

- You can help clients by identifying their past patterns and help them to plan for a different kind of ending.
- Preparation here can go a long way.
- Plan for termination during the first session, as your role is to help clients to be independent and empower them to succeed on their own.
- You and your clients will both have feelings about the ending:
  - It is important to be self-aware.
  - Anticipate for *both* of you what might be triggered.
  - Use supervision and consultation.
- Rituals can help celebrate and aid in the transition.
- Be careful of potential boundary and ethical issues.

CHAPTER 15

EVALUATION OF PRACTICE

Imagine you were going to be taking a course of some kind where you are hoping to improve your skills or knowledge in some area. It could be anything, such as an academic course, a cooking class, or an exercise class. You are paying for the course and going to all of the sessions, as well as doing whatever extra tasks are required outside the class time. Hopefully you are taking the course by choice, but even if you are not, imagine where you might be in terms of your skills or knowledge at the start of this imaginary course. By the end of it, you certainly would want to see that you had improved and gained something. Yet, how will you know if all that time and energy made a difference? If it is an academic course, you often receive a grade that may or may not reflect your knowledge and effort. If is not an academic course, such as a cooking course, how will you know that you are a better cook than when you started? On what basis will you make this judgment? Who will decide whether there has been improvement and based on what standard? Is it that you want to be better in learning how to cook a certain type of food, or are you more interested in knowing more about the chemistry of cooking and how ingredients fit together in general?

These are the same types of questions that you and your clients should be asking as you think about working together on their goals. Clients will come to you in hopes that something will change. It could be that they want to find safe housing or to have a better ability to manage their depressive symptoms to become more socially connected in their communities. Some of these desired changes or goals might have obvious benchmarks, such as finding safe housing. Yet, what does safe housing mean, particularly to the client? Does becoming more socially connected in the community mean having two acquaintances, or does it mean attending a community group once per month? As we discussed in Chapter 13 on treatment planning, it is critical that you and your client identify how you will *both* know when the changes that they are seeking have happened. By identifying these outcomes or objectives in the treatment-planning stage of the work with clients, you have done a bulk of the work in evaluating your practice, especially when it comes to termination.

In addition to deciding when to terminate work with clients as discussed in Chapter 14, it is critical that social workers conduct ongoing evaluations with clients to know whether the work together is heading in the right direction. Returning to the cooking class example, think about how it would feel to reach the end of the class and realize that you had not improved in your cooking. Now, think about how you would feel in the scenario where you discovered early in the course that you were not improving. Immediately, your instructor made an adjustment in his or her teaching to help you to make improvements in your cooking. Which experience would you rather have? Hopefully the latter one! If we are working with clients and we are not seeing that our work together is helping them get closer to their goals, then we need to step back and look carefully at what we are doing and find ways to shift the work so that it is more effective. Not only is this act a practical and common-sense response, but also it is identified by the National Association of Social Workers' (NASW, 2008) Code of Ethics as part of ethical practice. "Social workers should monitor and evaluate policies, the implementation of programs, and practice interventions" (Section 5.02.a). This chapter provides some easy-to-use tools in your work with clients to help you and your client determine when the goals have been met. We also introduce some ongoing evaluation tools that can be used to help you and your clients ensure that you are working effectively toward their goals.

METHODS FOR EVALUATING GOAL ACHIEVEMENT

According to Gambrill (2013), there are "10 Ways to Fool Yourself and Your Clients About Degree of Progress" (Table 15.1)So you do not fall into these traps, it is important to think about methods of evaluating the progress clients are making by keeping in mind the guidelines shown in Table 15.2 that we created to address Gambrill's list. We expand on these ideas in the chapter, but they serve as a quick checklist for you as you think about beginning your work with a client. Remember that the bulk of the work on how to evaluate your work with a client starts at the beginning.

The rest of this chapter highlights and elaborates on some of the major themes from this list.

TABLE 15.1: **What Not to Do in Evaluating Progress**

---

10 Ways to Fool Yourself and Your Clients About Degree of Progress

1. Focus on vague outcomes
2. Rely on testimonials
3. Rely on your intuition
4. Select measures that are easy to use even though they are not related to the intended outcome
5. Do not gather baseline data
6. Assess progress only in artificial settings, such as the office
7. Under no circumstances graph the data
8. Use only pre-/post-test measures (do not check in during the middle)
9. Use only postmeasures
10. Do not gather follow-up data (Gabmrill 2013, p. 491)

Guidelines for Evaluating Progress Toward Goals

1. Be specific regarding your goals and your objectives (remember SMART (specific, measurable, achievable, relevant, and with a time frame) goals from Chapter 12?)
2. Use measures to be completed by your client that include objective indicators that can also be paired with subjective measures.
3. Actually use evaluation tools rather than using your own ideas about how the work is going.
4. Ensure that the measures you use are relevant to the client's issues and needs.
5. Be specific with your client at the beginning of treatment about where they are in their work toward the goal—what is their baseline now?
6. Assess how the client is doing outside the setting in which you and the client work. Think about how to look at the progress of the goal(s) in multiple settings (i.e., within the foster home, at school, at the job site, with other residents in a shelter).
7. Use visual depictions of the progress. Graphs provide an easy method to measure progress on a goal.
8. Track the progress you and your client are making throughout your time with the client.
9. Use pre- and postmeasures, as well as continuous assessment tools.
10. When possible, gather information from your clients after the work has been completed. These time frames could range from 1 month to 2 years or beyond.

BE SPECIFIC WITH GOALS AND OBJECTIVES

As we emphasized in Chapter 13 on goal setting and in Chapter 14 on endings, there is a strong connection between treatment planning and termination. The clearer you and your client can be about where the client wants to be at the end of your work together, the easier it is to evaluate whether the client has met those goals. Of course, goals can change throughout treatment. Yet, we strongly recommend that with each new or altered goal, you put in the time to create that goal so it is clear what the intended outcomes will be at the end. Returning to the cooking class example, the more you are clear at the beginning of the course about what you hope to achieve, the more you will know about whether you have achieved your goal by the end.

USE A COMBINATION OF OBJECTIVE AND SUBJECTIVE MEASURES

It is critical that social workers use measurement strategies to assess the progress that clients are making in the work you are doing together. There are two main types of measures that are used in evaluating practice: objective and subjective. There are pros and cons to each approach, which is why advocate a combination of both for your work. *Objective measures* are not based on your own or your client's biases or opinions. These measures use concepts that evaluate an outcome based on a set standard. Examples of objective measures are a change in score on a standardized symptom checklist, the number of social contacts an assisted living resident has had in the last 3 weeks, the number of fights in school in a month, or the number of temper tantrums a 2-year-old has during a week. Each of these measures is not tied to anyone's perception so they indicate how the client has made shifts. These measures in theory are outside the bias of the client or the social worker.

Subjective measures are those that ask either the client or the social worker (or in some instances a third party, such as a parent or guardian) about their perceptions of the progress or changes that the client has made during the work. These measures ask different parties to share their opinions about any perceived changes and do not use an external method to gauge progress. Examples of subjective measures include a self-rating scale regarding anxiety levels, a social worker's assessment of the working alliance, or a parent's perception about what has contributed to their child's mood shifts. While these pieces of information help inform both the client and the worker regarding how they believe the work is progressing and what they believe has been helpful or not helpful so far, they do not provide an unbiased view of the progress to date.

We believe that both types of data are useful to social workers and should be included in the work with clients. What we want to emphasize here is that social workers need to do *something* to measure progress. Our Code of Ethics (NASW, 2008) requires it, and we believe it is simply good practice to ensure that the work with your client remains useful in helping him or her to reach personal goals.

Next, we provide brief summaries of different ways to include measures, both objective and subjective, that can be easily incorporated into your work with clients. These are easy to use, and we encourage readers to learn more about them from research textbooks and other similar resources that we have listed in the in the summary guide at the end of the chapter.

OBJECTIVE MEASURES

Standardized Instruments: One of the most common objective methods used to eliminate bias is to use standardized instruments. These instruments are measures that

> have uniform procedures for administration and scoring and are accompanied by certain kinds of information, including data concerning reliability, validity, and norms (average scores of certain groups). Standardized measures are used to: (1) describe populations or clients; (2) screen clients (e.g. make a decision about the need for further assessment or find out if a client is eligible for or likely to require a service); (3) assess clients (a more detailed review); (4) evaluate progress; and (5) make predictions about the likely futures of clients. (Gambrill, 2013, p. 395)

Given the number of ways that these measures are used, there are thousands of instruments that have been designed for countless settings, populations, symptoms, ages, languages, cultures, and other topics. Many of these instruments can be found online for free and with easily accessible instructions; others either require specialized training or are restricted by copyright laws. Therefore, it is important that you check first what the

TABLE 15.3: Standardized Instruments

Pros	Cons
Gather specific information about a client	Narrow in scope regarding what is assessed
Efficient methods of gathering information about a client or clients and not dependent on the social worker's memory regarding what to ask	May not be applicable or appropriate for your client(s) as the tests may not have been tested or evaluated using clients similar to yours
Have in theory been tested and evaluated for being unbiased and objective	Person administering them may not be adequately trained to obtain accurate information or to interpret the information correctly
Provide a succinct picture of an aspect of the client's life (e.g., level of functioning, amount of social supports)	Do not start where the client is; rather bring an external focus regarding the issues
Help to normalize for the client some of their struggles as they see that others have had similar ones	Often instruments that are designed to understand children and adolescents ask the adults for their feedback and not the child
Can provide a launching pad for more in-depth discussions of their struggles	Often do not assess for strengths but rather assess for deficits
Provide clients with information to help them link to additional information that may help them understand the struggles	Could bias the social worker about a particular client based on how the client "scores" on the instrument
Help to put their struggles in perspective compared to other individuals who are like them	Language used or questions included may be biased

restrictions are for any instrument you are interested in using. In addition, it is essential that you fully inform your clients of any risks or benefits, as well as how the instrument will be used and who will have access to it.

Depending on your setting, you may use such instruments for all or only one or two of the categories described previously. While there are many benefits to using standardized instruments, we would like to caution you also to consider some of the risks. "Many tests, for example, have biases, low reliability and poor validity; some are ill suited for certain clients and thus should be used with extreme caution" (Hepworth et al., 2013, p. 191). We listed in Table 15.3 some of the benefits as well as the cons as summarized by Grady and Drisko (2014).

We feel that Gambrill's (2013, p. 397) "Checklist for Reviewing Standardized Measures" is useful for new social workers who are starting to use these instruments (Table 15.4). We also want to add that many standardized instruments do in fact depend on subjective data. In other words, instruments that have been standardized on different populations rely on the client's report of how he or she is feeling, thinking, or behaving. It is therefore important to keep in mind that not all standardized instruments are completely objective. However, they are designed to take much of the bias out of client self-report.

For those who are interested in finding standardized measures that might be useful for their work, there are two primary resources that we recommend. The first is the database

TABLE 15.4: Standardized Instrument Checklist

Checklist for Reviewing Standardized Measures

1. Data are available showing that the measure is valid (measures what it is supposed to measure).
2. Data are useful in understanding client concerns.
3. Test-retest reliability (you can give in to someone twice in a short amount of time and get similar results) is high (in the absence of real change).
4. Easy to complete and does not take much time.
5. Acceptable to clients.
6. Required readings levels match client's skills.
7. Sensitive (small changes can be detected).
8. The user has the knowledge required to make effective use of the measure.
9. Norms are available for the populations of concerns (your client's demographics can be compared to others similar to him or her).
10. Data concerning reactive effects (clients are more likely to answer a particular way on subsequent administrations of the instrument based on their pre-test scores) are available.
11. Responses are quantifiable (you can count them).
12. The false positive is low (clients are incorrectly assumed to have a certain characteristic)
13. The false negative is low (clients are incorrectly assumed to NOT have a certain characteristic).
14. Biases are minimal (e.g. there is a way to tell if clients are just telling you what you want to hear).
15. Instructions for administration, scoring, and interpretation are clear
16. Cultural differences are considered in relation to content

Note: Adapted from *Social work practice: A critical thinker's guide* (3rd ed.), by E. Gambrill, Oxford University Press, p. 397.

Health and Psychological Instruments (HAPI), which is available through many school libraries. It has a long list of available instruments and important information about them, such as related studies on their strengths, appropriate populations, and scholarly articles that report on the use of the instrument in research and practice. Another key source is by Fischer and Corcoran (2013a, 2013b). This two-volume set includes numerous instruments with similar information as can be found in HAPI, but also often provides the complete instrument. The volumes are separated by developmental stages and outline those instruments for use with adults, children, adolescents, and families. These volumes are commonly found in most academic library settings.

Single-System Designs: Single-System Designs (SSDs) are also referred to as Single-Case Designs as they are an evaluation method used to assess one client system, which could be that of an individual, family, group, organization, or a community (Bloom, Fischer, & Orme, 2009). These evaluation methods can be simple as well as complex, with the more complex designs discussed in research methods courses. Here, we provide an overview of the basic ideas so that you can see how easily they can be incorporated into work with clients.

The overall aim of SSDs is to provide objective measures of the changes in the targeted issues over time. They allow you to show data before the start of the intervention, or the baseline, as well as during various parts of the intervention phase. As such, most SSD methods use a simple comparison between the baseline phase and the intervention phase to monitor any changes for the target issue. In SSD, the baseline phase of the work is indicated as Point A and the intervention phase is B. This comparison is then referred to as an AB design. As stated previously, there are more complex designs, but they all follow the same principles; each phase of the intervention is compared to other phases to see if there were changes in the desired directions. In this book, we only introduce the idea of an AB design.

The key to a useful SSD is to identify the most helpful outcome for that client in light of the context. One of the key areas that should be considered in deciding on the outcome is what exactly will be measured. This outcome could be the number of temper tantrums in a day, the score on a depression inventory, the number of social contacts a person has in a week, the number of times someone completes a rehabilitation task, or countless other examples. It is essential that the identified outcome is an accurate representation of the desired change, which could be an increase or a decrease in a particular event, and that everyone agrees on the exact definition of what will be "counted" and what will not be. The more specific regarding what counts that you, your client, and other involved parties can be in relation to what specifically will be counted, the more accurate and consistent your evaluation will be.

During the beginning part of the AB planning process, it is also important to identify the end goal. In other words, how will you and your client know that you have reached your goal? If someone has a pattern of 10 temper tantrums per day, is the goal to have zero? Or, is the goal to have 3 each week total? Is the goal to change the frequency of the temper tantrums, the intensity, or the duration? How you measure the targeted goal is directly related to how you will know if you have reached that goal.

Another important consideration is a realistic time frame for what is being measured. In other words, if the focus of the work is on something that occurs every day, such as a temper tantrum, then the measure should be one that accurately measures the daily or maybe even hourly rate of temper tantrums. However, if the goal of the work is to help someone increase their social contacts over the course of a week or a month, then the measure needs to reflect this time frame for the goal.

It is also important in the design of such a system for social workers to address the ease with which the event can be measured. For example, teachers who have 30 children in a classroom cannot easily fill out a behavioral chart every 15 minutes for 1 of these 30 students. So, while it may be helpful for the social worker to have a picture of each 15-minute increment during the day to see a detailed pattern, it is not realistic to expect the teacher to accurately record a child's behavior given the other demands in the classroom. Therefore, you must choose measurement strategies that are easy to execute and realistic given the context of the clients' lives.

Once you have considered all of these factors, the actual measurement begins. During the baseline and intervention phases, the same outcome measure should be used so that a clear comparison can be made between the various phases. The length of each phase is dependent on the issue and what is being measured. If the goal is to increase social interactions each week, then there is a shorter time frame to obtain more measures for that outcome, as compared to a monthly count. A daily count provides more points in time than weekly or monthly, but it may show only a "good week" and may not depict actual long-term trends. Therefore, it is important that social workers think through what is the most appropriate length of time to measure the outcome given what the goals of the intervention are.

Ideally, the baseline phase should be continued until "the pattern of behavior is fairly clear" (Gambrill, 2013, p. 501). While it is always ideal to have a "real-time" baseline, where clients begin to record the issue, if it is a long time frame (i.e., a month), it is possible to retroactively record the baseline by estimating. Again, this method is not ideal but may be necessary in some settings or situations. One example of such a situation is the number of hospitalizations an individual has had over the last 6 months. In this case, the client's records can be used to establish a baseline rather than waiting 6 months to create a baseline in real time. It is also important to note that some clients may begin to change the frequency of the issue simply due to recording it. These trends should also be recorded and included in the baseline counts.

The AB design allows you and the client to numerically and pictorially see if there have been any changes since the baseline phase began. Graphing changes is a wonderful way for you and your client to actually visualize the changes that are being made (Bloom et al., 2009; Engel & Schutt, 2014; Gambrill; 2013). Graphing can be done by hand, using a word-processing software program, or using a program like Excel that will make the graph for you. The graphs are set up to have the number of events of interest (i.e., number of temper tantrums or symptoms on a checklist) on the y axis (the vertical one) and the time on the x axis (the horizontal one). A line is created down the middle at the point of time when the baseline phase ends and the intervention phase begins. Figure 15.1 is an example of a graph of an SSD with an AB design for an individual who has been getting in fights at the homeless shelter where the individual is staying.

The graph in Figure 15.1 allows the social worker and the client to see if there is progress toward the goal. However, it is important that the worker and the client determine whether those changes are meaningful to the client. In other words, even if the shift is

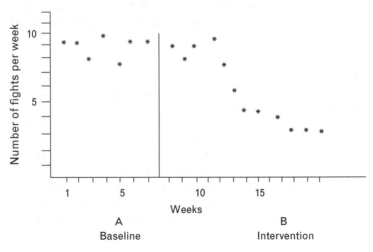

FIGURE 15.1: Single-system design graph.

going in the right direction, is it enough? Is it sustaining? The social worker and client will need to determine when they have reached the point in the work together at which the marks on the graph represent a meaningful change.

There is much more that could be said here about SSD. You are encouraged to look at the summary guide for other information on how to use them.

SUBJECTIVE MEASURES

Goal Attainment Scales: Goal Attainment Scales (GASs) are tools that are based on the client's own criteria for assessment, which means that they are individualized for that client's particular goals and capacities. Because they are specific to each client's needs, they are seen as more subjective measures rather than objective ones. GASs can be used for all "client systems (individuals, families, groups, organizations, and communities) to identify intervention goals and to specify expected outcome levels for each goal" (Miley, O'Melia, & DuBois, 2013, p. 421). One of the strengths of a GAS is that it focuses exclusively on stated goals rather than being problem focused, which fits well with social work values and ethics (NASW, 2008).

These scales are created as a grid or rubric to identify the various levels of goal achievement. Each level of achievement is given a score, generally ranging from –2 up to +2, with –2 representing "less than expected" and +2 representing "more than expected." Each score corresponds to a specific set of outcomes that have been identified by the social worker along with the client. Table 15.5 is an example of a GAS showing what one might look like for an individual who is living in an assisted living facility and is socially isolated.

The advantages of using GASs include how each can be individualized for each particular client's needs and context. They can also be used regardless of the size of the client system and are user friendly (Miley et al., 2013). Some of the disadvantages are that they are seen as subjective more than objective as they have not been tested for their validity or reliability as standardized measures have been (Miley et al., 2013). Yet, social workers may find these measures to be user-friendly tools that help the worker and the client identify concretely where the work is going and how they will know when they have reached those goals.

TABLE 15.5: Goal Attainment Scale

Level	Behavior
–2 = baseline	Does not engage in any social interactions with friends each week
–1 = less than expected outcome	Engages in 1 social activity/week
0 = expected outcome	Engages in 3 social activities/week
+1 = Greater than expected	Engages in 4 social activities/week
+2 = Much greater than expected outcome	Engages in 5+ social activities/week

---

Self-Anchored Scales: These are scales that are developed by the client and the social worker to monitor a particular feeling or experience. They are subjective because they use the client's words and perceptions both to create the scales and to complete them. Self-anchored scales are created by asking the client to think of two extremes of the issue he or she is facing, such as his or her level of anger. One "anchor" represents the most benign or mild experience of this issue, and the other anchor represents the highest level. For example, a 1 might represent least anger and a 10 represent the most anger. It is important for the terms to be consistent on the two anchors and for the client to help define what a 1 means or looks like for them, as well as a 10 or other midpoints along the scale. Table 15.6 is an example of a 7-point scale for anger.

Self-anchored scales can be useful in gathering information for an SSD or for teaching clients a skill related to self-monitoring. "Clients can use self-anchoring scales to record the extent of troubling internal states across specified time intervals (e.g. three times daily for seven days) in much the same way that they take frequency counts of overt behaviors" (Hepworth, Rooney, Dewberry-Rooney, & Strom-Gottfried, 2013, p. 359).

Session-Monitoring Scales: Another way to measure outcomes is to have an ongoing assessment of the client's feedback regarding how he or she feels in progressing toward the selected goals. This attempt to use client feedback in a systematic way is consistent with practice-based evidence, which "requires that practitioners adopt a highly individualized service delivery plan for each patient, acknowledging the patient's goals for treatment, ideas about how change occurs, and view of an effective therapeutic relationship" (Campbell & Hemsley, 2009, p. 1).

Real-time monitoring of the progress allows the client and social worker to make modifications quickly before the work becomes too off track. In addition, studies have shown that overall client outcomes improve when practitioners use assessment tools to obtain feedback from the client at the end of each session (Duncan et al., 2003). These tools assess how well the session addressed the client's needs, whether the client felt heard, whether the practitioner addressed the goals the client had for the session, as well as other areas (Duncan et al., 2003). These instruments can be user-friendly tools that practitioners can use to improve outcomes with their clients (Bringhurst, Watson, Miller, & Duncan, 2006; Campbell & Hemsley, 2009; Duncan et al., 2003).

Two of the most commonly used instruments are the Outcome Rating Scale (ORS) and the Session Rating Scale (SRS; Miller & Duncan, 2000). The ORS is designed to mainly measure the desired outcomes or level of distress by the presenting problem, whereas the SRS is designed to measure the alliance between the practitioner and the client (Campbell & Hemsley, 2009). These instruments have been shown to be valid and

TABLE 15.6: Self-Anchored Scale

1	2	3	4	5	6	7
Least angry (feel calm, relaxed)			**Moderately angry** (feel tension in body, breathing is getting faster, but still able to function)			**Most angry** (clenching fists, yelling, want to punch a wall)

reliable with a variety of populations and ages in multiple research studies (Campbell & Hemsley, 2009). They are very user friendly and take only a few minutes to complete. Depending on what information the social worker may find to be most useful, he or she may choose to use one or both of these instruments with clients. In addition, the authors have made them available to practitioners for free and have provided detailed instructions on how to use them as well as provided citations for the numerous studies that have been conducted using them. All of this information can be found online (https://heartandsoulofchange.com/), and multiple resources are provided to help practitioners improve outcomes.

CHAPTER SUMMARY

In this chapter, we discussed the importance of evaluating the progress the client is making toward personal goals. It is not only good practice but also consistent with our profession's code of ethics to continuously monitor how effective the services we are providing are in helping clients reach their goals. Practice evaluation should be viewed as an ongoing process, not just a task done at the end of the work. This process provides opportunities to determine if what you are doing is working and to change course if it is not. Returning to the cooking class example, if you went in hoping to learn how to cook a soufflé and realized at the end you could not do it, you will be disappointed and even angry. If you find out midway that you are off course, then you can correct that in time for a successful outcome. We have provided you with a number of user-friendly tools to measure outcomes. These can be easily woven into plans for intervention as well as into conversations with clients about termination when that time comes.

CHAPTER 15 RESOURCE GUIDE

RESEARCH TEXTBOOK REFERENCES

Bloom, M., Fischer, J., & Orme, J. G. (2009). *Evaluating practice: Guidelines for the accountable professional* (6th ed.). Boston, MA: Pearson.

Engel, R. J., & Schutt, R. K. (2013). *The practice of research in social work* (3rd ed.). Thousand Oaks, CA: Sage.

Lomand, T. C. (2012). *Social science research* (7th ed.). Glendale, CA: Pyrczak.

Ogles, B. M., Lambert, M. J., & Master, K. S. (1996). *Assessing outcome in clinical practice*. Boston, MA: Allyn & Bacon.

Pyrczak, F. (2013). *Evaluating research in academic journals: A practical guide to realistic evaluation* (6th ed.). Glendale, CA: Pyrczak.

Sederer, L. I., & Dickey, B. (Eds.). (1996). *Outcomes assessment in clinical practice*. Baltimore, MD: Williams & Wilkins.

PART IV

ONGOING ISSUES
FOR CONSIDERATION

CHAPTER 16

SUPERVISION

We hope that by now many of you have had the chance to experience a supervisory relationship that feels supportive as well as educational. We believe that for new practitioners such a relationship is at the core of learning how to be a professional social worker. Supervision plays a critical role in shaping one's developmental trajectory. As such, we believe it is essential to identify key characteristics of this relationship so that practitioners maximize the benefits and growth opportunities that can result from such an experience. Supervision styles differ across fields of practice; therefore, it is essential to find a good fit between supervisor and supervisee to create a safe professional relationship in which to grow and develop as a social work practitioner. In some settings, you may not get to choose your supervisors, which may be because of your assigned internship or because in a new position someone within the agency is appointed as your supervisor. When you are unable to choose your own supervisor, there may be a gap between what the supervisee wants from supervision and the supervisor's approach. The challenge becomes identifying and using the strengths of this relationship to maximize the learning potential.

This chapter explores how new practitioners can use supervision as part of their learning experience, how to use supervisor feedback in the learning process, and the nuts and bolts of supervision. We highlight the differences between one's own therapy for personal growth and the supervisory relationship for professional learning and the importance of keeping these relationships separate.

We strongly recommend that as you review each of the sections of this chapter, you reflect on what your supervisory experiences have been to date. Think about how these experiences compare to some of our advice, what you appreciated about those relationships, what you felt was lacking, and what you would wish for in the next experience or even a current one. If you are the supervisee, the supervision experience is really about you. The more you can identify what you want and need in this relationship, the more easily you will be able to articulate these wishes and have your learning needs met.

NUTS AND BOLTS OF SUPERVISION

There are many factors that have an impact on how supervisors provide supervision. The setting, the type of work that the practitioner will be doing, as well as the personal style of the supervisor will all influence how the supervisor delivers supervision. However, unlike what is often the case in a classroom or group setting where you "get what you get," in supervision, there are some norms and some legal requirements that can play a role in what the supervisor provides on a basic level, as well as other nuts and bolts that you should consider as the supervisee. You are your best advocate to get your needs met, so we encourage you to be clear about what you need and want.

LENGTH OF TIME OF SUPERVISION

The length of time and the frequency of supervision meetings vary depending primarily on the needs of the supervisee. In an internship setting, ideally supervision is held weekly, at a set time and place that is consistent from week to week, for 50 minutes to an hour. If an individual who has just graduated with his master's degree in social work (MSW) is hoping to obtain a clinical license, most jurisdictions require that the new MSW graduate receive an average of 1 hour of supervision per 40-hour work week. These meetings must be documented and then recorded and submitted to the jurisdiction where the supervisee is working to obtain a license. Most jurisdictions require about 2 years of supervision as part of the licensing requirements, which ends up being about 100 hours total (50 hours/year for 2 years). However, this number varies, and it is the supervisee's responsibility to know the requirements for wherever jurisdiction he or she is seeking licensure.

CREATING PROTECTED TIME

During supervision, both the supervisor and the supervisee should protect this time together. Protected time means that the meeting remains free from interruptions or distractions, and the supervisee has the supervisor's full attention. Unfortunately, many practitioners do not work in settings where the time feels protected. In these cases, supervision can often feel like it is being held "on the fly" or "catch-as-catch-can." Hallway check-ins, e-mail follow-ups, and brief meetings to discuss pressing matters are often provided in the place of regular supervision meetings in settings where finding a sacred 50- to 60-minute block of time is difficult.

When at all possible, we suggest that the supervisee request the following to increase the likelihood that the supervision time will be protected:

- Schedule the meeting for the same block of time each week. A regular time increases the likelihood that the time will be embedded in each person's schedule and will become more of a habit as a result.
- Request that phone calls, e-mail notifications, and other electronic interruptions be eliminated or reduced by turning off phones or computer notifications.
- Identify a quiet location, which may or may not be a personal office. It is important to be in a space that not only is not in the flow of the daily activities of the agency whenever possible but also allows for discussion of confidential material.
- Use a "do not disturb" sign if you are meeting in a room to reduce the number of interruptions during your meeting.

As stated previously, you are your best advocate to have your needs met in supervision. These logistical factors can play a significant role in accomplishing such a goal.

PURPOSES AND TASKS OF SUPERVISION

According to the National Association of Social Workers (NASW) and Association of Social Work Boards (ASWB) (2013), the three main tasks of social work supervision are addressing administrative tasks, overseeing client casework and attending to the education of new workers, and supporting the supervisee in his or her work. The first addresses *administrative* issues and tracks the worker's progress on paperwork, monitoring productivity, and addressing policies and procedures to ensure they are being followed. To address this, the supervisor will typically ask the supervisee how many clients he or she saw last week, whether all the required paperwork is complete, and questions about meeting funding requirements for the program (NASW & ASWB, 2013).

The second task of supervision is to address issues that arise in work with clients. These discussions are focused on particular clients or specific interactions with clients, and the supervisee looks for guidance and direction from the supervisor. The focus in these discussions is *educational*, as the two individuals discuss how to apply clinical theory, skills, and interventions with clients, and in doing so attempt to address any gaps in knowledge that may exist. In addition, during these conversations the supervisor may be assessing the practitioner's social work knowledge, skills, and abilities (NASW & ASWB, 2013).

The educational focus in supervision must be handled with care and empathy for the novice worker to avoid the supervisee feeling judged or criticized. The supervisor's role here is to help identify supports to fill in gaps in knowledge or skills and is a critical part of the supervisor's role and responsibility as a supervisor. It is the job of the supervisor to assist in providing feedback on areas where the worker excels, as well as identify areas for improvement. By providing such feedback, the practitioner can gain important information for his or her own professional development. In addition, the supervisor has a responsibility to the clients served by the supervisee. With this responsibility in mind, it is essential that the supervisor identify any areas in need of improvement to create better outcomes for the clients. The supervisor is ultimately responsible for the work of the supervisee and thus needs to ensure that the strongest and safest services are provided to the client. Giving the supervisee feedback on ways to improve his or her work is important not only for the individual supervisee's development as a practitioner but also for the clients served by the agency. To address any gaps, the supervisor may recommend that the supervisee attend particular trainings or spend time with that supervisee to reinforce knowledge and skills that need strengthening.

The final, and some might argue most essential, task of supervision is *support*. When social work practitioners feel that their supervisors are empathic and encouraging and want them to learn, grow, and be successful, supervisees reported decreased job-related stress and increased confidence (Davis, 2010). In many ways, the provision of supervision demonstrates an investment in the novice practitioner's development of a professional self. It is a commitment to the growth and development of that person for the good of both the individual's clients and his or her career. This relationship is a crucial one in this early stage of development and is strengthened when there is trust, support, and solid guidance during a vulnerable professional time (Bennett & Deal, 2009).

DIFFERENT SUPERVISION FORMATS

As discussed, during a social worker's training in school and in many settings after graduation, interns and new graduates must be supervised in their agencies. For recent graduates, this requirement is especially true for those who are providing direct practice or clinical services to clients. However, once someone is licensed, there are no requirements for supervision to continue. Yet, in our experience many practitioners opt to continue to have supervision beyond their license for a number of reasons:

- Continued supervision continues the learning process.
- Ethically, it is important to have another set of "eyes" on their work.
- It provides continued experiences of collegiality with other professionals.
- There may be a time in life (e.g., pregnancy, leaving a practice, personal or family illness) when the practitioner believes that due to their own personal situation, they may not trust their own judgment as strongly as they have outside the current circumstances.

Ongoing supervision can utilize many formats. Some practitioners continue with individual supervision. They may receive supervision for free in their job or see another practitioner outside their agency at their own expense. Some practitioners prefer to see someone outside their agency as they have more freedom to be imperfect because the outside supervisor is not involved in performance reviews that can be tied to merit pay increases or other performance-based interests. In addition, sometimes practitioners seek an outside supervisor because they have an interest in a particular population or topic area and want to learn from an expert with that body of knowledge. Finally, others seek outside supervision because no social worker is employed by the agency, and they want to see a social worker specifically for supervision, even beyond the licensing requirements.

An advantage of individual supervision is that the supervisee is able to receive one-on-one attention and training. The focus of the supervision is driven by the individual's specific interests and needs. In addition, the supervisee might feel less vulnerable sharing some "mess ups" or concerns about his or her work with one person versus a group of colleagues. A significant disadvantage is the potential cost of individual supervision if it occurs outside the agency. However, most supervisors offer reduced fees, especially to new practitioners. Do not be afraid to ask for fee reductions if you are interested in this format. Another disadvantage for individual supervision is the flip side of one of the strengths. By having the focus on him- or herself, the practitioner does not have the advantage of learning from peers who may have different perspectives from the supervisor, limiting the views or ideas discussed.

If you choose to seek outside supervision, we strongly recommend that you discuss this option with your assigned agency supervisor, even if that individual provides purely administrative supervision (vs. clinical). In our own practices, when we provide supervision for someone who works at a different agency, we require a signed contract between the supervisee, the agency supervisor, and ourselves, partly to ensure transparency among all parties. In the contract, we are also explicit that the agency-based supervisor is ultimately responsible for all of the client care, and that all client-related ideas that are developed within our supervision need to be discussed and approved by the agency-based supervisor, as the supervisor is ultimately responsible for the care and safety of the clients served by that agency.

In addition to individual supervision, an option is group or peer supervision. Group supervision is when several practitioners meet together and hire someone to serve as the supervisor/consultant. Group supervision can be a great option for newer practitioners as it can reduce costs because the group members split the costs of the supervisor's time. In addition, group supervision allows practitioners to learn from their peers. A significant disadvantage of this format is that, depending on how often the group meets and how many members there are, each individual's time on his own work is limited as the time is shared among the group members.

Peer supervision is another form of group supervision but generally does not involve an outside "expert" or supervisor. Rather, the individuals serve as each other's supervisors. Peer supervision can occur between people within the same agency or among people who work in different settings and contexts. One of the advantages of this format is that it is free. In addition, as each member is considered an equal, there is no hierarchy within the group. Because of the equal status, peer supervision can provide an important source of support, which has shown to be essential in decreasing burnout among practitioners (Kim, Ji, & Kao, 2011). One of the most commonly noted disadvantages that we have both experienced and heard about from other colleagues is that the groups can feel like "the blind leading the blind" as there is no one person who is the expert. Another disadvantage is similar to group supervision: Individual members share the space and time among their colleagues, limiting the focus on their own work.

MAXIMIZING THE LEARNING OPPORTUNITIES IN SUPERVISION

While there may be many variables in the supervisory relationship that are out of your control, there are some ways that you can optimize your own learning in this relationship. As we stated previously, you need to be your own advocate for getting what you want out of supervision. The more you are prepared for this relationship, the more satisfied you will be with how well it meets your expectations and professional goals.

IDENTIFY YOUR OWN LEARNING GOALS AND STYLE

One of the most effective strategies to get what you want out of the supervisory relationship is first to identify what your own learning goals are as well as your learning style. As supervisors, we can tell you that it is much easier to tailor our own style to the needs of our supervisees when they share with us how we can best meet their needs. We have found, for example, some supervisees prefer a much more formal or didactic/classroom teaching style of supervision, while others prefer to use their own cases as the main topic, with other information woven into the conversation. Other supervisees would like us to share articles or book chapters we feel might be relevant or useful, while others are burned out on academic-like materials. The following are some questions that might help you identify what it is that you want out of supervision:

- What is your learning style?
- What do you want to learn?
- Where are your gaps in training and experience?
- What style do you want? Didactic, process oriented, or mix?

TYPES OF QUESTIONS TO ASK IN SUPERVISION

In addition to asking yourself questions, another way to improve your odds at getting what you need in supervision is to be proactive and ask your supervisor questions. When there is an opportunity to choose a supervisor, you can gain a lot of information by asking a few pointed questions. First and foremost, it is essential to ask if the professional has the appropriate licensure and other qualifications for providing supervision. Many jurisdictions have requirements related to years of practice experience, completion of supervision coursework or trainings, and a process of becoming certified by the state board. Many of these states maintain databases that list the professionals they certify as meeting these requirements. We strongly recommend that supervisees determine their jurisdictions' requirements and confirm the credentials of any potential supervisor before beginning a supervisory relationship.

For practitioners who are being supervised to earn their own independent clinical license, it is crucial to ensure that the supervisor is appropriately licensed; those hours of practice will not count otherwise. You may want to use a conversational style to ask how long the person has been providing supervision, how and why they got started, how many people they supervise, and what kind of training and support they receive as a supervisor. It is also helpful to inquire about the type of practice they conduct. What are the types of clients and presenting problems with which they work? What theories and models of practice guide their interventions? Their answers to these questions should line up with your interests and needs for supervision. Here are some examples of potential questions:

- What is your supervision style?
- What is your fee? Do you have a sliding scale or reduced-fee time slot?
- What theories guide your work?
- How much do you incorporate the following into supervision:
  - Countertransference?
  - Diagnosis?
  - Theory?
  - Culture?
  - Or whatever your areas of interest are.

Even if you are not able to choose your own supervisor, it is important for supervisees to ask supervisors questions about how they approach supervision. Also, supervisees should inquire about their expectations of you as a supervisee. Once it is clear what the expectations are for this relationship, we strongly recommend that you and your supervisor develop a formal agreement or even a contract for how you will conduct supervision. This contract should also include the goals and tasks for this relationship, which can be helpful in providing clarity and structure to the meetings. In some jurisdictions, such a contract is a requirement for the supervision when the social worker is working toward obtaining a clinical license. For students, many programs require a learning contract between the student, the supervisor, the agency, and the educational program. These contracts can serve as a useful tool for tracking progress in supervision. In any case, the question "What are we doing here?" should be explored and answered by both parties.

HOW TO MAKE THE MOST OF A SUPERVISION MEETING

Once the supervisory relationship begins, some practitioners are unsure how to use the time effectively. Previously, we discussed the three main tasks of the supervisory relationship: administrational, educational, and support. Keeping these tasks in mind, it is important to then identify how to address these areas efficiently and walk away feeling like you have learned from the experience. To increase the likelihood of having such a feeling, we recommend that supervisees prepare an agenda (see summary guide for a sample agenda) and think through their questions ahead of time. In preparing your agenda, it may be helpful to keep in mind the three tasks and organize your questions into those three categories.

One of the best actions supervisees can take to maximize the learning that can take place in supervision is to be honest with their supervisors. While it is understandable to want your supervisor to see the best sides of your work and to provide praise for a job well done, most of the learning comes from exploring stuck points in your work or processing mistakes made with clients. Asking questions such as "What am I not seeing here?" and "How else could I have handled that situation?" are good places to start. You could also ask your supervisor to guide you toward readings or other resources on situations your clients are dealing with and interventions you would like to explore. It is often helpful to ask, "Where should I start in the next session?" This question can be particularly helpful in the early stages of working with a client and can help guide discussions on assessment, treatment planning, goal setting, and the beginning stages of the work. It is only through being honest about what you know and what you do not know that you will truly take advantage of all that supervision can offer.

BEING VULNERABLE AND RECEIVING FEEDBACK

We fully recognize that when supervisees ask for feedback and identify the areas where they are less confident in their knowledge or skills, they are placing themselves in a vulnerable position. It is for this reason that we return to the importance of creating a relationship that feels safe in order to reflect honestly on yourself, your work, and the client. When supervisees trust their supervisors, they are able to form such safe relationships (Bennett & Deal, 2009). A safe and trusting relationship is one in which the novice practitioner can discuss his or her reactions to the work (i.e., vicarious trauma), reactions to clients, and other personal feelings about the work.

In turn, a supervisor should work to provide, support, and empathize, while providing guidance and professional education, to earn a supervisee's trust. Yet, sometimes this guidance and feedback can feel critical and possibly even shaming. For some people, any sort of feedback from someone in authority can remind them of past occasions when they had a strong negative reaction. We hope that all supervisors will provide feedback in a sensitive and supportive manner. However, if you are someone who knows that you are especially vulnerable to having a strong negative reaction regardless of how gently it was given, we recommend that you explore this reaction outside the supervision as much as possible. There are times when you may find that sharing those past experiences with your supervisor may actually be possible.

In one of my (M.D.G.)own supervisory experiences, I had a supervisor who reminded me a great deal of someone is my own life who I worked hard to please and never felt fully successful in achieving that goal. This desire to please concerning academics especially was helpful in that it pushed me to strive to be successful in school. However, it also left me with a hyperawareness of any feedback that I perceived as negative, regardless of how innocuous it was. I was concerned that this interpersonal dynamic would negatively impact my relationship with the supervisor by leading me not to share my own perceived weaknesses in order to please this person. After much thought, I opted to share the dynamic I felt and why I felt it was emerging with this individual and asked for suggestions on how we could interact in a way that would allow me to feel more present rather than withdraw. Thankfully, this individual was receptive to the feedback, and I found that I could relax and be more forthcoming in our meetings. It is important to note here that the dynamic I described was fairly unique to this person, rather than to everyone. In other relationships, I was able to receive feedback without feeling so negatively about myself. I do not believe these feelings emerged because of the way the feedback was delivered. Rather, the feelings emerged due to the way I *received* the feedback based on my own personal experiences. Our take home from this experience is that it is important to look at patterns across relationships that make it difficult for you to receive feedback in a productive way. It is possible that you may find that sharing your own history with certain individuals can help you maintain a healthy dynamic and relationship with your supervisor.

It may be helpful to remember that not only does your supervisor have a personal investment in your success, as mentioned previously, but also the supervisor has a legal responsibility in the supervisory relationship. Unlicensed professionals are practicing under their supervisor's license. Your mistakes are their mistakes in the eyes of the law. Providing quality, ethical treatment to clients is their priority just as much as your professional growth and development. If you can remember that the supervisor's feedback comes from these dual foci, it can often feel more like professional guidance than personal criticism.

Another important point to remember about feedback is that direction and guidance given in supervision are not merely advice or suggestion. When a supervisor provides direct feedback about what to do about a particular situation, the supervisee should implement the feedback given and report back on how it went. When the supervisee is defensive or reluctant to trust the guidance of the supervisor, such visible defensiveness can result in a contentious supervisory relationship that is unproductive and not useful, most especially for the client. When you are open to feedback and exploring what you can learn and how you can grow professionally, supervision is the catalyst toward great work.

Due to the power imbalance, it is important to acknowledge that the supervisee can feel powerless to disagree or challenge the supervisor's recommendations. In this relationship, the supervisor often has a great deal of power over the supervisee's future. Obviously, if the supervisee is concerned about the feedback or has some reasons to suspect that the advice is not in the best interest of the client or the agency, then the supervisee should seek guidance from another colleague within the agency. However, in our experience these are rare occurrences. We find more often than not there is a rich and vibrant discussion between the supervisee and supervisor about different options and potential outcomes while exploring and dissecting each other's thoughts. These discussions can be rich learning experiences and fun.

HOW SUPERVISION IS DIFFERENT FROM THERAPY

We hope that we have communicated that supervision can be a wonderful opportunity for professional growth and development. As social workers, we often learn a great deal more about ourselves in our work with clients than we could have ever imagined. Supervision is the place to address the fact that you find it hard to work with a client who reminds you of your sister, but it is not the place to try to resolve this long-standing filial conflict. Supervision is different from your own personal psychotherapy in that practitioners should only be addressing their personal issues that are directly connected to the work. Exploring these dynamics with your supervisor should be done from the lens of how to manage your "stuff" while working on the client's stuff. You can see how it would be easy for supervision to devolve into therapy, so it is the responsibility of both parties to ensure that this boundary is held secure.

Keeping solid boundaries is essential for supervision. You are not friends, but you are friendly colleagues who often share personal information with each other. Supervision is not therapy. Rather, supervision is a relationship that serves to improve your work with clients through the exploration of how to remove barriers and strengthen assets in that relationship. Sometimes, the barriers originate from you as well as the client. Sometimes, your own assets are not being utilized effectively in addition to the client's. Supervision is the place to explore these dynamics to improve the *client's* life.

REFLECTIVE SUPERVISION

Due to the fast-paced environment of many social work settings, receiving supervision in a sacred 50-minute hour is difficult to sustain. This results in less time for practitioners to focus on self-reflection and awareness in the work, as was often done in more psychodynamic supervision. The standards for best practices in supervision say nothing about supervision as a place for supervisees to reflect on themselves in the work and gain insight into why they are engaging a client in a certain way or approaching a community project with a certain feeling (NASW & ASWB, 2013). As we have previously noted, self-reflection is important for every social worker. Therefore, we bring your attention to a method of conducting supervision that emphasizes greater self-reflection and self-awareness through the practice of reflective supervision (Wightman et al., 2007). In this method, the focus of supervision is to provide a space for supervisees to think not only about the work they are doing in their respective settings but also to reflect on how their feelings had an impact on the encounter. Reflective supervision encourages the supervisor and supervisee to address any impediments to progress that may be found in worker, client, or both. This method of supervision can be conducted individually or within a group. In addition, reflective supervision can take on different forms to suit the needs of the practice setting.

A reflective supervisor explores case material with the supervisee in such a way that they create the time and space to reflect on the relationship between worker and client, as well as addresses the administrative pieces of the job. In this way of working, the *relationship* is the foundation for reflective supervision that allows honest reflection to occur (Harvey & Henderson, 2013). This style of supervision requires that there is a strong working relationship that includes an agreement to work in an open, honest, and thoughtful way. Many methods of supervision tend to focus more on administrative tasks and education for novice practitioners and to spend less time on reflection and insight. In this style of supervision, there are explicit expectations for both the supervisor and supervisee that are stated prior to beginning their work together. These respective expectations, outlined by Wightman and colleagues (2007), are as follows:

A Reflective Supervisor
- Is consistent with meeting time and place;
- Is on time, open, curious, and emotionally available;
- Treats the time as sacred and guards against interruptions;
- Works with the supervisee to set the agenda;
- Respects strengths of supervisee and follows his or her pace;
- Observes and listens carefully, is reassuring, and gives specific feedback;
- Suspends harsh or critical judgment and focuses on increasing supervisees' awareness and insight;
- Invites the in-depth sharing of details about a particular situation;
- Listens for the emotional experiences of the supervisee;
- Is empathic in naming and responding to the experiences;

- Creates a safe space for the supervisee to have and talk about feelings;
- Maintains a shared balance of attention on client and supervisee; and
- Prepares for the next meeting by reflecting on previous ones.

A Reflective Supervisee

- Participates in setting up time and place of regular meetings and sticks to the schedule;
- Comes to supervision meetings open and emotionally available;
- Is prepared to discuss particular details of his or her work;
- Increases awareness of and reflection on feelings experienced in the work;
- Operates from a stance of openness to sharing those feelings with the supervisor;
- Explores the relationship between feelings and the work one is doing;
- Tells the supervisor what kind of support is needed and then is open to receiving that support;
- Remains curious and open to new interpretations;
- Suspends critical or harsh judgment of self and of others; and
- Prepares for the next meeting by reflecting on previous ones.

Some of you may be receiving this type of supervision if your supervisor is trained in psychodynamic theory and has had specific training in methods of supervision. If you do not, and this type of supervision is attractive to you yet not available in your setting, it is perfectly appropriate for your professional growth and learning to contract outside supervision.

FINAL THOUGHTS ON SUPERVISION

The relationship between supervisor and supervisee has the potential to provide powerful and rich learning and growth opportunities. Due to the power imbalance, there is the potential for supervisees to feel vulnerable within it. However, with support, trust, and empathy, this relationship has the potential to serve as a launching pad for significant professional development. Social workers are never truly "done" with supervision. When can you ever know all there is to know? When are you truly free from blind spots in your work? Even seasoned practitioners need the ongoing support that supervision brings. At its most basic, supervision provides a quiet time and space to reflect on the work we do, obtain feedback from another practitioner's point of view, and plan for the care of the clients we serve. While it is mandatory at the beginning of one's career, we encourage all readers to find ways to infuse supervision into their professional lives well beyond the mandatory period. Whether you use individual, group, or peer supervision, finding colleagues to whom you can turn for guidance and support in the work will be a treasured resource in your career. These relationships can last for years, even decades, and create communities of professional support that are invaluable.

CHAPTER 16 RESOURCE GUIDE

SUPERVISION GUIDE

National Association of Social Workers (NASW): D.C. Metro Chapter. (2013). *Best practice standards in social work supervision*. Retrieved from http://www.naswdc.org/practice/naswstandards/supervisionstandards2013.pdf

SAMPLE SUPERVISION AGENDA

The agenda can also serve as a record of what was discussed in supervision. It should be kept confidential, as it will often have client information on it. One example of an agenda is as follows:

Supervision Session
1:00–2:00 p.m.

 I. Review of the week: identify one success and one area for improvement
 II. Follow-up questions on motivational interviewing training
 III. Report on client contact this week
 IV. Questions about intervention plan for M.J.
 V. Debriefing of family session with C.K. and parents
 VI. Progress report on recruitment for support group
 VII. Planning of upcoming vacation—client coverage and office staffing needs
 VIII. Review of grant report
 IX. Plans for upcoming week

CHAPTER 17

TECHNOLOGY AND SOCIAL MEDIA

Before reading the rest of this chapter, think about your own presence on social media sites. Now, think about the clients you serve viewing that information. Would you show clients pictures from your vacation? Think about potential employers typing your name into a search on Google. What will they find? Would you want them viewing photos from your college reunion? While you have a right to your privacy and personal life, becoming a social worker also means projecting a professional image. We hope that as you read this chapter, you begin to think about your own use of the Internet and what information is available about you and how that information is consistent with the professional reputation and image you hope to establish and maintain in your career.

Social media is one of the most ubiquitous forms of interaction in our culture today. One in every nine people on Earth is on Facebook. Each Facebook user spends on average 15 hours, 33 minutes per month on the site. Twitter is adding nearly 500,000 users each day. Most communication is conducted via e-mail, text messages, instant messages, tweets, and other technology (Dombo, Kays, & Weller, 2014). Practitioners should have the freedom to participate in these forums for both personal and professional purposes. Practitioners should also be aware of how the use of these technologies has an impact on the clients they are serving. Conversely, if practitioners do not choose to utilize these forms of technology, we also believe they have an obligation to understand the cultural and relational significance of the modes of communication to better understand their clients.

Given these statistics, technology and social media are changing the landscape of social services and professional relationships. Beginning social work practitioners should be cognizant of ways their personal use of social media will have an impact on their clients, as well as how their professional use should be done in an ethical manner. Technological advancements have enabled clients to engage with practitioners and their services in new ways, raising a multitude of ethical dilemmas. While we cannot predict what the future holds in this area, we discuss the current ethical concerns, as well as some of the advantages and disadvantages of these technologies in working with clients.

ETHICS, TECHNOLOGY, AND SOCIAL MEDIA

Many social service organizations utilize social media to promote their programs, engage with the communities they serve, and raise their visibility to funders. However, the policies surrounding social media within these organizations may not be clear. As such, many ethical dilemmas arise in agencies surrounding their use of social media, especially when it comes to how social media is used in relation to the clients they serve. For example, consider the ethics of asking clients to "like" the website or become a "fan" of the Facebook page for your agency. Would it be a dual relationship for clients to write reviews of or testimonials regarding you or your agency on Yelp or other sites, whether solicited or not? Without clear statements on these issues by professional organizations, we must turn to our Code of Ethics(COE) to help in the decision-making process.

Unfortunately, the COE for social workers (National Association of Social Workers [NASW], 2008), like many other professions, has yet to catch up to the current cultural norms concerning use of technology. However, there are some guiding principles that can help the practitioner make choices about how to proceed. If you begin with the principle regarding the *importance of human relationships,* we see that the COE places an emphasis on human relationships between and among people; relationships are seen as central to the change process. While the current COE does not directly address the use of technology in relationships, it is possible that technology has the potential to be both a help and a hindrance to "strengthen relationships among people in a purposeful effort to promote, restore, maintain, and enhance the wellbeing of individuals, families, social groups, organizations, and communities" (NASW, 2008, p. 6).

PROFESSIONAL USE OF SOCIAL MEDIA

A social worker may use technology in an agency setting for a variety of reasons. For example, technology can make it easier to set up, change, or cancel appointments. It can also help with communication in a timely and economical manner to groups of people on particular issues. Many agencies have electronic newsletters, online scheduling for appointments, and blogs on issues such as mental health, social justice, and community organizing. In addition, many programs have transitioned to the use of electronic client records. These advances make it easier for social workers to communicate and connect with other professionals. However, there are risks associated with technology. For example, keeping client records on computers can leave the information at risk of hacking or being seen by others who are not the intended recipients of the communication, therefore violating a core principle of *confidentiality* (Reamer, 2013).

In addition to confidentiality concerns with client records, there are important considerations regarding the confidentiality of electronic communications with clients. E-mail has become a common form of communication among professionals and between social workers and their clients. However, when communicating by e-mail, it is important to consider whether it is being sent to the correct person. Who will see it? Does it in any way contain sensitive or confidential information such as why the person is meeting with you, what agency you represent, or other information that could indicate the person is a client of your agency?

The use of telephones for communication involves a form of technology. When placing a telephone call, does your agency name appear on caller identification? When I (E.D.) worked at a rape crisis center, our phone number was not tied to the name of the agency for purposes of confidentiality. So, when we would call a client, "Rape Crisis Center" would not come across a caller ID system. Many agencies have similar policies. However, if someone autodialed a return call to that number, the person answering the phone would say "Rape Crisis Center, this is Eileen, how can I help you?" This response would mean that a call from the center was placed to that phone number. There were many occasions when I would answer the phone and someone would say: "Why did someone from a rape crisis center call my house?" Obviously this person did not know that someone in his or her home, such as a spouse, child, or roommate, was receiving services from the center. This example demonstrates that even the most earnest attempts at keeping agency and client contact information confidential can be thwarted by technology.

Concerns about confidentiality and fostering connection in relationships with clients are also related to the principle of *cultural competence* (NASW, 2008). The culture of many of our clients is to communicate through the use of e-mail, FaceTime, text, and so on. If we do not utilize these means of communication, are we disrespectful of our clients' culture? However, some clients due to financial restraints may not have access to various technologies, and we may have to work with them to find a compromise solution that protects and supports them in the work while protecting your own boundaries.

Striking a balance between being accessible via technology and keeping the boundaries of the professional relationship is vital, yet difficult to navigate. Most practitioners need to find their own comfort level with this balance and be consistent with all clients. We strongly recommend discussing your use of technology with clients at the beginning of the helping relationship as a part of the informed consent discussion. This is particularly important to be in compliance with the Health Insurance Portability and Accountability Act of 1996 (HIPAA). HIPAA calls on us to safeguard client information, including case notes, particularly related to information stored electronically. This also means that we cannot share client information, or even acknowledge that someone is a client at our agency, without written consent. If your agency provides services using technology, then you should discuss these parameters with your supervisor and be sure that clients are made aware of the potential threats to confidentiality (Santhiveeran, 2009).

We recommend that you and your supervisor discuss the agency norms regarding technology and then discuss how those norms fit with your own comfort level. For example, many agencies that provide community-based services do not have landlines for their workers because they are out in the field more than in the office. As a result, many of the workers may use their personal cell phones as their primary form of communication with other agency workers *and* their clients. While this may be the norm, you should consider what sharing your personal cell phone number with clients might mean. It may mean that now, for all of eternity, even when your internship or position ends, your clients will have your personal cell phone number and can reach you no matter where you go. They can then text, call, or send you pictures any time they like for as long as you have that phone number. Therefore, it is important to process and think through how to balance the needs of your clients as well as your own.

Finally, technology has made it easier to enact the principles of *public participation* and *social and political action*. The COE states that professionals should "ensure that all people have equal access to the resources, employment, services, and opportunities they require to meet their basic human needs and to develop fully. Social workers should be aware of the impact of the political arena on practice and should advocate for changes in policy and legislation to improve social conditions in order to meet basic human needs and promote social justice" (NASW, 2008, p. 27). Social media is used by organizations to engage in advocacy toward this end. Sending out e-mail blasts, tweeting the results of studies, and organizing thousands of people through one touch of a smartphone are examples of positive ways technology is advancing social work values (Csiernik, Furze, Dromgole, & Rishchynski, 2006).

PERSONAL USE OF SOCIAL MEDIA

Like it or not, social workers' personal use of social media can have professional implications. The COE (NASW, 2008) states that we must comport ourselves in our *private conduct* in such a way that it does not interfere with our professional responsibilities. We also must take care to avoid *misrepresentation* of our personal beliefs and practices as our own and not representative of our profession or agency. Finally, our behavior should reflect positively on the *integrity of the profession*. These ethical standards highlight that, in the course of our personal lives, we are still viewed by the public and our clients and communities we serve as a social worker who represents the profession. This representation is true in the online community as well. Our personal use of social media should be done in such a way that is respectful of our profession, our colleagues, and the clients and communities we serve. We strongly encourage that professionals make use of privacy settings or develop an alternative name for personal Facebook pages or Twitter accounts as these strategies can help create a boundary between the personal (private) and the public (professional). For example, professionals who use Twitter accounts have been found to tweet at handles that cross personal and professional lines, such as @socialjerkblog or @fatsocialworker. What are the implications of this for the profession? How savvy can we expect the public to be in making distinctions between our online personal selves and our professional selves (Dombo et al., 2014)?

It is important to remember, however, that technology changes rapidly, and one cannot ever be assured that his or her private pages are not being hacked or accidently made public (Dombo et al., 2014). If you would not show your clients photos from your vacation, think about where you are posting them online. While some self-disclosure is inevitable in our increasingly technological world (McWilliams, 2004), we have an ethical responsibility to our professional community and the communities we serve to set boundaries and limits with our own personal use of social media.

CLIENTS' USE OF TECHNOLOGY

Our clients' use of technology is also important to consider. For example, many clients who seek services from social workers and other practitioners will turn to the Internet to see what information they can find on a variety of topics. Some intentionally look for personal information about the practitioner they are planning to see, while others find this information accidentally. In exploring how often clients seek and find information about a therapist with whom they are working, researchers found that 70% of the study participants reported having found personal information about their therapist on the Internet (Kolmes & Taube, 2011). Of those who found personal information, 87% found it intentionally, and only 13% found it accidentally. Finally, for those who participated in this study, most of the participants did not disclose that they had done this (Kolmes & Taube, 2011).

The Kolmes and Taube (2011) study also reported that the majority of the clients stated that their reaction to finding such information was either positive or neutral. The participants also reported feelings of curiosity, interest, and reassurance when they found information about their therapists. Nonetheless, in addition to these positive feelings, participants also frequently reported feelings of guilt, awkwardness, and embarrassment. In one particular case, a client experiencing erotic transference with a therapist saw pictures of his therapist in a bathing suit online and was so distressed that he left therapy (Kolmes & Taube, 2011). Depending on what the client found, as in the previous example, we are fairly confident that these experiences influenced the relationship with the practitioner in multiple ways and distracted from the focus on the client's presenting issues.

In addition to using the Internet to gather information, clients provide information on the Internet through the use of blogs (Glassgold, 2007). Clients have shared publicly what it felt like when they found information about their therapists regarding confidentiality, what it was like to learn information they did not want to know, and how that information complicated and entangled boundaries and led to greater difficulties detaching after termination. The clients used words such as *awkward* and *creepy* with regard to learning about their therapists online. While some approaches to boundaries with online interactions are viewed as too rigid or cautious (Glassgold, 2007), it is the social worker's responsibility to make every attempt to keep private information private.

Another ethical issue that we mentioned is inviting clients to comment on the agency's social media sites. To avoid conflicts of interest (NASW, 2008) in working with clients, practitioners and their agencies should think carefully before asking clients to endorse the services on a website or Facebook page. Asking clients to do this could be seen as being in the agency's best interest, but not the client's. In addition, such requests have the potential to exploit the professional relationship. Also, asking clients to post blogs on the agency website about their experiences could be viewed as either empowering to the client or as creating a dual relationship (Dombo et al., 2014; NASW, 2008). These kinds of arrangements can create ethical dilemmas that need to be carefully considered with supervisors and agency leaders before making decisions about how to proceed.

USE OF TECHNOLOGY TO DELIVER SERVICES

There are many settings that are using technology to deliver services to clients. This is commonly referred to as *telehealth* and is particularly beneficial for people living in rural or hard-to-reach areas, people who are homebound, or people who require a sense of anonymity to reach out for support (Reamer, 2013). There are many online support groups, crisis hotlines, and self-help resources that clients can access in lieu of traditional face-to-face counseling meetings.

Technology is also being used in the form of smartphone apps and self-guided interventions that can be used as adjuncts to traditional counseling or on their own (Barak & Grohol, 2011). While there are benefits to this mode of delivering services such as those we have listed, there are drawbacks as well. For example, it can be difficult to build rapport and engage clients when each person is unable to read nonverbal cues. Also, another downside to the use of telehealth is that there is the potential for the meaning of e-mails and text messages to be misconstrued because there is no context provided with these forms of communication (Menon & Rubin, 2011).

If your setting is providing services utilizing technology, we strongly encourage you to be sure that clients are made aware of the limitations of this form of service delivery as a part of *informed consent* processes (NASW, 2008). An important aspect of professional competence is knowing about the range of services that exist and being appropriately trained and supervised in carrying out these interventions (NASW & Association of Social Work Boards, 2005). In addition, social workers must evaluate the client's appropriateness for interventions that are delivered via technology. Kraus, Stricker, and Speyer (2011) stated that there are a few situations in which this modality is contraindicated:

- Client has thoughts or hurting him- or herself or others
- Client is in an emergency situation
- Client has a history of suicidal, violent, or abusive tendencies
- Client is having delusions or hallucinations
- Client is an active alcohol or drug abuser

These types of situations require more intensive work, and the worker may need to have more direct interaction with the client to monitor such cases. In addition, by not taking a more direct approach, social workers may be putting themselves in a legally vulnerable position if they continue to use telehealth technology knowing that their clients require more intensive supervision. These potentially risky situations raise a concern with regard to licensing and technology. Many states do not have specific regulations regarding the delivery of services utilizing technology or specify education and training requirements, leaving many social work practitioners with little guidance and information regarding how best to manage such client situations. See Dombo et al. (2014) for a full listing of this information by state.

FINAL THOUGHTS ON TECHNOLOGY

Because you are at the beginning of your career as you read this, you can enter your career in such a way that it is responsive to the trends in social media use personally and professionally. By setting good habits early, you will feel confident that your professional reputation will be protected when viewed through the eyes of the Internet. Some suggestions (Dombo et al., 2014) are presented here to start your thinking about this:

- Regularly monitor your representations on the Internet (e.g., set up a Google Alert for yourself).
- Clean up your online presence to eliminate information that may be dated or problematic for clients to find.
- Become educated about privacy settings on social media sites you participate in, their limits to privacy protections, and risks of hacking and other unintentional breaches in privacy.
- Be as thoughtful in your digital presence as you are in the "real world" (e.g., ask yourself before you post something, "Would I be comfortable saying this to a client directly?").
- Review your state's regulations and ongoing legal changes relevant to the delivery of social work services through technology and other online activity.
- Be prepared for how you to handle situations where clients bring up information they have found about you online; integrate this into sound clinical practice, just as you would discussions about race, gender, religion, and culture.
- Create online practices and policies that account for online issues and boundaries (see summary guide for examples) and integrate them into your informed consent procedures or using client contracts.
- Use an alternative name for your personal online presence that is significantly different from your professional one.
- Establish guidelines and principles to help guide online use by social workers if you are the head of an agency or a supervisor.

CHAPTER 17 RESOURCE GUIDE: SUGGESTIONS FOR CREATING A POLICY ON TECHNOLOGY

It is strongly suggested that all social service organizations as well as independent practitioners create policies for use of technology by workers as well as for interactions with clients utilizing technology (Dombo et al., 2014). Some suggestions for what to include are as follows:

- Organizations should indicate who can and who cannot post official messages on social media sites.
- There should be specific people designated to handle Twitter accounts to both send and respond to messages.

- It is generally not recommended to ask clients to "friend" or "fan" an organization's Facebook page as this can create a dual relationship. Instead, ask other providers who are referral sources to do this.
- Employees should be given clear guidelines regarding how to protect client information in databases and computerized health records systems and should know under what circumstances they can share protected information.
- Clients should be told about electronic health records or other use of technology as part of informed consent.
- If using e-mail to communicate with clients, the policy should clearly state the threats this format can pose to confidentiality.
- Parameters concerning sending and receiving e-mails or text messages from clients should be clearly stated.
- Consider setting policies about not accepting friend requests or LinkedIn requests from current or former clients to protect their privacy.
- Consider specifying the type of videoconferencing software used to provide teletherapy or conduct clinical supervision if applicable. The software utilized should be secure.

CHAPTER 18

BEGINNING KNOWLEDGE OF THE BRAIN AND ITS FUNCTIONS

As with virtually every chapter so far, it is beyond the scope of this book to cover everything you need to know about the brain. However, we frequently hear how often practitioners feel pressure to understand and include more knowledge of neurobiological factors in their assessments and interventions with clients. To alleviate some of this pressure, this chapter provides an overview of the concepts that they may hear about in their work. This content includes some of the essential features of psychological testing and a summary of what is currently known about neurobiology and brain functioning.

In addition, regardless of the practice setting, many nonmedical helping professionals work with clients who are prescribed at least one psychiatric medication by their primary care provider or a psychiatrist. Given that social workers are often the individuals who may hear from the clients about their experiences with these medications, we feel strongly that, at a minimum, social workers should know the broad categories of the families of medications so that they are attuned to any medication-related concerns expressed by their clients. We recognize that this knowledge is continually evolving. As such, we provide general guidelines and encourage readers to continue to seek new knowledge.

NEUROBIOLOGY

WHAT IS NEUROBIOLOGY?

The study of neurobiology in fields such as social work and psychology has increased in the last few decades, yet what we know is still only a drop in the bucket. We study the brain and nervous system to better understand how they influence human behavior. The brain has been described as "the social organ of the body" (Siegel, 2007, p. 48) because it is connected to the other organs of the body *and* connects us with other individuals. In this way, our knowledge of brain functioning can help us comprehend the behavior of our clients, and perhaps more important, it can be used to help clients better understand themselves.

WHAT IS THE BRAIN?

Weighing in at 3 pounds, the brain is the most powerful organ in the human body. There are many models of the brain in textbooks (e.g., Farmer, 2009; Siegel, 2007), and you can find some great images and videos with a quick Google search on the brain (see the summary guide for recommended sites). You can also find workshops, seminars, or short courses on neurobiology in continuing education or postgraduate educational programs. However, the following provides a beginning understanding of the brain (Farmer, 2009; Siegel, 2007):

1. The **cerebral cortex** is the outside of the brain; it handles the complex functions of attention, perception, and planning. Within the cortex are a number of different areas called lobes that have different functions, such as those related to motor activity. Also within the cortex are several columns responsible for activities such as seeing and hearing and that connect through neurons to transfer information. The cerebral cortex is divided into right and left hemispheres, which are connected by the *corpus callosum*:
   a. The right brain regulates affective experiences then transfers that knowledge to the left brain.
   b. The left brain controls verbal and analytic functions.
2. The **prefrontal cortex** is the frontal lobe and is considered to be the "executive center" of the brain that addresses regulating, and controlling emotions and behaviors.
3. The **limbic system** is under the cerebral cortex and houses a number of structures, including the amygdala, hippocampus, thalamus, and hypothalamus, which are primarily responsible for the creation of emotions and moods, the appraisal of meaning, the creation of emotional attachment, and implicit memory.
4. The **brainstem** (also known as the "reptilian brain") regulates basic processes of the heart and lungs and sleeping and waking states and is the conduit of information from the spinal cord. This part of the brain is where our fight-flight-freeze reactions are housed. It is seen as the most primitive part of the brain because it is dedicated to our basic survival instincts.
5. **Neurons** are the nerve cells within the brain that communicate with one another using signals. The neurons signal to one another and create feelings, thoughts, and memories.
6. **Neurotransmitters** are the chemicals neurons use to signal and communicate with one another. There are two types of neurotransmitters with a variety of functions. Those that are *inhibitory* (e.g., serotonin) help to calm and balance

mood. Excitatory neurotransmitters, such as dopamine, stimulate the brain and help individuals to focus.

7. **Mirror neurons** are considered to be a certain type of neuron that takes a perception of what you see and then prepares you to imitate that behavior in the same way. These special neurons are crucial to social and emotional functioning because they help us anticipate the feelings and intentions of others. Mirror neurons are linked to the development of empathy and the ability to interpret social cues. They "connect the observed and the observer" (Farmer, 2014, p. 268).

WHY CARE ABOUT NEUROBIOLOGY?

Although our understanding of how the brain works is limited, the knowledge that is available can be an important part of understanding human behavior. Neuroscience is seen as the "missing link" in the helping professions because knowledge of the brain fills in gaps in our understanding of mental health and illness (Farmer, 2009, p. 1). In other words, this knowledge has transformed practice. Whether you work with children in foster care, older adults with Alzheimer disease, women with substance use issues, communities recovering from a natural disaster, or federal policy initiatives for veterans, it is essential for social workers to have a basic knowledge of the role of the brain in the bio-psycho-social-spiritual framework of human behavior. This knowledge helps us more fully understand the human experience (Badenoch, 2008; Farmer, 2009).

Understanding the structure and various functions of the brain has great utility across a number of fields of practice. For example, research on autism spectrum disorders is currently exploring potential deficits in mirror neurons (Fan, Decety, Yang, Liu, & Cheng, 2010). Researchers seeking to better understand substance abuse disorders are investigating the role of the neurotransmitter dopamine in these disorders (Bennett & Petrash, 2014). Another example comes from trauma research, where there are attempts to determine the impact of trauma on the development of the limbic system in children (Weber & Reynolds, 2004). Practitioners can utilize knowledge of the brain to help clients who struggle with these issues, both in understanding the origins of these issues and how to address them. What is most encouraging about much of this research is that as clients learn new ways of being in the world or have new experiences, their brains can change. This change process can be explained and understood through the concept of *plasticity* (Siegel, 2007).

In my (E.D.) work with trauma survivors, it is particularly helpful to explore the role of the fight-flight-freeze response with their behavior. When a client asks questions such as "Why didn't I just run?" or "Why couldn't I speak up?" I am able to talk with them about the way our brains are wired to respond to distress. The same is true for talking with clients about memory and dissociation and the more recent understanding about how traumatic memory is stored in the brain, and when we avoid remembering, it weakens that memory. When a client wonders why they dissociate when overwhelmed by traumatic experiences, I can explain that it is the brain's way of protecting the client from what is happening. While they cannot physically escape, the brain provides a way to mentally shut down to avoid the experience.

BRAIN PLASTICITY

Brain plasticity is a term that explains the way new experiences can have an impact on the brain. In essence, the concept means that the brain changes. The idea of brain plasticity is a relatively new concept (Farmer, 2009); until recently, the prevailing thought was that the human brain stopped developing in adolescence. It seems like such an antiquated notion now, akin to doctors treating a cold with leeches. The evolving scientific understanding of the brain tells us two important things: (a) The plasticity of the prefrontal limbic cortex makes the brain particularly vulnerable to disorganization that results from negative experiences; and (b) the prefrontal cortex is also the area of the brain amenable to reordering, restructuring, and repatterning through supportive counseling and therapy (Farmer, 2009; Montgomery, 2002). Therefore, plasticity means that the brain is *both* negatively and positively impacted by experiences. What is especially important for social workers to remember is that the brain changes in response to environmental conditions. The concept of plasticity speaks to the role of an individual's environment and how it has an impact on his or her brain's structure; harmful environments wire neurons a certain way, while safe and nurturing environments create different pathways.

For example, research on the brain has demonstrated a connection between traumatic stress and brain development. Specifically, early trauma has been shown to negatively impact attachment, coping skills, and emotional regulation (Allen, 2001). These experiences then have an impact on the organization of the limbic system, which then has an impact on an individual's future ability to adapt to new and changing environments (Cohen, Tottenham, & Casey, 2013; Garland & Howard, 2009; Schore, 2001; Weber & Reynolds, 2004).

One of the ways adaptation is difficult relates to the challenges faced by individuals who have a trauma history. These folks often struggle to describe their trauma in a cohesive narrative. The reason for this challenge is because traumatic experiences inhibit neural integration of the events. In other words, the brain cannot process the information from such an overwhelming event, and some information is lost and fractured in how the person remembers the event. Therefore, one of the goals of an intervention is to help the client create a more cohesive narrative of their past traumatic experiences. Research continues to show that the brain, as a result of plasticity, can be altered, most often through the experiences of a supportive and reparative relationship (Siegel, 2003). Neural integration is the outcome of attuned relationships we have with our clients (Siegel, 2003). This research reinforces the importance of forming effective relationships we discussed in Chapter 2. In these relationships, we are not only helping our clients to gain new ways of being in the world through the development of new patterns, but also helping to change the brain and the way their brain functions on a physical level.

NEUROSCIENCE AND MACRO PRACTICE

Neuroscience is not just relevant for social workers in direct practice or clinical settings. A critical connection also exists between social justice issues and neuroscience. The stress that often results from a lack of medical and mental health coverage, as well as experiences of oppression in various forms, can have serious negative effects on the brain. This information can be useful to clients who are struggling to understand their own challenges. Through psychoeducation, social workers can help clients understand how their environment has played a role in their mental health conditions. From a macro lens, this knowledge directly speaks to the need to work for societal change to reduce negative environmental forces in the lives of our clients (Ivey & Zalaquett, 2011). Therefore, macro interventions, such as community organizing and policy advocacy, should address the impact that oppression, trauma, and stress have on brain development.

Neuroscience research is critical to bridge the micro and macro efforts of our work. Advocates for mental health research and services can use knowledge developed from neuroscience to show how the processing of events, memories, and feelings with a social worker or other professional in a safe holding environment grows new dendrites in the brain and strengthens neural pathways that would otherwise atrophy. Neuroscience provides solid evidence to support that what we do as practitioners has positive effects on the brain (Ivey & Zalaquett, 2011; Matto & Strolin-Goltzman, 2012; Montgomery, 2002).

PSYCHIATRIC MEDICATIONS: UNDERSTANDING YOUR ROLE

There is a clear connection between medications for psychiatric conditions and neurobiology. Practitioners whose clients are taking psychotropic medications must attend to these connections to best understand and serve the client (Farmer, 2014). For practitioners who work on macro-level issues, understanding the connection between medications and mental well-being is crucial to advocating on behalf of these populations. For practitioners who work directly with clients who use prescription or nonprescription drugs, it is essential to explore the impact they are having on brain functioning, emotional well-being, and ability to be attuned with others in their lives and with their internal processes.

Many clients helped by social workers and other practitioners have chronic mental health diagnoses that require ongoing medication monitoring and compliance. Referring to psychiatrists and coordinating care with these providers are some of the most common tasks performed by social workers in clinical settings (Bentley, Walsh, & Farmer, 2005). These tasks are in line with the code of ethics for social workers, particularly the principles of social justice, dignity and worth of the person, valuing the central importance of human relationships, and striving for competence in our practice domains (Bentley & Walsh, 2006). When working with clients who rely on access to psychiatric care and affordable medications to live independently and manage their mental health challenges with dignity and grace, it is incumbent on practitioners working with these populations to collaborate closely with psychiatrists to coordinate care.

Your role with regard to medications will depend in large part on your practice setting. However, you will likely be advocating on behalf of the client; consulting with family members about the need for medications; supporting the physician's recommendations; counseling the client about the struggles of medication compliance; and monitoring the medication side effects. In other settings, you may be providing psychoeducation about medications and conducting research on the psychosocial effects of medications on particular client populations (Bentley & Walsh, 2006). In all instances, to be a competent practitioner, you will need a good working knowledge of psychotropic medications (Farmer, Bentley, & Walsh, 2006).

Your settings and populations may require other types of skills and knowledge. For example, when working in settings where the clients have a substance use disorder and a chronic mental health diagnosis that requires psychotropic medication (often referred to as a "dual diagnosis"), your role will include carrying out integrated treatment to help the client understand the interactions between prescription and nonprescription substances (Drake & Mueser, 2000). When working with diverse populations, you will also need to educate yourself about the differences in effects of psychotropic medications depending on the ethnic, social, and cultural differences of your clients (Ruiz, 2000). This is an all-too-often overlooked issue, as many medications are tested on Caucasian study participants and not adjusted for other populations (Farmer, 2014). Finally, there are some groups viewed to have specific needs related to psychotropic medications. If you are working with older adults, children, adolescents, and pregnant or postpartum women, you will need specific education related to these specific concerns (see the National Institute of Mental Health [NIMH] link in the summary guide).

In the role of counselor, your main job is to understand the common side effects of the medications your client is taking, empathize with the difficulties of compliance, and work together for the best possible outcome. It is beyond the scope of this chapter to address all the side effects of all the medications and how they will differ for each individual and address the potential interactions of psychotropic drugs with other medications the client is taking. However, it is crucial to understand that many clients struggle with adherence to the prescribed medication regime. Often, the experience of feeling better due to the effects of the medication leads the person to believe he or she is better and does not need it any more. Stopping the medication on one's own without the help of the psychiatrist can be dangerous. Each individual has his or her own unique experience of a medication, and this subjective interpretation can have an impact on adherence and therefore the outcome of services you are providing (Bentley, 2010).

In my (E.D.) practice experience, many clients grapple with the negative side effects of medications and wonder if they outweigh the benefits of adhering to them. For example, one of my clients was experiencing clinical depression as the result of a history of childhood sexual abuse trauma. Her depression was connected to her inability to feel safe being sexually intimate with her husband, and she was beginning to feel hopeless about her ability to overcome these dynamics. One of the side effects of her antidepressant medications was a decrease in sexual arousal and interest. This was greatly distressing to her as she felt it would make her presenting problem worse, not better. In this situation, the client and I spoke at length about her dilemma. I encouraged her to share these concerns with her psychiatrist, and she was able to work with the doctor to find a medication that was a better fit.

If the client had not felt able to convey these concerns to her psychiatrist, I would have asked her to sign a release of confidentiality so I could speak on her behalf and advocate for her needs. These types of situations draw attention to the need to develop good working relationships with psychiatrists, as well as all practitioners from other disciplines. In the summary guide, you will find recommendations for referring clients to psychiatrists and developing working alliances with them. As an advocate for the client's needs, you can demonstrate that psychiatrists are typically more than willing to collaborate on their care and want the best outcome for their mental health. Over time, you can encourage clients to ask specific questions, such as the following:

- How long will it take for me to feel the effects of the medication?
- Is this a generic label or trade label? Is there a difference?
- What should I do if I forget a dose?
- Are there programs or resources available to help defray the cost of medications?
- Are there any negative interactions with my other medications?
- What food or drink (including alcohol) should I avoid while on this medication?
- Is there a fact sheet on this medication that I can take home with me?
- What are the common side effects?
- If I decide to stop taking this medication, will you talk with me about safe and effective ways to do this?

The goal is for the client to become the leader of this team, which includes you and the psychiatrist, working together to manage the symptoms of the client's presenting problems toward the best outcomes possible.

FINAL THOUGHTS ON NEUROBIOLOGY AND MEDICATIONS

It is normal to feel confused and overwhelmed by the content of this chapter. You do not need to be a neuroscientist or psychiatrist to embrace your role as a practitioner who understands these complex ideas. Part of competent practice is staying current on the brain science behind mental health and the psychotropic medications designed to be part of a comprehensive treatment approach for wellness. Do not shy away from this content. Spend time becoming familiar with the classes of medications listed in the summary guide and the basic parts and processes of the brain that relate to mental health. You will feel more prepared for your work, whether it is advocating for funding for research, creating policies on mental health treatment, linking clients with psychological testing, or helping a client's family understand the role of medications in the management of symptoms.

CHAPTER 18 RESOURCE GUIDE

This guide provides some links to web resources on the brain and neurobiology, as well as links to current information about psychotropic medications. Finally, we present some guidelines for collaborating with psychiatrists and general information about the major classes of drugs.

NEUROBIOLOGY

Center for Neuro Skills (CNS). (2014). *Brain function.* Retrieved from http://www. neuroskills.com/brain-injury/brain-function.php

Cold Spring Harbor (CSH) Laboratory. (2005–2009). *Genes to cognition.* Retrieved from http://www.g2conline.org/2022

Dr. Dan Siegel. (2010). *Resources.* Retrieved from http://drdansiegel.com/resources/

Inside the Brain: Weekly Neuroscience Updates (n.d.). Retrieved from http://inside-the-brain.com

Alzehimer's Association (n.d.). Inside the brain: An interactive tour. Retrieved from http://www.alz.org/alzheimers_disease_4719.asp

Society for Social Neuroscience. (2010). *Links & resources.* Retrieved from http://s4sn.org/links/

YouTube. (2010). *Dr. Daniel Siegel presenting a hand model of the brain.* Retrieved from http://www.youtube.com/watch?v=DD-lfP1FBFk&noredirect=1

MEDICATIONS

National Institute of Mental Health. (n.d.). *Mental health medications.* Retrieved from http://www.nimh.nih.gov/health/publications/mental-health-medications/index.shtml?utm_source=rss_readers&utm_medium=rss&utm_campaign=rss_full

U.S. Food and Drug Administration. (2014). *Information by drug class.* Retrieved from http://www.fda.gov/Drugs/DrugSafety/InformationbyDrugClass/

U.S. Food and Drug Administration. (2014). *Medication guides.* Retrieved from http://www.fda.gov/drugs/drugsafety/ucm085729.htm

U.S. Food and Drug Administration. (2014). *MedWatch: The FDA safety information and adverse event reporting program.* Retrieved from http://www.fda.gov/Safety/MedWatch/default.htm

WebMD. (2005–2014). *Drugs and medications a-z.* Retrieved from http://www.webmd.com/drugs/index-drugs.aspx

GUIDELINES FOR PSYCHIATRIST REFERRAL AND COLLABORATION

1. Research psychiatrists in your area. Find out what insurance they take and if they have low-cost or sliding scale services. Many community mental health agencies employ psychiatrists for their clients, so this can be a good place to start. Ask colleagues about the psychiatrists to whom they refer; many have specialties, such as working with trauma survivors or children. This is important information to know before making a referral.

2. Visit the offices of those to whom you will be making referrals. Make a brief appointment to introduce yourself and your agency or practice. Keep it short and simple, but make a connection.

3. When making the referral, be sure the client is ready to make an appointment to avoid diminishing the goodwill of the psychiatrist. While some resistance is to be expected, unless the client is ready for a serious discussion about medications, both client and psychiatrist will feel frustrated by the meeting.

4. After the meeting, if the psychiatrist has not followed up with you, be sure to contact the psychiatrist to say thank you for meeting with the client and to ask if there is information to share that will help with the coordination of services to the client. If you both have a confidentiality release signed by the client, than this collaboration is not violating any previous confidentiality agreements.

5. Check in regularly with your client about adherence to the medications prescribed. Explore side effects and any complicating factors that may be prohibiting the client from taking the medication as needed.

6. Find out when the client has his or her next appointment with the psychiatrist and encourage the client to prepare for the appointment with questions for feedback that will help the medication regime. You can spend time with your client role-playing any interactions with the doctor the client may feel apprehensive about.

7. Keep in regular contact with the psychiatrist throughout the working relationship to check in regularly and coordinate care. Even if you terminate your work with the client, be sure to terminate the coordination with the psychiatrist appropriately.

These guidelines were adapted from Bentley, Walsh, and Farmer (2005).

CLASSES OF PSYCHOTROPIC MEDICATIONS

Class of Medication	Some Examples of Common Generic Drugs (Trade Name in Parentheses When Applicable)	Used to Treat
Antipsychotics	Aripiprazole (Abilify), chlorpromazine (Thorazine), haloperidol (Haldol), perphenazine, fluphenazine, risperidone (Risperdal), olanzapine (Zyprexa), quetiapine (Seroquel), ziprasidone (Geodon), paliperidone (Invega), clozapine (Clozaril), iloperidone (Fanapt), loxapine (Loxitane), molindone (Moban)	Schizophrenia and related disorders
Antidepressants	**Selective serotonin reuptake inhibitors:** Citalopram (Celexa), escitalopram (Lexapro), fluoxetine (Prozac), paroxetine (Paxil), sertraline (Zoloft) **Tricyclic antidepressants:** Amitriptyline (Elavil), imipramine (Tofranil/Tofranil-PM) **Monoamine oxidase inhibitors:** Bupropion (Wellbutrin)	Depression
Mood stablizers	Some antipsychotics (see antipsychotic section) Lithium, divalproex sodium (Depakote), carbamazepine (Tegretol), lamotrigine (Lamictal), oxcarbazepine (Trileptal)	Bipolar disorders
Antianxiety medications	Some antidepressants (see antidepressant section) Lorazepam (Ativan), buspirone (BuSpar), clonazepam (Klonopin), chlordiazepoxide (Librium), clorazepate (Tranxene), diazepam (Valium), alprazolam (Xanax)	Post-traumatic stress disorder; obsessive compulsive disorder; generalized anxiety disorder; panic disorders; social phobia
Psychostimulants	Methylphenidate (Ritalin, Concerta), amphetamine (Adderall), dextroamphetamine (Dextrostat), dexmethylphenidate (Focalin), atomoxetine (Strattera)	Attention deficit hyperactivity disorder

Source: Bentley &Walsh, 2006; National Institutes of Mental Health.

CHAPTER 19

FINAL THOUGHTS

We hope by the end of this book you feel more confident and excited about your work as a social worker or other helping professional. As we stated in the introduction, we cannot imagine another profession for ourselves, and we hope that you feel the same level of connection and passion for your future profession. We have shared our practice experiences with you throughout the book for three main reasons. First, it is our hope that you will have a better sense of what you will face in working in the multiple roles and settings. Second, we want you to think through some common pitfalls that can occur in the early years of working in the helping professions so you can begin to gather specific ideas about how to avoid them if possible. Finally and most important, we hope that by thinking through and avoiding some common difficulties, you will have a greater likelihood of helping your clients achieve their goals.

With these goals in mind, it is fitting that we end this book with some general words of advice that stem from our own years as practitioners and from our years of teaching courses to graduate-level students in social work. These pieces of advice are also based on our own errors and missteps. We wished someone had passed on to us this advice as we were beginning our careers. Remember, the journey of developing your professional self never ends, but these are some good places to begin.

- **Practice regular self-care.** Identify your own personal needs to stay emotionally, mentally, and physically healthy. Each person has his or her own methods to take care of him- or herself. I (M.D.G.) get up superearly so I can exercise as I know, without exercise, I do not sleep as well or eat as well, and I am moodier. On the other hand, I (E.D.) like to find ways to add humor to my days by finding time to laugh with colleagues or enjoy a comedy on television or in the movies. Laughter helps me balance out all the other emotions that arise in me from the work.

- **Try to remember what you can change in the world and what you cannot.** We both entered social work with large hopes for our capacity to be change agents. Yet, we learned quickly that we are one piece in a large puzzle. We do not mean to imply that we cannot do anything and are powerless. If we believed that idea we would not be in the field this long. We just want to communicate that it is important to take the gains and setbacks of our clients in stride. For example, we always hope that we can help our clients feel more confident that there are people who can help them. We hope that this experience with us increases the likelihood that they are more likely to obtain help in the future. Maybe this level of change is all we can hope for with some clients.

- **Be humble.** As mentioned, there are many aspects of a client's life that influence what changes he or she is able to make in your work together. As such, it is also important to remember that when the client does make changes, it was a team effort. Clients will often thank you and give you all the credit for success in reaching their goals. Our clients own their work. It is always wonderful to feel that you are effective in helping a client to reach his or her goals. However, if we cannot take all the "blame" for when clients do not reach their goals, we also cannot take all of the credit when they do.

- **Create a strong peer group of colleagues.** We cannot emphasize enough the importance of finding a group of colleagues with whom you can share, cry, vent, or be vulnerable. While this work can be invigorating, it can also be frustrating and humbling. It is essential to have a group of colleagues with whom you can share these moments. As you move on in your career, a peer group can support you through peer supervision, help you continue to learn and grow through the sharing of new research and practice, and create a community of supportive people who understand the challenges and rewards of the work. I (E.D.) have been part of a peer supervision group for years, and I truly value the ability to be vulnerable with them. I look to this group of seasoned professionals to help me see my blind spots and teach me something new each time we meet.

- **Be honest about what you know, what you do not know, and when you make mistakes.** We are not perfect. We have both been practicing for about 20 years, yet we still are surprised about what we do not know. Social workers are ethically mandated to work within our practice areas, which means we need to be honest about what we know and what we do not know. When we make mistakes, it is important to talk through these mistakes with a colleague or supervisor and own them. We cannot emphasize enough the importance of being honest in supervision. Your learning will be so much greater if you can be honest with your supervisor about what is going on in your work with clients so that he or she can help you to gain the knowledge and skills that you need to be more effective. We all have gaps in our professional knowledge.

- **Celebrate difference.** Throughout your career, you will work with colleagues, communities, and clients who are different from you. Do not fear this difference or pretend it does not exist. Do not feel as though you need to read everything ever written about every cultural group you might ever encounter in your work. Approach difference by valuing it. Embrace the richness that comes with different beliefs, value systems, and cultures. By approaching working across cultures with a stance of *not knowing*, you avoid a more defensive or hubristic stance of knowing it all when you really do not.

- **Find your niche.** Social work is an incredibly broad field, which is one of its strengths. However, we have found that when we stumbled through trial and error and we found populations and settings that matched our passions and intellectual curiosities, we were more satisfied professionally. You may be surprised by where you end up. We encourage you to be open to all sorts of different experiences, as you never know what will pique your interests. I (M.D.G.) wanted to learn more about group work, and the only group that was happening in my agency at the time was a group for adjudicated adolescent sex offenders. Never in a million years did I think I had an interest in working with this population. I had always (and still do) worked with survivors of trauma, including sexual trauma. However, the work was fascinating, and I realized that if I really wanted to stop sexual violence from happening, it was this population with whom I needed to work. My work in this group led me back to school for my doctorate and has been a main focus of my research ever since. You just never know what will strike you until you try it.

- **Keep learning.** We encourage you to use one-on-one supervision, peer supervision, and continuing education to keep learning. When you graduate, it is easy to recognize that there is so much more to learn. However, once people get more comfortable with their role as a professional social worker, it can be easy to stay in your comfort zone and just do what you do without challenging yourself to incorporate new or different knowledge and skills into your work.

- **Stay balanced.** Social work provides ample opportunities to work directly with clients, take on administrative roles, address unjust policies, and much more. We have found that having a balance of different roles, tasks, and challenges keeps us energized. We have both had times when we were solely doing direct service with clients. While this work was rewarding, it was also tiring. We both felt the need to incorporate different roles and activities in our work, such as providing supervision or an in-service training for our agency. If you can, try to diversify your work, which also includes your caseloads if you are working directly with clients. As much as you can, try to work with clients who present with a variety of issues and needs. Having variety in your work life is helpful in preventing compassion fatigue.

- **Remember to maintain a work–life balance.** We discussed self-care previously, but work–life balance is worthy of a separate discussion. It is important to remember that although you are a social worker, you have other roles in life, such as friend, partner, sibling, daughter/son, parent, and many others. To protect those, it is important not only to incorporate self-care into your daily life but also to draw boundaries around your work and personal lives. You can incorporate self-care into your professional day in many ways. Leaving the office at 5:00 p.m. in order to meet a friend for dinner is not the only way to practice self-care. Keeping a work–life balance, means taking time off, not checking work voice mails or e-mails when you do not need to, not discussing your work outside work hours, and trying as much as possible to be present in your life outside work. Yes, you are important to your clients, but you are not solely responsible for their care, and it is important for *your* life to nurture and attend to the people and activities that you will have in your life beyond your career.

- **When in doubt, don't!** We stated previously in the book concerning self-disclosure that when in doubt, don't. However, we believe that this phrase is appropriate for all aspects of your work with clients. This statement is not meant to imply that you should never do anything when you have doubts. We use the phrase to emphasize how important it is to give yourself time to think through your options before making a decision. For example, clients may ask you for a ride, if you can attend a special event for them, or if you would be willing to complete a task for them. We encourage you to take the time to think these choices through with another before making any decision. Take your time to think through your response.

- **Be curious.** One of the most important messages you can communicate to your clients is your curiosity about their lives, their choices, their worlds, and their wishes. Curiosity implies interest in the whole story and should be done without judgment. Maintaining a stance of curiosity conveys an ever-present interest in your clients' experience. The more you know about them, the more you will be able to empathize and respond appropriately to their needs.

- **Celebrate and acknowledge even small achievements.** Social workers are trained to look at individual and macro issues. As such, our scope of professional interest is vast. As a result, we can become overwhelmed by the problems and barriers in the world. Therefore, we encourage you to look for and celebrate every change that you see in the work you do as social workers, from the large to the small. Acknowledging and celebrating any form of change is a way to help stay invigorated and motivated in your work. When working with client systems of all sizes, you will often only see a small part of a larger arc of change and growth. In many ways, it can feel like walking into a movie in the middle or losing a book before you finish it. We do not always get to see how the story turns out or what came before our work. Celebrating the small steps and accomplishments helps validate these important milestones toward the larger goals.

- **Be proud to be a social worker.** You may find that when you meet different social workers in the field, they introduce themselves by their role versus their profession (i.e., a therapist versus a clinical social worker). By using other labels to describe their role, these social workers are not acknowledging our profession and providing the opportunity for others to learn about our profession and all of the diverse roles of social workers. We always introduce ourselves as social workers, even though much of our professional lives has been spent "doing psychotherapy." We could easily say that we are therapists or professors. Yet, we both proudly introduce ourselves as social workers. We are each proud to be one and happy to shout from the rooftops that this is who we are.

There is much to learn in our work about the world, people, and ourselves. The work we do as social workers is challenging, frustrating, and exhilarating. We have every hope and expectation that you will have a fulfilling and satisfying career as a social worker. Good luck!

REFERENCES

CHAPTER 2

Burkard, A. W., Knox, S., Groen, M. Perez, M., & Hess, S. A. (2006). European American therapist self-disclosure in cross-cultural counseling. *Journal of Counseling Psychology, 53*(1), 15–25.

Cameron, M. (2014). This is common factors. *Clinical Social Work Journal, 42*, 151–160.

Dewane, C. J. (2006). Use of self: A primer revisited. *Clinical Social Work Journal, 34*, 543–558.

Dombo, E. A., & Gray, C. G. (2013). Engaging spirituality in addressing vicarious trauma in clinical social workers: A self-care model. *Social Work & Christianity, 40*(1), 89–104.

Edwards, J. K., & Bess, J. M. (1998). Developing effectiveness in the therapeutic use of self. *Clinical Social Work Journal, 26*(1), 89–105.

Figley, C. R. (1999). Compassion fatigue: Toward a new understanding of the costs of caring. In B. H. Stamm (Ed.), *Secondary traumatic stress: Self-care issues for clinicians, researchers, and educators* (2nd ed., pp. 3–28). Lutherville, MD: Sidran Press.

Graybeal, C. (2014). The art of practicing with evidence. *Clinical Social Work Journal, 42*, 116–122.

Katz, J. M. (2003). Tales of a therapist: Unexpected self-disclosure in couple therapy. *Journal of Couple & Relationship Therapy, 2*(1), 43–60.

Mackey, R. A., & Mackey, E. F. (1993). The value of personal psychotherapy to clinical practice. *Clinical Social Work Journal, 21*(1), 97–110.

Mahoney, M. J. (2003). *Constructive psychotherapy: A practical guide.* New York, NY: Guilford Press.

McCracken, S., & Marsh, J. (2008). Practitioner expertise in evidence-based practice decision making. *Research on Social Work Practice, 18*, 301–310. doi:10.1177/1049731507308143

Meichenbaum, D. (2007). *Self-care for trauma psychotherapists and caregivers: Individual social and organizational interventions.* Melissa Institute Conference, Miami, FL.

Richardson, J. I. (2001). Guidebook on Vicarious Trauma: Recommendations Solutions for Anti-Violence Workers. Centre for Research on Violence Against Women. Ontario, Canada: Author.

Safran, J. D. (2011). Theodor Reik's *Listening With the Third Ear* and the role of self-analysis in contemporary psychoanalytic thinking. *Psychoanalytic Review, 98*, 205–216.

Schneider, D. A., & Grady, M. D. (2015). Conscious and unconscious use of self: An evolutionary process. *Psychoanalytic Social Work, 22*(1), 52–70.

Stamm, B. H. (2002). Measuring compassion satisfaction as well as fatigue: Developmental history of the Compassion Satisfaction and Fatigue Test. In C. R. Figley (Ed.), *Treating compassion fatigue. Psychosocial stress series, no. 24* (pp. 107–119). New York, NY: Brunner-Routledge

Trippany, R. L., Kress, V. E. W., & Wilcoxon, S. A. (2004). Preventing vicarious trauma: What counselors should know when working with trauma survivors. *Journal of Counseling and Development, 82*, 31–37.

CHAPTER 3

Blow, A., Davis, S., & Sprenkle, D. (2012). Therapist–worldview matching: Not as important as matching to clients. *Journal of Marital and Family Therapy, 38*(1), 13–17.

Bryan, L. A., Dersch, C., Sterling, S., & Aredondo, R. (2004). Therapy outcomes: Client perception and similarity with therapist view. *The American Journal of Family Therapy, 32*(1), 11–26.

Coleman, D. (2006). Therapist–client five-factor personality similarity: A brief report. *Bulletin of the Menninger Clinic, 70*, 232–241.

Corneau, S., & Stergiopoulos, V. (2012). More than being against it: Anti-racism and anti-oppression in mental health services. *Transcultural Psychiatry, 49*, 261–282.

Dybicz, P. (2010). Confronting oppression not enhancing functioning: The role of social workers within postmodern practice. *Journal of Sociology & Social Welfare, 37*(1), 23–47.

Erdur, O., Rude, S., & Baron, A. (2003). Symptom improvement and length of treatment in ethnically similar and dissimilar client–therapist pairings. *Journal of Counseling Psychology, 50*(1), 52–58.

Farsimadan, F., & Draghi-Lorenz, R. (2007). Process and outcome of therapy in ethnically similar and dissimilar therapeutic dyads. *Psychotherapy Research, 17*, 567–575.

Hall, J., Guterman, D., Lee, H., & Little, S. (2002). Counselor–client matching on ethnicity, gender, and language: Implications for counseling school-aged children. *North American Journal of Psychology, 4*, 367–381.

Lee, E. (2011). Clinical significance of cross-cultural competencies (CCC) in social work practice. *Journal of Social Work Practice, 25*, 185–203.

Murphy, M., Faulkner, R., & Behrens, C. (2004). The effect of therapist–client racial similarity on client satisfaction and therapist evaluation of treatment. *Contemporary Family Therapy, 26*, 279–292.

Perez Foster, R. (1999). An intersubjective approach to cross-cultural clinical work. *Clinical Social Work Journal, 26*, 269–291.

Rosenblum, K., & Travis, T. M. C. (2008). *The meaning of difference: American constructions of race, sex and gender, social class, sexual orientation, and disability.* New York, NY: McGraw Hill.

Safran, J. D. (2000). Resolving therapeutic alliance ruptures: Diversity and integration. *Journal of Clinical Psychology, 56*, 233–243.

Schmitz, C. L., Stakeman, C., & Sisneros, J. (2001). Educating professionals for practice in a multicultural society: Understanding oppression and valuing diversity. *Families in Society, 82*, 612–622.

Smith, L., Li, V., Dykema, S., Hamlet, D., & Shellman, A. (2013). Honoring somebody that society doesn't honor: Therapists working in the context of poverty. *Journal of Clinical Psychology, 69*, 138–151.

Spencer, M. (2008). A social worker's reflections on power, privilege, and oppression. *Social Work, 53*, 99–101.

Taber, B., Leibert, T., & Agaskar, V. (2010). Relationships among client–therapist personality congruence, working alliance, and therapeutic outcome. *Psychotherapy, 48*, 376–380.

Williams, E., & Barber, J. (2004). Power and responsibility in therapy: Integrating feminism and multiculturalism. *Journal of Multicultural Counseling and Development, 32*, 390–401.

Yoon, E., Moulton, J., Jeremie-Brink, G., & Hansen, M. (2012). Own group oppression, other group oppression, and perspective taking. *International Journal for the Advancement of Counseling, 35*, 203–215.

Walker, R., & Staton, M. (2000). Multiculturalism in social work ethics. *Journal of Social Work Education, 36*, 449–463.

Williams, D., & Levitt, H. (2008). Clients' experiences of difference with therapists: Sustaining faith in psychotherapy. *Psychotherapy Research, 18*, 256–270.

Williams, E., & Barber, J. (2004). Power and responsibility in therapy: Integrating feminism and multiculturalism. *Journal of Multicultural Counseling and Development, 32*, 390–401.

Zane, N., Sue, S., Chang, J., Huang, J., Lowe, S., Srinivasan, S., . . . Lee, E. (2005). Beyond ethnic match: Effects of client–therapist cognitive match in problem perception, coping orientation, and therapy goals on treatment outcomes. *Journal of Community Psychology, 33*, 569–585.

CHAPTER 4

Bogo, M. (2006). *Social work practice: Concepts, processes, and interviewing.* New York, NY: Columbia University Press.

Carroll, L. (1962). Alice's adventures in wonderland. Harmondsworth, Middlesex: Penguin. (Original work published 1865)

Duncan, B. L. (2010). Prologue: Saul Rosenzweig: The founder of common factors. In B. L. Duncan, S. D. Miller, B. E. Wampold, & M. A. Miller (Eds.), *The heart and soul of change* (2nd ed., pp. 3–22). Washington, DC: American Psychological Association.

Gambrill, E. (2013). *Social work practice: A critical thinker's guide* (3rd ed.). New York, NY: Oxford University Press.

Hepworth, D. H., Rooney, R. H., Dewberry-Rooney, G., & Strom-Gottfried, K. (2013). *Direct social work practice: Theory and skills* (9th ed.). Belmont, CA: Brooks/Cole.

Hubble, M. A., Duncan, B. L., Miller, S. D., & Wampold, B. E. (2010). Introduction. In B. L. Duncan, S. D. Miller, B. E. Wampold, & M. A. Miller (Eds.), *The heart and soul of change* (2nd ed., pp. 49–82). Washington, DC: American Psychological Association.

Kirsch, I. (1985). Response expectancy as a determinant of experience and behavior. *American Psychologist, 40*, 1189–1202. doi:10.1037/0003-066X.40.11.1189

Lambert, M. J., & Barley, D. E. (2002). Research summary on the therapeutic relationship and psychotherapy outcome. In J. C. Norcross (Ed.), *Psychotherapy relationships that work: Therapist contributions and responsiveness to patients* (pp. 17–36). New York, NY: Oxford University Press.

Teyber, E., & McClure, F. H. (2011). *Interpersonal process in therapy: An integrative model* (6th ed.). Belmont, CA: Brooks/Cole Publishing Company.

Walsh, J. (2013). *Theories for direct social work practice* (3rd ed.). Belmont, CA: Thompson Brooks/Cole.

Wampold, B.E. (2010). *The basics of psychotherapy: An introduction to theory and practice.* Washington, DC: American Psychological Association.

Weinberger, J., & Rasco, C. (2007). Empirically supported common factors. In S. G. Hofmann & J. Weinberger (Eds.), *The art and science of psychotherapy* (pp. 103–129). New York, NY: Routledge.

CHAPTER 6

American Psychiatric Association. (2013). *Diagnostic and statistical manual of mental disorders* (5th ed.). Washington, DC: Author.

Berry, K. (2011). The ethnographic choice: Why ethnographers do ethnography. *Cultural Studies—Critical Methodologies, 11*, 165–177.

Bisman, C. (1994). *Social work practice: Cases and principles.* San Francisco, CA: Thompson Brooks Cole.

Corcoran, J., & Walsh, J. M. (2014). *Mental health in social work: A casebook on diagnosis and strengths based assessment* (2nd ed.). Boston, MA: Pearson.

Drisko, J. W., & Grady, M. D. (2012). *Evidence-based practice in clinical social work: Essential clinical social work series.* New York, NY: Springer Science+Business Media, LLC.

Forsey, M. G. (2010). Ethnography as participant listening. *Ethnography, 11*, 558–572.

Fraser, M., Richman, J., & Galinsky, M. (1999). Risk, protection, and resilience: Towards a conceptual framework for social work practice. *Social Work Research, 23*(3), 131–144.

Gambrill, E. (2013). *Social work practice: A critical thinker's guide* (3rd ed.). New York, NY: Oxford University Press.

Haight, W., Kayama, M., & Korang-Okrah, R. (2014). Ethnography in social work practice and policy. *Qualitative Social Work, 13*(1), 127–143.

Heller, N. R., & Gitterman, A. (2011). Introduction to social problems and mental health/illness. In N. R. Heller & A. Gitterman (Eds.), *Mental health and social problems: A social work perspective* (pp. 1–17). New York, NY: Routledge.

Hutchison, E. (2013). *Essentials of human behavior: Integrating person, environment, and the life course.* Thousand Oaks: Sage Publications.

Karls, J. M., & O'Keefe, M. (2008). *Person-in-environment system manual* (2nd ed.). Washington, DC: NASW Press.

Kline, P. (2013). *Handbook of psychological testing* (2nd ed.). New York, NY: Routledge.

Kondrat, M. E. (2008). Person-in-environment. In T. Mizrahi & L. E. Davis (Eds.-in-Chief), *Encyclopedia of social work* (20th ed., pp. 348–354). Washington, DC, and New York, NY: NASW Press and Oxford University Press.

Lambert, M. C., Rowan, G. T., Kim, S., Rowan, S. A., An, A. S., Kirsh, E. A., & Williams, O. (2005). Assessment of behavioral and emotional strengths in Black children: Development of the Behavioral Assessment for Children of African Heritage (BACAH). *Journal of Black Psychology, 31*, 321–351.

Lambert, M. C., Markle, F., & Bellas, V. F. (2001). Psychopathology and assessment in African American children and families: A historical, ecological, and strength-based perspective. In A. Neal-Barnett, J. Contreras, & K. A. Kerns (Eds.), *Forging links: A clinical developmental understanding of African American children* (pp. 1–26). Westport, CT: Prager.

Lee, S., & Kleinman, A. (2007). Are somatoform disorders changing with time? The case of neurasthenia in China? *Psychosomatic Medicine, 69*, 846–849.

Leigh, J. W. (1998). *Communicating for cultural competence.* Toronto, Canada: Allyn and Bacon.

PDM Task Force. (2006). *Psychodynamic diagnostic manual.* Silver Spring, MD: Alliance of Psychoanalytic Organizations.

Probst, B. (2013). "Walking the tightrope": Clinical social workers' use of diagnostic and environmental perspectives. *Clinical Social Work Journal, 41*, 184–191.

Riemann, G. (2005). Ethnographies of practice—practising ethnography: Resources for self-reflective social work. *Journal of Social Work Practice, 19*(1), 87–101.

Saleeby, D. (2012). *The strengths perspective in social work practice* (6th ed.). Boston, MA: Pearson.

Sheafor, B. W., & Horejsi, C. R. (2011). *Techniques and guidelines for social work practice* (9th ed.). Boston, MA: Pearson.

Wakefield, J. C. (2013). DSM-5 and clinical social work: Mental disorder and psychological justice as goals of clinical intervention. *Clinical Social Work Journal, 41*, 131–138.

World Health Organization. (1992). *The ICD-10 classification of mental and behavioral disorders: Clinical descriptions and diagnostic guidelines.* Geneva, Switzerland: Author.

World Health Organization. (2014). *Mental health: Strengthening our response.* Fact sheet no. 220. Retrieved from http://www.who.int/mediacentre/factsheets/fs220/en/

CHAPTER 7

Courtois, C. A., & Ford, J. D. (2012). *Treatment of complex trauma: A sequenced, relationship-based approach.* New York, NY: Guilford Press.

Cunningham, M. (2012). *Integrating spirituality in clinical social work practice: Walking the labyrinth.* Boston, MA: Pearson.

Drake, R. E., & Mueser, K. T. (2000). Psychosocial approaches to dual diagnosis. *Schizophrenia Bulletin, 26,* 105–118.

Farmer, R. L. (2014). Interface between psychotropic medications, neurobiology, and mental illness. *Smith College Studies in Social Work, 84,* 255–272.

Heller, N. R., & Gitterman, A. (Eds.). (2011). *Mental health and social problems: A social work perspective.* New York, NY: Routledge.

Jamison, K. R. (1999). *Night falls fast: Understanding suicide.* New York, NY: Knopf.

Tanner, T. B., Wilhelm, S. E., Rossie, K. M., & Metcalf, M. P. (2012). Web-based SBIRT skills training for health professional students and primary care providers. *Substance Abuse, 33*(3), 316–320.

Walsh, B. W. (2006). *Treating self-injury: A practical guide.* New York, NY: Guilford Press.

Witkiewitz, K., & Marlatt, G.A. (2004). Relapse prevention for alcohol and drug problems. *American Psychologist, 59*(4), 224–235.

CHAPTER 8

Ainsworth, F. (2002). Mandatory reporting of child abuse and neglect: Does it really make a difference? *Child and Family Social Work, 7,* 57–63.

Antle, B., Barbee, A., Yankeelov, P., & Bledsoe, L. (2010). A qualitative evaluation of the effects of mandatory reporting of domestic violence on victims and their children. *Journal of Family Social Work, 13,* 56–73.

Bennice, J. A., Resick, P. A., Mechanice, M., & Astin, M. (2003). The relative effects of intimate partner physical and sexual violence on post-traumatic stress disorder symptomatology. *Violence and Victims, 18*(1), 87–94.

Briere, J., & Elliott, D.M. (2003). Prevalence and symptomatic sequelae of self-reported childhood physical and sexual abuse in a general population sample of men and women. *Child Abuse and Neglect, 27,* 1205–1222.

Cox, L., & Speziale, B. (2009). Survivors of stalking: Their voices and lived experiences. *Affilia, 24*(1), 5–18.

Dass-Brailsford, P. (2007). *A practical approach to trauma: Empowering interventions.* Thousand Oaks, CA: Sage.

Donovan, K., & Regehr, C. (2010). Elder abuse: Clinical, ethical, and legal considerations in social work practice. *Clinical Social Work Journal, 38,* 174–182.

Jamison, K. R. (1999). *Night falls fast: Understanding suicide.* New York: Knopf.

Jobes, D. A., Rudd, M. D., Overholser, J. C., & Joiner, T. E. (2008). Ethical and competent care of suicidal patients: Contemporary challenges, new developments, and considerations for clinical practice. *Professional Psychology: Research and Practice, 39*(4), 405–413.

Lawson, D. M. (2009). Understanding and treating children who experience interpersonal maltreatment: Empirical findings. *Journal of Counseling & Development, 87*(2), 204–215.

Meloy, J. R., Davis, B., & Lovette, J. (2001). Risk factors for violence among stalkers. *Journal of Threat Assessment, 1*(1), 3–16.

National Association of Social Workers. (2008). *Code of Ethics.* Available from: http://www.socialworkers.org/pubs/code/code.asp

Reamer, F. G. (2005). Documentation in social work: Evolving ethical and risk—management standards. *Social Work, 50*(4), 325–334.

Reamer, F. G. (2006). *Ethical standards in social work* (2nd ed.). Washington, DC: NASW Press.

Sinwelski, S. A., & Vinton, L. (2001). Stalking: The constant threat of violence. *Affilia, 16*(1), 46–65.

Spinazzola, J., Ford, J. D., Zucker, M., van der Kolk, B. A., Silva, S., Smith, S. F., & Blaustein, M. (2005). National survey evaluates complex trauma exposure, outcome, and intervention among children and adolescents. *Psychiatric Annals, 35*, 433–439.

Spitz, M. (2003). Stalking: Terrorism at our doors—How social workers can help victims fight back. *Social Work, 48*(4), 504–512.

Tower, L. E. (2003). Domestic violence screening: education and institutional support correlates. *Journal of Social Work Education, 39*(3), 479–494.

Tufford, L., Mishna, F., & Black, T. (2010). Mandatory reporting and child exposure to domestic violence: Issues regarding the therapeutic alliance with couples. *Clinical Social Work Journal, 38*, 426–434.

Walsh, B. W. (2006). *Treating self-injury: A practical guide.* New York, NY: Guilford Press.

Webster, S. W., O'Toole, R. O., O'Toole, A. W., & Lucal, B. (2005). Overreporting and underreporting of child abusers: Teachers' use of professional discretion. *Child Abuse and Neglect, 29*, 1281–1296.

Zellman, G. L., & Fair, C. C. (2002). Preventing and reporting abuse. In J. E. B Meyers, L. A. Berliner, J. N. Briere, C. T. Hendrix, T. S. Reid, & C. A. Jenny (Eds.), *The APSAC Handbook on Child Maltreatment* (2nd ed., pp. 449–476). Thousand Oaks, CA: Sage.

CHAPTER 9

de Becker, G. (1999). *The gift of fear and other survival signals that protect us from violence.* New York, NY: Dell.

Harkey, J. (n.d.). *Be careful: Personal safety for social workers.* Billerica, MA: CEU School.

Jongsma, A. E. (2004). *The suicide and homicide risk assessment and prevention treatment planner.* New York, NY: Wiley.

National Association of Social Workers. (2013). *Guidelines for social worker safety in the workplace.* Washington, DC: Author.

National Association of Social Workers Center for Workforce Studies. (2006). *Assuring the sufficiency of a front line workforce: A national study of licensed social workers.* Washington, DC: Author.

Occupational Safety and Health Administration. (2004). *Guidelines for preventing workplace violence for health care and social service workers.* Retrieved from https://www.osha.gov/Publications/osha3148.pdf

Shields, G., & Kiser, J. (2003). Violence and aggression directed toward human service workers: An exploratory study. *Families in Society, 84*(1), 13–20.

Smith, M. (2006). Too little fear can kill you. Staying alive as a social worker. *Journal of Social Work Practice, 20*(1), 69–81.

Spencer, P., & Munch, S. (2003). Client violence toward social workers: The role of management in community mental health programs. *Social Work, 48*(4), 532–544.

Tapp, K., & Payne, D. (2011). Guidelines for practitioners: A social work perspective on discharging the duty to protect. *Journal of Social Work Values & Ethics, 8*(2), 2–13.

Weinger, S. (2001). *Security risk: Preventing client violence against social workers.* Washington, DC: NASW Press.

Winstanley, S., & Hales, L. (2008). Prevalence of aggression towards residential social workers: Do qualifications and experience make a difference? *Child Youth Care Forum, 37*, 103–110.

CHAPTER 10

Arends, I., Bruinvels, D. J., Rebergen, D. S., Nieuwenhuijsen, K., Madan, I., Neumeyer-Gromen, A., . . . Verbeek, J. H. (2012). Interventions to facilitate return to work in adults with adjustment disorders. *Cochrane Database of Systematic Reviews 2012, 12.* Art. No.: CD006389. doi:10.1002/14651858. CD006389.pub2

Drisko, J. W., & Grady, M. D. (2012). *Evidence-based practice in clinical social work: Essential clinical social work series.* New York, NY: Springer Science+Business Media.

Grady, M. D., & Drisko, J. W. (2014). Thorough clinical assessment: The hidden foundation of evidence-based practice. *Families in Society, 95*(1), 5–14. doi:10.1606/1044-3894.2014.95.2

Graybeal, C. (2014). The art of practicing with evidence. *Clinical Social Work Journal, 42*, 116–122.

Haynes, R., Devereaux, P., & Guyatt, G. (2002). Clinical expertise in the era of evidence based medicine and patient choice. *Evidence-Based Medicine, 7*, 36–38.

Isaac, S., & Michael, W. B. (1971). *Handbook in research and evaluation.* San Diego, CA: Educational and Industrial Testing Services.

National Association of Social Workers. (2008). *Code of ethics.* Retrieved from https://www.socialworkers.org/pubs/code/code.asp

Sackett, D., Rosenberg, W., Muir Gray, J., Haynes, R., & Richardson, W. (1996). Editorial: Evidence based medicine: What it is and what it isn't. *British Medical Journal, 312*, 71–72.

Thyer, B. A. (1991). Guidelines for evaluating outcome studies on social work practice. *Research on Social Work Practice, 1*(1), 76–91.

CHAPTER 11

Beck J. (2011). *Cognitive therapy: Basics and beyond* (2nd ed.). New York, NY: Guilford Press.

Drisko, J. W., & Grady, M. D. (2012). *Evidence-based practice in clinical social work: Essential clinical social work series.* New York, NY: Springer Science+Business Media.

Goin, M. K. (2005). A current perspective on the psychotherapies. *Psychiatric Services, 56*, 255–257.

Grady, M. D. (2009). Sex offenders part I: Theories and models of etiology, assessment and intervention. *Social Work in Mental Health, 7*, 353–371. doi:10.1080/15332980802052456

Hubble, M. A., Duncan, B. L., Miller, S. D., & Wampold, B. E. (2010). Introduction. In B. L. Duncan, S. D. Miller, B. E. Wampold, & M. A. Hubble (Eds.), *The heart and soul of change* (2nd ed., pp. 23–46). Washington, DC: American Psychological Association.

Hutchinson, E. (2013). Setting the stage: A multidimensional approach. In E. D. Hutchison (compiler), *Essentials of human behavior: Integrating person, environment, and the life course* (pp. 3–34). Los Angeles, CA: Sage.

MacDonald, D., & Webb, M. (2006). Toward conceptual clarity with psychotherapeutic theories. *Journal of Psychology and Christianity, 25*(1), 3–16.

Norcross, J. C. (2002). Empirically supported therapy relationships. In J. C. Norcross (Ed.), *Psychotherapy relationships that work: Therapist contributions and responsiveness to patients* (pp. 3–16). New York, NY: Oxford University Press.

Norcross, J. C., Hedges, M., & Castle, P. H. (2002). Psychologists conducting psychotherapy in 2001: A study of the Division 29 membership. *Psychotherapy: Theory, Research, Practice, Training, 39,* 97–102.

Prochaska, J. O., & Norcross, J. C. (1999). *Systems of psychotherapy: A transtheoretical analysis* (4th ed.). New York, NY: Brooks/Cole.

Segal, Z. V., Williams, J. M. G., & Teasdale, J. D. (2012). *Mindfulness-based cognitive therapy for depression* (2nd ed.). New York, NY: Guilford Press.

Walsh, J. (2013). *Theories for direct social work practice* (3rd ed.). Belmont, CA: Thompson Brooks/Cole.

Wampold, B. E. (2010). *The basics of psychotherapy: An introduction to theory and practice.* Washington, DC: American Psychological Association.

CHAPTER 12

Bateman, A. W., & Fonagy, P. (2011). *Handbook of mentalizing in mental health practice.* Washington, DC: American Psychiatric Publications.

Beck J. (2011). *Cognitive therapy: Basics and beyond* (2nd ed.). New York, NY: Guilford Press.

Bratton, S., Landreth, G., Kellam, T., & Blackard, S. R. (2006). *CPRT package: Child parent relationship therapy (CPRT) treatment manual: A 10-session filial therapy model for training parents.* New York, NY: Routledge Press.

Greene, G. J., Kondrat, D. C., Lee, M. Y., Clement, J., Siebert, H., Mentzer, R. A., & Pinnell, S. R. (2006). A solution-focused approach to case management and recovery with consumers who have a severe mental disability. *Families in Society: The Journal of Contemporary Social Services, 87,* 339–350.

Miller, W. R., & Rollnick, S. (2012). *Motivational interviewing: Helping people change* (3rd ed.). New York, NY: Guilford Press.

Norcross, J. C. (2002). Empirically supported therapy relationships. In J. C. Norcross (Ed.), *Psychotherapy relationships that work: Therapist contributions and responsiveness to patients* (pp. 3–16). New York, NY: Oxford University Press.

Teyber, E., & McClure, F. H. (2011). *Interpersonal process in therapy: An integrative model* (6th ed.). Belmont, CA: Brooks/Cole Publishing Company.

Walsh, J. (2013). *Theories for direct social work practice* (3rd ed.). Belmont, CA: Thompson Brooks/Cole.

Wampold, B. E. (2010). *The basics of psychotherapy: An introduction to theory and practice.* Washington, DC: American Psychological Association.

CHAPTER 13

Deegan, P. E. (1988). Recovery: The lived experience of rehabilitation. *Psychosocial Rehabilitation Journal, 11,* 11–19.

Doran, G. T. (1981). There's a S.M.A.R.T. way to write management's goals and objectives. *Management Review, 70*(11), 35–36.

Hepworth, D. H., Rooney, R. H., Dewberry-Rooney, G., & Strom-Gottfried, K. (2013). *Direct social work practice: Theory and skills* (9th ed.). Belmont, CA: Brooks/Cole.

Meyer, P. J. (2003). What would you do if you knew you couldn't fail? Creating S.M.A.R.T. goals. In *Attitude is everything: If you want to succeed above and beyond.* Waco, TX: Meyer Resource Group.

Miller, W. R., & Rollnick, S. (2012). *Motivational interviewing: Helping people change* (3rd ed.). New York, NY: Guilford Press.

Spiegler, M., & Guevremont, D. (2010). *Contemporary behavior therapy.* Belmont, CA: Thompson/Wadsworth.

Yemm, G. (2012). *Essential guide to leading your team: How to set goals, measure performance and reward talent.* New York, NY: Pearson Education.

CHAPTER 14

Applegate, J. S., & Bonovitz, J. M. (1995). The transitional process. In *The facilitating partnership: A Winnicottian approach for social workers and other helping professionals* (pp. 157–177). New York, NY: Rowman & Littlefield.

Beck, J. (2011). *Cognitive therapy: Basics and beyond* (2nd ed.). New York, NY: Guilford Press.

Bogo, M. (2006). *Social work practice: Concepts, processes and interviewing.* New York, NY: Columbia University Press.

Cameron, M., & Keenan, E. K. (2013). *The common factors model for generalist practice.* Boston, MA: Pearson.

Conner, K., & Grote, N. (2008). Enhancing the cultural relevance of empirically-supported mental health interventions. *Families in Society: The Journal of Contemporary Social Services, 89,* 587–595. doi:10.1606/1044-3894.3821

Corcoran, J. (2011). *Helping skills for social work direct practice.* New York, NY: Oxford University Press.

Fontes, L. A., & Plummer, C. (2010). Cultural issues in disclosures of child sexual abuse. *Journal of Child Sexual Abuse: Research, Treatment, & Program Innovations for Victims, Survivors, & Offenders, 19,* 491–518.

Gambrill, E. (2013). *Social work practice: A critical thinker's guide* (3rd ed.). New York, NY: Oxford University Press.

Hepworth, D. H., Rooney, R. H., Dewberry-Rooney, G., & Strom-Gottfried, K. (2013). *Direct social work practice: Theory and skills* (9th ed.). Belmont, CA: Brooks/Cole.

Kenny, J. (2008, January 28). The last session: Quitting therapy. *The New Yorker.* Retrieved from http://www.newyorker.com/magazine/2008/01/28/last-session

Miley, K. K., O'Melia, M. W., & DuBois, B. L. (2013). *Generalist social work practice: An empowering approach* (7th ed.). Boston, MA: Pearson.

National Association of Social Workers. (2008). *Code of ethics.* Washington, DC: Author.

Norcross, J. C. (2002). Empirically supported therapy relationships. In J. C. Norcross (Ed.), *Psychotherapy relationships that work: Therapist contributions and responsiveness to patients* (pp. 3–16). New York, NY: Oxford University Press.

Ow, R., & Katz, D. (1999). Family secrets and the disclosure of distressful information in Chinese families. *Families in Society: The Journal of Contemporary Human Services, 80,* 620–628. doi:10.1606/1044-3894.1783

Shulman, L. (2012). *The skills of helping individuals, families, groups, and communities* (7th ed.). Belmont, CA: Brooks/Cole.

Steen, C. (2001). *The adult relapse prevention workbook*. Branford, VT: Safer Society Press.

Wampold, B. E. (2010). *The basics of psychotherapy: An introduction to theory and practice*. Washington, DC: American Psychological Association.

Xiong, Z., Tuicomepee, A., LaBlanc, L., & Rainey, J. (2006). Hmong immigrants' perceptions of family secrets and recipients of disclosure. *Families in Society: The Journal of Contemporary Social Services, 87*, 231–239. doi:10.1606/1044-3894.3516

Zayas, L., Torres, L., & Cabassa, L. (2009). Diagnostic, symptom, and functional assessments of Hispanic outpatients in community mental health practice. *Community Mental Health Journal, 45*, 97–105.

CHAPTER 15

Bloom, M., Fischer, J., & Orme, J. G. (2009). *Evaluating practice: Guidelines for the accountable professional* (6th ed.). Boston, MA: Allyn & Bacon.

Bringhurst, D., Watson, C., Miller, S., & Duncan, B. (2006). The reliability and validity of the Outcome Rating Scale: A replication study of a brief clinical measure. *Journal of Brief Therapy, 5*(1), 23–30.

Campbell, A., & Hemsley, S. (2009). Outcome Rating Scale and Session Rating Scale in psychological practice: Clinical utility of ultra-brief measures. *Clinical Psychologist, 13*(1), 1–9.

Duncan, B., Miller, S., Sparks, J., Claud, D., Reynolds, L., Brown, J., & Johnson, L. (2003). The Session Rating Scale: Preliminary psychometric properties of a "working" alliance measure. *Journal of Brief Therapy, 3*(1), 3–12.

Engel, R. J., & Schutt, R. K. (2014). *Fundamentals of social work research* (2nd ed.). Los Angeles, CA: Sage.

Fischer, J., & Corcoran, K. (2013a). *Measures for clinical practice and research: A sourcebook. Vol. 1: Couples, families, and children* (5th ed.). New York, NY: Oxford University Press.

Fischer, J., & Corcoran, K. (2013b). *Measures for clinical practice and research: A sourcebook. Vol. 2: Adults* (5th ed.). New York, NY: Oxford University Press.

Gambrill, E. (2013). *Social work practice: A critical thinker's guide* (3rd ed.). New York, NY: Oxford University Press.

Hepworth, D. H., Rooney, R. H., Dewberry-Rooney, G., & Strom-Gottfried, K. (2013). *Direct social work practice: Theory and skills* (9th ed.). Belmont, CA: Brooks/Cole.

Miley, K. K., O'Melia, M., & DuBois, B. (2013). *Generalist social work practice: An empowering approach* (7th ed.). Boston, MA: Allyn & Bacon

Miller, S. D., & Duncan, B. L. (2000). *Outcome Rating Scale (ORS)*. Retrieved from: http://www.scottd-miller.com/srs-ors-license/

National Association of Social Workers. (2008). *Code of ethics*. Washington, DC: Author.

CHAPTER 16

Bennett, S., & Deal, K. H. (2009). Beginnings and endings in social work supervision: The interaction between attachment and developmental process. *Journal of Teaching in Social Work, 29*(1), 101–117.

Davis, R. T. (2010). Constructing a profession of social work: The role of social work supervision. *Social Work Review, 9*(1), 20–30.

Harvey, A., & Henderson, F. (2013). Reflective supervision for child protection practice: Reaching beneath the surface. *Journal of Social Work Practice, 28,* 343–356.

Kim, H., Ji, J., & Kao, D. (2011). Burnout and physical health among social workers: A three-year longitudinal study. *Social Work, 56*(3), 258–68.

National Association of Social Workers & Association of Social Work Boards. (2013). *Best practice standards in social work supervision.* Washington, DC: NASW.

Wightman, B., Weigand, B., Whitaker, K., Traylor, D., Yeider, S., & Hyden, V. (2007). Reflective practice and supervision in child abuse prevention. *Zero to Three, 28*(2), 29–33.

CHAPTER 17

Barak, A., & Grohol, J. A. (2011). Current and future trends in internet-supported mental health interventions. *Journal of Technology in Human Services, 29,* 155–196.

Csiernik, R., Furze, P., Dromgole, L., & Rishchynski, G. M. (2006). Information technology and social work: The dark side or light side? In J. M. Dunlop & M. J. Holosko (Eds.), *Information technology and evidence-based social work practice* (pp. 9–25). Binghamton, NY: Haworth Press.

Dombo, E. A., Kays, L., & Weller, K. (2014). Clinical social work practice and technology: Personal, practical, regulatory, and ethical considerations for the 21st century. *Social Work in Health Care, 53,* 900–919.

Glassgold, J. (2007). Redrawing the boundaries of psychotherapy: Is it ethically possible? *PsycCritiques, 52,* 978–979.

Kolmes, K., & Taube, D. (2011). *Summary of client–therapist encounters on the web: The client experience.* Retrieved from http://drkkolmes.com/research/#therapist%20survey

Kraus, R., Stricker, G., & Speyer, C. (2011). *Online counseling: A handbook for mental health professionals.* San Diego, CA: Elsevier.

McWilliams, N. (2004). *Psychoanalytic psychotherapy: A practitioner's guide.* New York, NY: Guilford Press.

Menon, G., & Rubin, M. (2011). A survey of online practitioners: Implications for education and practice. *Journal of Technology in Human Services, 29,* 133–141.

National Association of Social Workers. (2008). *Code of ethics.* Washington, DC: Author.

National Association of Social Workers & Association of Social Work Boards. (2005). *NASW & ASWB standards for technology and social work practice.* Retrieved from http://www.socialworkers.org/practice/standards/naswtechnologystandards.pdf

Reamer, F. G. (2013). Social work in a digital age: Ethical and risk management challenges. *Social Work, 58,* 163–172.

Santhiveeran, J. (2009). Compliance of social work e-therapy websites to the NASW code of ethics. *Social Work in Health Care, 48*(1), 1–13

CHAPTER 18

Allen, J. G. (2001). *Traumatic relationships and serious mental disorders.* New York, NY: Wiley.

Badenoch, B. (2008). *Being a brain-wise therapist.* New York, NY: Norton.

Bennett, S., & Petrash, P. (2014). The neurobiology of substance use disorders: Information for assessment and clinical treatment. *Smith College Studies in Social Work, 84,* 273–291.

Bentley, K. J. (2010). Psychiatric medications and meaning-making in a residential program for adults with serious mental illness. *Qualitative Social Work, 9,* 479–499.

Bentley, K. J., & Walsh, J. (2006). *The social worker and psychotropic medication* (3rd ed.). New York, NY: Brooks/Cole.

Bentley, K. J., Walsh, J., & Farmer, R. (2005). Referring clients for psychiatric medication: Best practices for social workers. *Best Practices in Mental Health, 1*(1), 59–71.

Cohen, M. M., Tottenham, N., & Casey, B. J. (2013). Translational developmental studies of stress on brain and behavior: Implications for adolescent mental health and illness?. *Neuroscience, 249,* 53–62.

Drake, R. E., & Mueser, K. T. (2000). Psychosocial approaches to dual diagnosis. *Schizophrenia Bulletin, 26*(1), 105–118.

Fan, Y., Decety, J., Yang, C., Liu, J., & Cheng, Y. (2010). Unbroken mirror neurons in autism spectrum disorder. *Journal of Child Psychology and Psychiatry, 51,* 981–988.

Farmer, R. L. (2009). *Neuroscience and social work practice.* Thousand Oaks, CA: Sage.

Farmer, R. L. (2014). Interface between psychotropic medications, neurobiology, and mental illness. *Smith College Studies in Social Work, 84,* 255–272.

Farmer, R. L., Bentley, K. J., & Walsh, J. (2006). Advancing social work curriculum in psychopharmacology and medication management. *Journal of Social Work Education, 42,* 211–229.

Garland, E. L., & Howard, M. O. (2009). Neuroplasticity, psychosocial genomics, and the biopsychosocial paradigm in the 21st century. *Health & Social Work, 34*(3), 191–199.

Ivey, A. E., & Zalaquett, C. P. (2011). Neuroscience and counseling: Central issue for social justice leaders. *Journal for Social Action in Counseling and Psychology, 3*(1), 103–116.

Matto, H. C., & Strolin-Goltzman, J. (2010). Integrating social neuroscience and social work: Innovations for advancing practice-based research. *Social Work, 55,* 147–156.

Montgomery, A. (2002). Converging perspectives of dynamic theory and evolving neurobiological knowledge. *Smith College Studies in Social Work, 72,* 178–196.

Ruiz, P. (2000). *Ethnicity and psychopharmacology: Review of psychiatry series,* Vol. 19. London: Eurospan Group.

Schore, A. N. (2001). The effects of early relational trauma on right brain development, affect regulation, and infant mental health. *Infant Mental Health Journal, 22*(1–2), 201–269.

Siegel, D. (2003). An interpersonal neurobiology of psychotherapy: The developing mind and the resolution of trauma. In M. Soloman & D. Siegel (Eds.), *Healing trauma: Attachment, mind, body, and brain* (pp. 1–56). New York, NY: Norton.

Siegel, D., (2007). *The mindful brain.* New York, NY: Norton.

Weber, D. A., & Reynolds, D. R. (2004). Clinical perspectives on neurobiological effects of psychological trauma. *Neuropsychology Review, 14,* 115–129.

INDEX

Note: Page numbers followed by italicized letters indicate *figures* or *tables*.

MacDonald, D., conceptual syncretism, 113, 114
Mahoney, M. J., *Constructive Psychotherapy: A Practical Guide.*, 13
mandated reporting
  and client confidentiality, 44–45
  compiling report, 81
  discrepancies in, 74
  legal and ethical issues, 75
  meaning of, 73–74
mandated treatment, motivating clients for change, 136–137
mandated *vs.* voluntary clients, and initial client session, 47
marginalization, awareness of issues, 21–23, 23–24, 27–28
Measures for Clinical Practice and Research (Fischer & Corcoran), 163
medications
  classes of, 200
  psychiatric, 195–197
meditation, to address vicarious trauma, 19–20
Meichenbaum, D., *Self-care for Trauma Psychotherapists and Caregivers*, 16
mental health
  areas of practitioner expertise, 107
  mental status exam, 57–58
  neuroscience and issues of mental health care, 195
  World Health Organization (WHO) definition, 51
Michael, W. B., *Handbook in Research and Evaluation*, 104–106
middle phase of treatment
  developing new patterns, 132–133
  explaining patterns, 130–132
  four main steps of, 124
  influence of theories and models on, 123–124
  linking patterns to presenting concerns, 128–130, 128t, 129t
  and pattern identification, 125–128
    using charts, 125–126, 126t, 127t
    using journals, 126–128
midrange theory, used by social workers, 108
mirror neurons, 193
modality, used in planning for change and setting goals, 142
models
  definition of, 109
  influence on middle phase of treatment, 123–124
mood stabilizers, 200
Motivational Interviewing
  and developing new patterns of behavior, 132
  and planning for change, 137
Muir Gray, J., definition of evidence-based medicine, 96

National Association of Social Workers (NASW)
  code of ethics
    duration of treatment, 149
    evaluating progress, 161
    mandated reporting, 75
    personal boundaries, 155
    private conduct, 186
    the professional self, 8
    social and political action, 186
    use of social media, 184–187
    use of technology, 184
  and supervision, 173
  use of evidence-based practice, 95–96
  workplace safety report, 85
neglect, identifying in clients, 75–76
neurobiology
  anatomy and physiology of the brain, 192–193
  defined, 191–192
  significance of in client care, 193–194
neurons
  definition of, 192
  mirror neurons, 193
neuropsychological testing, use in assessment, 60
neuroscience, and macro practice, 195
neurotransmitters, definition of, 192–193
Night Falls Fast: Understanding Suicide (Jamison), 80

objective measures
  examples of, 160–161
  standardized instruments, 161–163
objectives
  specifying, 160
  use in planning for change, 140, 141t, 142
Occupational Safety and Health Administration (OSHA), 90–91
oppression and power, awareness of, 21–23, 23–24, 27–28
oral communication, and the professional self, 7
organizational theories, overview of, 121
Outcome Rating Scale, 167
outcomes, client
  common factors in, 34–35
  the "dodo verdict," 33–34
  and a working alliance with clients, 35–36

paperwork, attending to, 45
participant listening, and assessment, 55
pathology, balancing with strengths, 54
patterns'
  developing new, 132–133
  development and purpose of, 130–132
  identifying during intervention, 124, 125–128

waiting room, greeting clients in, 42
Walsh, J.
    consistency between theory and intervention, 110
    theories used by social workers, 107–108
Webb, M., conceptual syncretism, 113, 114
Wightman, B., reflective supervision, 180–181
working alliance
    and social worker-client relationship, 35–36
    strengthening, 37
work-life balance, maintaining, 203
workload
    and compassion satisfaction, 15

    diversifying, 203
    impacts of on individual social
        workers, 13–16
    and rewards of social work profession, 16–17
workplace and professional self-care,
        assessing, 19
workplace safety, assessing, 87–88
World Health Organization (WHO)
    definition of mental health, 51
    International Classification of Diseases, Tenth
        Revision (ICD-10), 60, 61
written communication, and the professional self, 7